W9-CNR-730

THE ART OF STAND UP PADDLING

The Naish Ohana cruising in Kaneohe Bay on the southeast side of Oahu. Katie Naish is on a Naish Alana 9'5" wood while Robbie and Christina are on a Naish Nalu 10'10" AST.
Stephen Whitesell, courtesy Naish SUP

THE ART OF
STAND UP
PADDLING

A COMPLETE GUIDE TO SUP ON LAKES, RIVERS, AND OCEANS

Second Edition

Ben Marcus

FALCONGUIDES

GUILFORD, CONNECTICUT
HELENA, MONTANA

FALCONGUIDES®

An imprint of Rowman & Littlefield
Falcon, FalconGuides, and Outfit Your Mind are registered trademarks of Rowman & Littlefield.

Distributed by NATIONAL BOOK NETWORK

Copyright © 2016 by Ben Marcus
A previous edition of this book was published by The Globe Pequot Press in 2012.

Photos by Alexandra Westmore unless otherwise noted.

All rights reserved. No part of this book may be reproduced in any form or by any electronic or mechanical means, including information storage and retrieval systems, without written permission from the publisher, except by a reviewer who may quote passages in a review.

British Library Cataloguing-in-Publication Information Available

Library of Congress Cataloging-in-Publication Data is available.

ISBN 978-1-4930-0832-2 (pbk.: alk. paper)
ISBN 978-1-4930-1466-8 (electronic)

∞™ The paper used in this publication meets the minimum requirements of American National Standard for Information Sciences—Permanence of Paper for Printed Library Materials, ANSI/NISO Z39.48-1992.

The author and Rowman & Littlefield assume no liability for accidents happening to, or injuries sustained by, readers who engage in the activities described in this book.

CONTENTS

ACKNOWLEDGMENTS

From First Edition

Dorothy Parker once said: "I hate writing, I love having written." Which is true, because finishing a complicated mother of a book is a good feeling. However, the end game of writing a book is always a little traumatic when it's time to wade back through months and thousands of e-mails to compile a list of thank-yous and acknowledgments. Traumatic because it brings back to memory how complicated books are to put together and how many people I had to pester with dozens and hundreds of e-mails.

Traumatic to remember many people were kind enough to contribute their experience and photos. A lot of photos. Thousands of dollars' worth of photos from individuals and companies—almost all of them donated by big companies like Surftech, Starboard, and Naish, and from dedicated SUP enthusiasts like Ken Hoeve, Charles MacArthur, Mike Sandusky, Dane Jackson, Caroline Gleich, and David Adams, who donated personal photos and/or affixed GoPros to their boards and paddles and made it all look good.

Traumatic because of the responsibility of remembering to thank everyone who contributed—and not leave anyone out.

The first e-mails for this book began around September 13, 2010. If it's okay to use a steelhead metaphor in a SUP book: I hand-tied a flashy book proposal and drifted it in front of several publishers. John Burbidge at FalconGuides was the first to take the bait and now here we are—exhausted and gasping after a long fight.

This is my fifteenth book, but the first book I ever pitched to a publisher that was accepted. I quote Captain Willard from *Apocalypse Now*: "I wanted a mission, and for my sins, they gave me one."

Books aren't easy. They don't write themselves. Nor do they research themselves, interview and transcribe interviews by themselves, or fact-check or copyedit themselves. Books are a lot of work, but they are made easier with input from a lot of people.

It's now July of 2011, ten months after that first cast, and this book is almost *finito*. It wouldn't have happened without the following people:

First of all thanks to John Burbidge for wrestling this monster into order. Wasn't easy. It's almost over—all he has to do now is edit 1,500 words of thank-yous down to something that will fit.

Thanks to instructor Skylar Peak, Beckers Malibu retail dude Mitch Taylor, and students Noam and Michelle Geft and their lovely children, Daniel Dolphin and Evan Eagle, for their time and dedication in laying down the instructional part. The best decision I made in the last year was to ask the Gefts if they wanted to be the models. That part worked out perfectly.

Of course thanks to Alexandra "Aflex" Westmore for shooting all the instructional stuff, and just for being a righteous babe in general. Thanks to Bill Miller at Malibu Kitchen for the bench space. (It's 12:43 p.m. as I write this and time to clear out!)

Also thanks to Janet Macpherson and Steve Farbus for the tool shed—sorry about the water bottles.

And to Sue Peck for the PCH space. And John Ortiz for the peace and quiet on Malibu Road.

Clay Feeter, Steven Sjuggerud, and Glenn Dubock at *Standup Journal* were stand-up guys in helping this book along from go to whoa. They were a big help in laying down a lot of history, pointing me to a wide range of stand up paddlers from Maui to the Mediterranean, and providing me with contact lists of people in the SUP industry.

In *SUP Magazine*, Sam George talked about this book as it was still being created and said something to the effect of, "The history of SUP is too new to lay down." *Au contraire*: Laying down history as it's happening is important to the future, and the part of this book I like best is the history of SUP.

Might not be perfect, but a solid base for others to mutate however they like.

Thanks to Laird Hamilton for dedicating some water time to a couple of long phone calls to lay down his history and philosophy of stand up paddling. I hope I got it right.

And to Jane Kachmer for connecting me to the Coconut Wireless.

Thanks to Jack McCoy and "Gravey Davey" for taking the time to e-mail that "missing link" image of Duke on the Australian surf ski circa 1939 and thanks to DeSoto Brown, Sandy Hall, Geoff Cater, Scott Starr, Nick Carroll, and Jack McCoy for unraveling where that board came from, and its significance—if any. If anyone has anything earlier: Send it! Thanks also to Don Love for permission to use the image.

Also to Geoff Cater for the *khasake* clue-in.

Almost too late, Michael Ah Choy delivered two scoops on the impact of John "Pops" Ah Choy and his brothers Bobby and Leroy on the history of standing up on a big surfboard and propelling it with a paddle. Almost missed that. Glad we didn't.

Gerry Lopez contributed in ways he was aware of and not aware of. He gave a long interview that didn't make it into the book, and that's a shame, but fifty years from now, some SUP historian will love finding a transcript of Gerry's words.

Many others contributed to the history, including Duke Brouwer and Randy French at Surftech. Thanks to them for the historical input, technical information, and for opening their photo files. And thanks to Ty Zulim and the crew in HB for equipment support, and Steve Cranston in Hawaii for letting Noam and Michelle tour the warehouse and borrow some boards.

Also thanks to Dave Parmenter and Todd Bradley at C4 Waterman/Pohaku Paddles for laying down the west side/Makaha side of the story. Even if we couldn't use all the best stuff.

Cameron Farrer was a big help with his eyewitness account of stand up paddling around Privates in the early 1990s. Sam George supported Cameron's accounts with his own of the early days, as did Scott Bass, who laid down an early history of SUP in San Diego County.

Many others contributed to the history, including Felipe Pomar, Marshall Coben, Gerry Lopez, Jay Butki, Loch Eggers, Ambrose Curry, Mike Waltze, Jimmy Lewis, Ken Russell and Marlon Lewis, Mickey Eskimo, Roger Mansfield, Chris Power, Charlie Force, Blane Chambers, Chris Malloy, Gary Lynch, Joe Bark, Ron House, Steve Sjuggerud, Clay Feeter, Mickey Munoz, Don King, and Sam George.

Who else? I'd better look through it right now. I did a FIND for "said" in the history chapter and found Nik Zanella for the China angle, Patrice Grenoule for the Podoscaphe photo, Tom Moore, Ray Kleiman, and also nonagenarian SUP'er John "Zap" Zapotocky—although his quotes and stories were taken from other sources.

For the retail chapter, apologies to Scott and Leslie Ruble at CoveWater in Santa Cruz—sorry we didn't make it up there. Same to Jim Smiley at Paddle Power in Newport. We didn't make it down there either, and stayed close to home.

Thanks to Mitch Taylor (again) at Beckers Malibu and also Travis Collings for letting us invade the shop and disrupt their shockingly solid SUP sales.

Also thanks to Gary Stone at Isthmus Sailboards/Paddleboards and probably a couple dozen other SUP retailers I pestered along the way for information—and am now rudely forgetting.

Caroline Gleich, Ken Hoeve, Charlie MacArthur, Dane Jackson, Mike Sandusky, Jim and Elizabeth Terrell of Quickblade, and Karen Chun all pitched in with equipment advice in the retail section.

For the fitness chapter, thanks to Laird Hamilton, Karen Seade, Suzie Cooney, Paddle Diva Gina

Bradley and all her Divas, and Brody Welte. And although they didn't know they were contributing: Rick Rubin, Chris Chelios, Marissa Miller, and many other athletes and trainers who were quoted about the fitness benefits of SUP in other media.

For the etiquette chapter, thanks to M_____ R_____, Patrick Stoker, Skylar Peak, Tinker Blomfield, Josh Kuntz, and Dr. Ken Siporin. And Simone Harrar for that sequence of Skylar and crew.

From the industry side, "taak" to Svein Rasmussen and Margareta Engstrom at Starboard for opening their treasure chest of photos from around the world. I've always said Norway is the best-run country in the world, and it was nice to see some Scandinavian efficiency from Svein and Margareta. They said they would do something and then they did it—right away.

And the same to Surftech: more good stuff than we could use.

Jim and Elizabeth Terrell at Quickblade were quick to respond to countless e-mails and also to let us use some of their cool graphics.

Thanks to Julia Schweiger, who does the marketing for Naish, for photos and input.

Thanks to Karen Chun, spokeskahuna for Malama Chun, maker of quality paddles on Maui.

As noted, this book came together with a lot of generous contributions of photos from a lot of people, professional and amateur. Thanks to Mike Nixon for his sequence of Laird doing the helicopter and to Bill Parr for the windy Malibu Christmas card image and *Malibu Magazine* cover. Thanks to Janice Burns for finding it and Jason Rouse for letting us use it. Thanks to Dylan Fish, Jon Roseman, Rick Isbell, Dave Clark, and Scott Winer at Tavarua for some crystal-clear Fiji photos. Thanks to Dan Tucker for the Mitch Taylor photos and Strider "Raspberry" Wasilewski for the Cam Farrer photo. Thanks to Fernando Aguerre and the International Surfing Association for the Peru *caballito* photos, and to Michael Ah Choy and Todd Bradley for the Zapotocky photo—and for getting the date right. Scott Hulet, Steve Pezman, and Sylvain Cazenave get thanks for the sequence of Laird and Dave at Mudflats. Thanks to Gary Lynch for sending that Tom Blake "gator gun" photo from the 1930s and the Surfing Heritage Foundation for letting us use it—along with the Blake quiver photo. And to David Collyer and Richard Merryman for the photos of Skylar getting shacked and getting whacked. To Wingnut for the fishy photos, Patrick Stoker for the injury photos, and Joel T Smith for his *caballito* photos. To Suzie Cooney and Thomas Barwick for her photos, and to Pat Huber, Michael Cassidy, and Rainbow Sandals for their Battle of the Paddle pix and the Duke poster art.

Thanks to Dashama and Aflex for the yoga moves on the water.

For the "Branching Out" chapter, a lot of paddlers from ocean to inland chipped in with stories and photos: Norm Hann from BC with photos from Taylor Kennedy and Brian Huntington. Mike Sandusky from Ontario, Canada, with photos from Michael Shin and Grant Kennedy. Caroline Gleich and Dane Jackson for the words and photos. Eric Stiller and Erik Olsen for the Manhattan visuals. Ken Hoeve from Colorado with his cool GoPro photos—wish we could have run more. And Skylar, Christian, and Morgan for their photos of the adventure from S___ C___ to W___. Hope Tofino goes good, too. (Christian's playing at Malibu Inn right now. Should I finish this or go?)

Thanks to Lili Foster and Lucia Griggi, who shot photos of the Gefts in Hawaii at Waikiki, Pua'ena, and Waimea: That worked great.

Thanks and apologies to anyone I left out.

Noam Geft is standing at Malibu Kitchen right now, telling me to finish this later and head out to L___ P___ because the tide is dropping and the wind is coming up. He'd never been on a stand up paddleboard prior to September of 2010, and now he's all surf stoked and has it wired. That is the effect SUP is having on people, and I hope this book helps put them on the right path.

All of that for one little ol' book. Hope you enjoy it and learn from it, and please: Don't venture into the surf until you have your skills down. It's very dangerous.

For Second Edition

It is 18:00 on Tuesday, the third of March 2015. After lagging big time on this book—it was due in November of 2014—I am reading it through one more time and turning it in tomorrow. Yay. I could have finished the book a long time ago, but in some ways it's good I didn't because I have seen and experienced things in Seattle and Hawaii during that lag time that have made this revision more complete.

For the 2015 revision of *The Art of Stand Up Paddling*, muchos mahalos to Steve Cranston for hiring a depressed, burned-out writer to work in the warehouse at Surftech Hawaii, and to D___, Carl, and Rance for putting up with my spacey sloppiness. Special thanks to David Legere and the powers that be at FalconGuides for not sending out a hit squad, and then lighting a fire under me to get 'er done. The history chapter was revised with help from Mike Waltze's SUPumentary *That First Glide* and also the 2014 *SUP the Mag Gear Guide*.

One of the good things that happened during the lag time was Dashama showing up on Oahu in late March, exactly when I needed her. Thanks to her sister Jophiel for driving them both to Ala Moana Park, and to both of them for doing the sunset to twilight paddle. That was fun. And big thanks to Dashama for turning around the SUP yoga chapter in two days. Thanks to the photographer(s) who took all the yoga photos of Dashama, and also to GoPro for making the ultimate selfie machine. Thanks to Jodi Caplan for looking through her yoga photos of Annelise and to both of them for letting me use them in the book.

For the competition chapter, thanks to Barrett Tester, Mike Ishikawa, Fernando Aguerre, Liam Ferguson, Tristan Boxford, Shannon Delaney, Todd Bradley, Carlos Escaba, Chris Parker, Ron House, Pat Huber, Karen Baxter, Connor Baxter, Zane Schweitzer, and Reid Inouye for input on the evolution of competitive SUP. Thanks to Ben Thouard and Starboard for providing the photos and also to Shannon Delaney, Molokai-2-Oahu, Kuty Hoy, Erik Aeder, and Johann Meya for opening their files. Also thanks to Sarah Euler at Pau Hana for their photos.

Thanks to Duncan Norris for driving me around Hawaii and to Greg Martin for letting me stay on the *Gemini*—that was a sublime month in Kewalo Harbor, watched over by Orion, protected by F-22 Raptors, swimming Ala Moana channel in the morning and surfing the reef at night. Thanks to Angel at the Jamba Juice on Ward for the oatmealoha. Also thanks to Barb and George Gronseth for hiring me at Issaquah Paddle Sports for the summer of 2014 and giving me an eye-opener to how popular the sport has become. And thanks to Laird Hamilton and Gabrielle Reece-Hamilton for the interview and photos. Now it's 18:03 and I have 298 pages to read and proof before my battery gives out and the sun goes down. No shore power on the *Gemini*. I hope you enjoy the revision.

INTRODUCTION
WHY SUP?

The original version of *The Art of Stand Up Paddling* was written between October 2010 and February 2011. Three years later, in March of 2014, FalconGuides asked for a revision, wondering if much had changed in the world of stand up paddling in those three years. That revision was supposed to

have been written over the summer of 2014 and submitted in September of 2014.

But now here it is December 20, 2014, and I'm just getting started on revising this book.

That's bad, because I have written seventeen or so books since 2001 and I have never lagged on

Issaquah Paddle Sports on Lake Sammamish in east Seattle, where the author worked during the summer of 2014 and saw how popular stand up paddling had become. Ben Marcus, with thanks to the Gronseths

one as badly as this. Lagging is bad, but it's also good because in that gap from March of 2014 to now—when I was supposed to be writing this revision—I spent a lot of time in Seattle and took short trips to Southern California, New York, and Hawaii and experienced and saw a lot of things in the brave new world of SUP that, added up, justify this revision.

Stand up paddling really didn't exist until as recently as September 12, 2002—when Laird Hamilton went public at First Point Malibu with this new thing he and his friends had been working on. So everything that has happened in SUP has happened in just twelve years, but the popularity of the sport and the development of new techniques and facets has increased dramatically in the last three years.

Clearly, SUP is a big sensation.

From March to September of 2014 I worked at Issaquah Paddle Sports (IPS) on Lake Sammamish near Issaquah, Washington, in east Seattle. The people who own IPS are longtime kayakers, and their rental place on the lake began as a kayak rental. But as the summer progressed it became very clear that kayaks and pedal boats were now a sideshow, and SUP was the go.

Over the course of the summer, Issaquah Paddle Sports increased their SUP fleet to about sixty boards—a combination of Liquid Shredders from Peru, Pau Hana from Los Angeles, and a few boards from Imagine, Surftech, and other brands.

The people of Seattle cherish their sunny weather, and when the sun comes out, they do all they can to get out in it. And during the summer of 2014, I saw just how popular stand up paddling had become, on one corner of one lake in east Seattle.

Very, very popular. On a busy, sunny weekend, all sixty of those SUPs would be rented, and there would be fifteen people in line—in various states

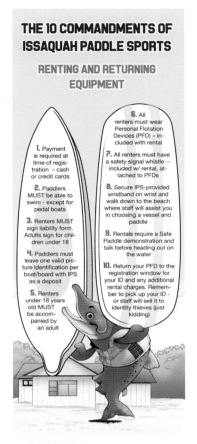

Signage for Issaquah Paddle Sports with Sammy the Sammamish Salmon laying down the law.
Signage courtesy Issaquah Paddle Sports

of sweaty and grumpy—all fiending to try this new sensation.

Mothers and fathers with eager children, teenagers running up with fun in their eyes, older couples wanting to exercise their aching bones, deskbound Microsoft hackers and supply-chain gurus from Costco headquarters taking long lunch breaks from the shady turf of their offices—they all came for the waters, to catch some rays on Lake Sammamish using this new sensation of SUP.

Some SUPistas were first-timers who didn't have a clue, and we would get them started on their first steps—making sure they didn't have their fins jammed into the sand when they climbed aboard,

Why SUP? Because it's a way to connect with nature and get quality time with loved ones. Pro kayaker Elaine Campbell and friend on a Pau Hana Big EZ Air. Photo: Pau Hana

and giving them basic instruction: Don't be sideways to the wind, paddle on your knees to get a feel for the board, have some speed when you get to your feet, place your feet close to the carry handle to find the sweet spot, place your hand over the top of the paddle, pull with your core, not your arms.

Newbies climbed aboard thinking they were going to suck, going to fall, going to drown, going to be rescued. We reassured them: "You'll go out shaky and come back strong." That was our advice to one and all, and it proved to be true. What I learned on Lake Sammamish in the summer of

2014 is that SUP is a very flattering sport. Beginning SUPistas might go out like newborn colts on shaky legs, but within an hour they come flying in like Laird Hamilton, skim the boards right up to shore, and hop off like World War II fighter pilots. All jaunty-like. Got it dialed in, in an hour.

And the reason they SUP was right there on their sunburned faces: smiles. Stand up paddling is a lot of fun. More fun than kayaks or pedal boats, apparently. Some people would go out in the middle of the lake, fall off, and have splashing paddle battles. Others would paddle over to the sandbar to the left of the beach and goof around on that all day.

Others looking for adventure were instructed to try their skills on Issaquah Creek: walk their boards over the sandbar that separates the lake from the creek, get back on their board in the creek, and paddle up-creek until they heard banjos. On Issaquah Creek there was a submerged log they had to paddle over, and then an arched "limbo log" they had to paddle under. There was a bit of current and some forks in the creek, and it was all pretty adventurous. Issaquah Creek presented an interesting challenge course for people on SUPs. They came back all smiles and said they would return soon—with friends.

Issaquah Paddle Sports had a lot of repeat customers throughout the summer and especially into the dog days of August, when the weather in Seattle is sublime. A lot of the customers were Microsoft workers who made a lot of money and could most likely have bought their own boards, paddles, leashes, and accessories, but they didn't. They came to IPS to try the variety of boards and paddles—and also for instruction.

There was a small platoon of ardent paddlers who would come to Lake Sammamish and launch their own boards. Some of these were serious competitors, training for the Around the Rock SUP

Why SUP? Because in this crowded world, five guys on one board on one wave makes economic sense. Photo courtesy Starboard

Why SUP? Ask the steersman in back. Photo courtesy Starboard

Lindsay Lambert throws down a scorpion on Lake Sammamish during the summer of 2014.
Photo courtesy Lindsay Lambert and her cell phone

race event in the fall. Others were just workers and parents wanting to clear their heads. Over the summer I got an eyeful of how many SUP brands are out there, and the bewildering array of boards that are being produced for cruising, wave-riding, racing, tandem—even SUP fishing.

And even SUP yoga. When I was assigned this book, I asked around to people who know, wondering what was new in stand up paddling. The answer I got more than any other was: yoga on stand up paddleboards. In lakes, bays, rivers, swimming pools, and reservoirs around the world, men and women are liberating themselves from the confines of sweaty, stinky yoga studios and taking to the water on stand up paddleboards to try their asana.

That was happening on Lake Sammamish this summer, as a shockingly limber yogini named Lindsay Lambert lead SUP yoga classes in the morning and afternoons. But it wasn't just Lake Sammamish, as SUP yoga appears to have spread around the world, from Malibu to Maui to Monaco to the Maldives.

I was busy at Issaquah Paddle Sports all summer—which is why I didn't write this revision—but during that time I also took three road trips to do signings for a book called *365 Surfboards*: I did a signing at the Coronado Library in Southern California in June, the Patagonia store in New York City and Water Brothers Surf Fest in Newport, Rhode Island, in July—by way of Long Island—and then Waikiki in August.

Three short trips, but guess what I saw everywhere?

Stand up paddlers all over Southern California, from Malibu to Huntington Harbor to Dana Point to Coronado Bay. Cruising, racing, riding waves in harbors, lakes, and out to sea. And doing SUP yoga in quiet harbors and out in the surf.

I'd never been to Long Island, and when I got there in July, I found it was a target-rich environment for stand up paddling: from the calm summer waters of Peconic Bay, to the ferocious tidal race of Shinnecock Inlet, and back to the calm waters of Lake Montauk. Long Island has a zillion nooks and crannies for stand up paddling on both

Why SUP? This is Billy Rossini, founder of Nocqua Adventure Gear, maker of SUP lighting accessories. He is on the Pau Hana Big EZ Angler, which is a SUP made for fishing.
Photo courtesy Pau Hana

sides and through the middle. And in the summer of 2014, there were stand up paddlers all over Long Island.

Clearly, stand up paddling is a big sensation from coast to coast and a lot of places in between.

In August I went to Waikiki, rented a board, and paddled out at Publics—the same place where Greg Brady wiped out in that long-ago episode of *The Brady Bunch*. Although Publics is in Waikiki, it's a little hairier than I thought. Like Greg Brady I wiped out, lost my board, and had to swim over coral heads. Fun.

At Waikiki I got a lot of stinkeye from surfers at Queens as I wobbled around on my rented SUP. It was obvious there was more than a little friction between stand up paddlers and surfers along the reefs and beaches where stand up paddling evolved.

Waikiki put a hook in me, so I went back to Seattle to finish up at Issaquah Paddle Sports and then moved to Hawaii, mostly to escape those dreary Seattle winters, but also to do further exploring along the Oahu coast—and maybe start writing the revision to this book.

I now work in the warehouse at Surftech, a company that made the first production stand up paddleboards back in the early twentieth century and now makes a wide variety of high-tech SUPs for cruising, racing, wave-riding, even yoga.

I have been in Hawaii for two months now, working in the warehouse at Surftech, living on a sailboat in Kewalo Basin, and enjoying the perfect weather and warm water of Hawaii.

At Surftech I am getting an up-close and personal look at the state of the art in stand up paddleboard design, and at who are using what boards. The beach services and resorts like Disney's Aulani love the Surftech Universals and Softops, because those boards can take a beating from weather and *malahini* and keep on ticking.

And on the other end, I have had to unload shipping containers loaded with Surftech Dominators, Downwinders, D2s, and other high-end racing boards as big as 14 feet that fly out of the warehouse, bought by men and women training for the Molokai-2-Oahu Paddleboard World Championship, the Catalina Classic, the Battle of the Paddle, and other long and short races in Hawaii and around the world.

Along with SUP yoga, SUP racing is a facet of the sport that has skyrocketed in popularity in the last couple of years. And so that too will be detailed in this book.

In the morning and evening I paddle from Kewalo Basin to Ala Moana Park to clear my head, and on weekends I go all the way to Waikiki by way of Ala Moana, the Ala Wai Canal, and Ala Moana Bowls and spend the day riding waves, soaking up the sun, getting exercise, feeling better.

Waikiki is the spiritual and physical home of stand up paddling, and so it's perfect that I will be paddling there every day as I write this revision to *The Art of Stand Up Paddling*. In fact, I just got out of the water at Ala Moana and that left me clear-headed enough to get started and write this introduction.

I saw and did a lot in the last six months: I helped Dashama write a press release for her new SUP yoga inflatable from Starboard. In August a giant swell hit Southern California. The waves at Malibu were scarcely to be credited, and it was cool to see Laird Hamilton catch a bomb and ride it through the pier, almost twelve years after he first paddled out there on that 12' × 24" tandem board with the American flag attached to his paddle handle.

Laird Hamilton uses his paddle and fancy footwork to spin a helicopter on his SUP in the surf at a private surf break. Mike Nixon

If this intro reads a bit jumbled, it's because I've seen a lot in the last six months and talked to a lot of people, and now it's time to quit lollygagging and making excuses and get to folding all of that into a revision of *The Art of Stand Up Paddling*. In the following pages—laid over the exceptional original—you will read updated chapters about history, equipment, and instruction, and fresh chapters on SUP yoga, SUP racing, and anything new about SUP that has emerged in the past three years.

Sorry it took so long, but I was busy out having fun on my SUP.

Ben Marcus

The Surftech offices at Queen and Ward

December 20, 2014

The author paddling around Pillar Point Harbor, toward Pillar Point and the Air Force station that overlooks the surf spot Mavericks.
Marc "Dad" Marcus

A tupista *at Huanchaco, Peru, dropping into a wave on a reed boat the residents of northern Peru called a* tup *and the Spanish conquistadores renamed* caballito de totora. *This modern man standing up and paddling into a wave on a reed boat is practicing something that goes back at least 5,000 years.*
International Surfing Association (ISA)

CHAPTER 1

THE (CONTROVERSIAL, UPDATED) HISTORY OF
STAND UP PADDLING

1777: The Most Supreme Pleasure

In 1777 Captain James Cook was on the island of Tahiti in the Polynesian archipelago he dubbed "the Society Islands" when he made the first comment on Polynesian wave riding by a European person—which is still one of the best comments on wave riding by any person (and is attributed by some to William Anderson, the ship's surgeon on Cook's *Resolution*):

I could not help conclude that this man felt the most supreme pleasure while he was driven on, so fast and so smoothly, by the sea. . . .

Well said, Cap'n (or Surg'n). Was that Tahitian man standing up in his canoe and stroking into waves using a paddle? Maybe yes, maybe no. Whether it was Captain Cook or Surgeon Anderson who recorded this incident, they wrote "sat motionless," so it's probably no, he wasn't standing.

The form and function of standing up and propelling a small watercraft with an oar, paddle, or pole are being proven with plastics and carbon fiber here in the twenty-first century, but these sensations are not new. Stand up paddling is called "beach boy surfing" by some, as it has roots that go back to the Waikiki beach boys some time in the early or mid-1900s. What the Hawaiian beach boys innovated on large surfboards as a way to watch over tourists and photograph them—and keep their hair and cigarettes dry—is a small craft technique that goes way back: to the gondoliers of Venice, to the hasake riders of Israel and Arabia in the eighth century AD, to the paddlers of the *caballito de totora* of 3000 BC, and maybe all the way back to the beginning of humans making small boats.

3000 BC: Caballitos de Totora

Along the coast of Peru, and especially at a beach called Huanchaco, modern-day Peruvians and adventurous travelers practice a form of stand up paddle surfing (SPS)—that dates back as far as 5,000 years. At Huanchaco local residents use paddles to propel reed boats in and out of the surfline. The Peruvians typically paddle on their knees or in a sitting position and do not stand until they are riding a wave. Children will often stand, but the *caballito*'s stability will not allow comfortable standing until it picks up speed.

According to Peruvian surfing champion Felipe Pomar, the northern Peruvian name for the reed boat was *tup*.

Odd that the local name going back thousands of years is one letter away from SUP, but the craft were rebranded when Europeans arrived

in northern Peru, according to Pomar: "When the Spanish *conquistadores* arrived and saw the fishermen riding on the waves, they called it *caballito de totora* (little reed horse) because they were used to riding on horses."

The *tup* was designed to ride waves and used for fishing and for sport. Different designs and sizes were used according to the size of the waves. On bigger days riders took smaller *tups* and paddled with their arms. On smaller days they used the bigger *tups* and paddled with a paddle.

Ancient Peruvians riding waves standing up or sitting down or kneeling or whatever are problematic to surf historians, as claims by the *caballistos* that surfing began in Peru in 3000 BC

Still in Peru but 5,000 years later, a modern stand up paddler takes the drop at Chicama, considered the longest left point in the world and a surf spot on the SUP-it list of many.
Photo Margareta Engstrom

are troublesome to the vast majority of surfers, who prefer to think of their family tree planted in soil on the shores of Polynesia and the Hawaiian Islands: "Good luck selling the idea that anchovy-trolling Peruvians were the first wave-riders," Matt Warshaw wrote in his *History of Surfing*. "Surfers choose their collective past and when it comes down to Hawaii or Peru, the tropics or the desert, the sport of kings or the sport of fishermen—well, that's hardly a choice at all."

(above) A modern tup / caballito de totora wows a mob of Peruvians with flashes from their ancestry during the Billabong World Surfing Games at Punta Hermosa, Peru, in October 2010. International Surfing Association (ISA)

Joel Smith with a quiver of caballitos de totora at Huanchaco, Peru. An average caballito is 12' × 2' and weighs 90 pounds—which makes them 1 inch shorter, 7 inches narrower, and 60 pounds heavier than the Surftech / Ron House Laird Hamilton Tuflite model, which is 12'1" × 31" and 30.5 pounds. Photo courtesy of Joel T. Smith

Eighth Century AD: The *Hasake*

Fast-forward halfway around the world and 3,000+ years from 3000 BC Peru to the Mediterranean coast around the eighth century AD: "Here's the *hasake*," Arthur G. Klein wrote in his 1965 book *Surfing.*

A rather distant cousin of the [Australian surf] ski, the hasake *or* hasaki *is found off beaches of Israel at the eastern end of the Mediterranean, which the Romans once called, with a justified smugness,* Mare Nostrum *[our sea].* Hasake, *which comes from the Arabic, is pronounced something like "khasakay"; the first sound is a guttural, throat-clearing one.*

This craft, suited to gentler surfs, is used more for pleasant paddles through and beyond the surf than for actual surf riding toward shore. A full-sized hasake, *such as the author has often watched meandering among the swells, may be 12 to 13 feet long and 3½ to 4 feet wide at the center and weigh 130 to 155 pounds. In construction it resembles a small sailboat hull or a large, hollow surfboard.*

Riders stand erect, wielding paddles of great length—as long as 10 feet—with rather small paddling surfaces at either end. A solo rider usually stands aft of the center. Two paddlers stand so as to maintain trim and keep out of each other's way.

The *hasake* as described here is about the same length as a stand up paddleboard, but much wider at 42" to 48", and also much heavier. At 130 to 155 pounds, the *hasake* is closer to a boat than a stand up paddleboard, and the width suggests a very stable platform: for transporting goods, rescuing, and fishing. What the ancient riders of the *hasake* understood is the same thing modern-day stand up paddleboarders are learning—there is a world of difference between sitting astride a board or in a boat and standing tall on your own two feet. The difference in elevation is only a couple of feet, but the difference in what you can see is everything.

WITCH SUP

According to historian Sandra Kimberely Hall, during the English civil war of 1643, a woman was seen doing something similar to stand up paddling across the River Newbury. The troops of the army of Essex were confounded when they saw her riding: "a plank overshadowed with a little shallow water."

The woman was a witch, obviously, and in the 1600s witches were still fair game in the UK and not protected as they are now: "She's a witch, shoot her!" But the soldiers were further confounded when they fired their rifles to no effect: "But with a deriding and loud laughter at them she caught their bullets in her hands and chew'd them."

Laughing at soldiers and chewing their precious, hand-poured bullets is a bad idea at any time, but especially during a time of civil war, which can be fatally uncivil.

As the woman approached shore, one soldier gamely dispatched her with a handgun: ". . . discharge[s] a pistoll beneath her eare, at which she straight sunk down and dyed, leaving her carcass to the worms. . . ."

That would not be the last act of incivility shown to a stand up paddler.

Twelfth Century AD: One-Legged Paddlers of Inle Lake, Burma

Inle Lake is a shallow lake in the Shan Hills of Myanmar, the military dictatorship formerly known as Burma. The depth of the lake is between 7 and 12 feet in the dry season, and it is home to a culture of fishermen who propel their canoes standing up, with one leg wrapped around their paddle.

The practice dates to the twelfth century, according to Debbie Jefkin-Elnekave, who wrote about these fishermen in *Inle Lake: A Magical World Afloat*:

If there is one aspect of Inle Lake that fully captures its spirit, it is the legendary fishermen. They are best known for their standing, one-legged rowing technique. The origin of the technique is uncertain, but it

A fisherman on Inle Lake, Myanmar (Burma), paddles his small boat with one leg wrapped around a paddle, as his ancestors did 900 years ago. Shutterstock

is believed that the practice began in the 12th century to enable the fishermen to navigate their flat-bottom wooden boats above the floating gardens.

. . . Now just past dawn, it is time for the fishermen to leave the cold solitude of the lake and return to their villages with last night's catch. With one leg firmly planted on the stern and the other leg extended to power the oar, they make their way toward the lacy network of canals that will lead them home. They row with such mesmerizing grace that they appear to dance to a timeless tune.

1866: Mark Twain Goes Hawaiian—and Venetian

Mark Twain was something of a waterman himself. His real name was Samuel Clemens, but his nom de plume came from his work as a river pilot on the Mississippi River from 1859 to 1861. By 1863 Clemens was working as a newspaperman in Virginia City, Nevada, when he used his handle for the first time: "Mark Twain" was an expression he brought west from his days working on the Mississippi, because those are the two words the leadsman would call when his leadline showed they were moving over 2 fathoms (12 feet) of water.

In 1866 the *Sacramento Daily Union* sent Twain to the Sandwich Islands (later called the Hawaiian Islands), where Twain wrote one of the earliest descriptions of the wave-riding sport the residents of this northern Polynesian franchise called *he'e nalu*:

In one place we came upon a large company of naked natives, of both sexes and all ages, amusing themselves with the national pastime of surf-bathing. Each heathen would paddle [by hand] three or four hundred yards out to sea (taking a short board with him), then face the shore and wait for a particularly prodigious billow to come along; at the right moment he would fling his board upon its foamy crest and himself upon the board, and here he would come whizzing by like a bombshell! It did not seem that a lightning express-train could shoot along at a more hair-lifting speed.

Round round get around, Mark Twain got around. After his three-week trip to the Sandwich Islands, Twain went the other way, from the sport of Kings to the Queen of the Adriatic. Venice, Italy, is a city built on and around the water, and a Mississippi kid like Twain most likely felt a kinship with people who lived on the water and got around in boats large and small.

At first, Twain was disappointed by the gondoliers of Venice, whose tradition could date back before the establishment of the Church of San Jacopo in AD 421, when the Romans identified the *incolae lacunae*—lagoon-dwelling fishermen populating the marshy islands that would become the city of Venice. Twain wasn't digging the romance, as he wrote in chapter 22 of *The Innocents Abroad* (1869):

We reached Venice at eight in the evening, and entered a hearse belonging to the Grand Hotel d'Europe. At any rate, it was more like a hearse than anything else, though to speak by the card, it was a gondola. This the famed gondola and this the gorgeous gondolier! The one an inky, rusty old canoe with a sable hearse-body clapped on to the middle of it, and the other a mangy, barefooted guttersnipe with a portion of his raiment on exhibition which should have been sacred from public scrutiny.

Twain sounds as if he is describing the 1860 version of a hip-hop kid walking around with his pants falling down and his underwear showing. But he spoke too soon—maybe it was ship lag or culture shock—and he soon got swept away by the romance of Venice, and the men who paddled their boats around, standing tall:

But I was too hasty. . . . The gondolier is a picturesque rascal for all he wears no satin harness, no plumed bonnet, no silken tights. His attitude is stately; he is lithe and supple; all his movements are full of grace. When his long canoe, and his fine figure, towering from its high perch on the stern, are cut against the evening sky, they make a picture that is very novel and striking to a foreign eye.

Had Mark Twain seen a parallel between the stand up gondoliers of Venice and anything he had seen the "heathens" doing over the reefs of Waikiki that same year, that comparison would have provided a missing link in the evolution of stand up

(above) A modern-day gondolier works the waters of Venice.
Lucia Griggi

(left) A stand up paddler, or supoliere, cruises the byways of Venice, going places the gondoliers can't go.
Photo courtesy of Starboard

paddling: proof that Hawaiians were doing it as far back as the 1860s.

But Twain didn't find a parallel between the gondoliers of Venice and the *hui o he'e nalu* wave riders of the Sandwich Islands, because in the 1860s the gondoliers had been there for centuries, while the Waikiki beach boys were still about fifty years away. When Twain traveled to the middle of the Pacific in the 1860s, a trip to the Sandwich Islands was like a trip to the moon. Only people with time and money on their hands—and a sense of adventure that disregarded danger and discomfort—traveled to that part of Polynesia. And it wasn't until the turn of the twentieth century that an increase in tourism to what was now called the Hawaiian Islands inspired the need for the Waikiki beach boys—whom the Romans would have identified as *magnus felix icis brunneo mocae*, or swarthy, brown happy braddahs.

1900: Hawaii and the Waikiki Beach Boys

By 1900 the Sandwich Islands were called the Hawaiian Islands and the centuries-old monarchy had been overthrown by American commercial, military, and spiritual interests. In 1900 Hawaiian exports, mostly sugar, were valued at $20 million. In current dollars, that is more than $500 million worth of sugar in one year. The Hawaiian Islands were a giant ATM in the middle of the Pacific, and Uncle Sam had decided to steal the entire building. Matt Warshaw detailed the demise of the Hawaiians—and of surfing as a part of Hawaiian culture—in his *History of Surfing*:

By any measure, the nineteenth century was a disaster for surfing. By 1890, however, the worst was over. The Hawaiian immune system had toughened up. The missionaries were gone. The sport now entered a second incubation. It lasted just a few years. There were no big changes in technique, or board design, or the number of participants. But the sport and its practitioners looked different somehow—at least to the world at large. Surfing had been described by Reverend Hiram Bingham in 1820 as the pastime of "chattering savages." Now it was about to be reintroduced by swashbuckling writer Jack London as nothing less than "a royal sport for the natural kings of the earth."

The population of the Hawaiian Islands fell from an estimated 400,000 to 800,000 when Captain Cook arrived, to less than 40,000 only 130 years later, and surfing died with the natives.

By the turn of the twentieth century, surfing was practiced in only a few places in Hawaii, with Waikiki being the main spot. And it was at Waikiki in the early 1900s that a different breed of *haole* breathed life into the sport of kings: the Waikiki beach boys.

So, at what point did the beach boys of Waikiki pick up paddles and step onto oversized surfboards and begin to innovate "beach boy–style surfing" with paddles?

To answer that question, it might first make sense to determine when they *weren't* seen doing it.

In 1907 Jack London sailed to Hawaii aboard the *Snark* and updated the surfing experience in a story for *Woman's Home Companion* depicting the "royal sport for the natural kings of earth." London was taken under the wing of George Freeth, a Hawaiian-Irish waterman who was one of the first of the beach boys, a loose affiliation of canoeists, sailors, surfers, swimmers, and ukuleleists who took tourists into the pounding surf, showed them some Hawaiian-style thrills, and made sure they stayed safe.

Jack London wrote about surfing with Alexander Hume Ford and then George Freeth. He had his successes and failures, but nowhere did he describe Ford or Freeth hovering around him, standing on a big board, and propelling it with a paddle.

London's stories of surfing and his other adventures in the Hawaiian Islands were serialized in American magazines and also in his 1911 adventure book *The Cruise of the Snark*. They inspired a great deal of interest in travel to Hawaii, and as hotels filled, the need for the beach boys' services grew.

The Royal Hawaiian was the second major hotel to open in Waikiki, in 1927. By then, the beach boys were well known, and the promoters of

Podoscaphe in France, early 1900s.
Photo courtesy of Patrice Guenole

SUP in France today. Photo courtesy of Starboard

FRANCE CIRCA 1900—PODOSCAPHE

Patrice Guenole is a dedicated stand up paddler who runs Gong SUP in Bastia, on the Mediterranean island of Corsica. Contacted for this book about how SUP made it to the home of Napoleon Bonaparte, Patrice sent an intriguing image of a stand up paddle-board–like device from France: "Look at this sport in the 1900s," Patrice said in an e-mail. "It is called *podoscaphe.* They did it with a double paddle or a single like we do in SUP. Funny, no?"

Funny, *oui. Très amusant* and more proof—going back to the turn of the twentieth century in France—that the more *sportif* were propelling themselves through the rivers, canals, and maybe even on the beaches, standing up with a paddle. These days, the French are getting into stand up paddling along with the rest of the world. The surf photo was taken somewhere along the Basque coast of France, a place famous for its smooth, glassy beach breaks.

Hawaiian tourism used photographs and illustrations of Hawaiians surfing and canoeing, often with screaming tourists on the waves with them.

In Hawaii's Bishop Museum there are hours and hours of moving images of the Waikiki beach scene available for viewing—and also on YouTube. Sit through those hours and hours of moving images from 1906 through the 1930s, and you will see images of Hawaiian beach boys in the water with tourists: paddling and steering canoes, riding tandem with *haole* girls, and teaching honeymooners how to surf.

But in all of those moving images and still photos from 1906 until World War II, there is not one image of a beach boy—or anyone—standing up on a big surfboard and propelling it through the water with a paddle or an oar.

Until you watch *Blue Horizon*, that is.

1939: Blame Australia? Duke Does Stand Up

Blue Horizon is a 2004 surf movie made by Jack McCoy for the Billabong clothing company. In the history section of that movie, there is a vintage black-and-white clip of Duke Kahanamoku doing something that looks a lot like stand up paddling. At first he is seated on the bow of what appears to be a very large surfboard, because there are three other people seated on the board behind him.

Duke clowns for the camera a bit, then stands, holding a two-bladed paddle in his hand. There appears to be a leash from the nose of the board to Duke's waist, or maybe the paddle. He paddles forward as his three passengers balance behind him. Then Duke shows some serious skills paddling a huge board with four people into a wave, and riding the wave until one of the three passengers shifts their weight wrong, and the board wipes out, out of frame.

Duke Kahanamoku with a two-sided paddle in his hand and a leash connected from the paddle to the nose of the surf craft, doing something pretty close to modern-day stand up paddling on an Australian kayak (surf ski), circa 1939.
Image courtesy of Don Love, Malama Pono Ltd.

Is this the missing link showing one of the origins of stand up paddling on a surfboard?

A YouTube clip of Duke doing that went out in an e-mail sent to Hawaiian/Australian filmmaker Jack McCoy, California film historian Scott Starr, Australian journalist Nick Carroll, Australian surf historian Geoff Cater, Australian surf historian and Duke Kahanamoku expert Sandra Kimberely Hall, and Hawaiian Bishop Museum archivist DeSoto Brown.

It returned very fast responses: "Australian Kayak, Not a Surfboard GET IT STRAIGHT!" Jack McCoy stated emphatically in the e-mail subject line:

Yeah mate. . . . I got that clip off of a news reel I bought. . . . It's stretching the truth that it's SUP, the board was an Australian kayak that was taken to HI and obviously got the Duke's attention. I've got photos of Aussie guys standing up on their kayaks too—way before the Duke if you want to open that can of worms.

CROATIA, 1938

Svein Rasmussen is the founder of Starboard, a Norwegian company that morphed from sailboards to become one of the leading innovators and suppliers of stand up paddleboards.

Svein Rasmussen submitted this odd photo and explained that it's not the fjords of his native land but something even stranger: "This is Delnice Creek in Croatia, around 1938. It was January 5, 1938, to be exact."

Curiouser and curiouser. Sven didn't have much of an explanation for why a well-dressed man was stand up paddling in a reservoir surrounded by other well-dressed men, in a Croatian reservoir in 1938—but there it is.

A stand up paddler on Delnice Creek in Croatia, 1938. Photo courtesy of Svein Rasmussen/Starboard

Scott Starr has an enviable collection of vintage surf movies and knows his surf history. He confirmed McCoy's thoughts in an e-mail a few minutes later:

That footage you saw of Duke is from about 1939. I actually have color footage of Duke on a stand up around the same time . . . same board, probably different day . . . he is riding by himself. Oh also these stand ups were big in Australia around the same time. I have footage of guys riding them there in the '30s too. In my head I can see them sitting down riding them. Not sure if the footage actually shows someone standing up after catching a wave . . . but maybe . . . they were, I think, sit down paddle boards but Duke and others would stand up.

And then this e-mail from Nick Carroll, one of the top surf historians Down Under in God's Own Lucky Country:

What you're seeing is an Australian surf ski. This craft was invented by a bloke in Port Macquarie, New South Wales, around 1912, after he'd become intrigued by the idea of riding waves and discovered his uncle's open canoe wasn't too good at it. (In bumpy Australian sandbar waves, canoes fill with water.) The surf ski was a hollow, wood-constructed craft which was paddled with a twin blade paddle from a sitting position, but a lot of ski riders got into standing up on 'em while riding waves. . . . Duke was given one by a touring Aussie surf team in 1939.

Sandra Kimberely Hall is a resident of Hawaii and one of the foremost experts on the life of Duke Kahanamoku. Sandy was kind enough to proof this history and added this:

Nick Carroll is right, except it wasn't a surf team. They were handpicked surf life savers, many of whom Duke knew from his Olympic appearances and his Down Under Tour of 1914–1915. People like Harry Hay, who was the team captain in 1939, and Lou Morath. The team was sponsored by AMPOL (petrol)

and they brought their humungous surfboats and surf skis with them [easier to do when you traveled by ship].

Geoff Cater is another dedicated historian of Australian and all surf history, and he filled in some of the blanks:

When SUP first appeared in the media sometime in the 1990s, one company or commentator suggested that this was the re-introduction of an ancient Hawaiian technique. At the time I viewed this as unsupportable and simply a marketing attempt to give the product some historical credibility.

As for the film of Duke Kahanamoku standing up on a board. Rather than a "giant surfboard," the craft is undoubtedly the Australian surf ski that was sent to him by the Walker brothers from Manly Beach sometime in the 1930s. Judge Adrian Curlewis, a longtime president of the Surf Life Saving Association and Palm Beach boardrider, noted: "The Walker Brothers sent a surf ski to Duke Kahanamoku at Honolulu and members of the Australian Pacific Games team which visited Honolulu in 1939 say Duke was often seen paddling around on his 'ski from Australia."

DeSoto Brown is the collections manager for the Bishop Museum in Hawaii, home to tens of thousands of still images and hundreds of hours of moving images of old Hawaii. Brown has looked at most of it, and he has also written a book about surfing, using the images from the Bishop Museum collection:

The shot of Duke comes from a 1938 Hawaii travelogue produced by Castle Films. He's not identified in the film; it's just a generic surfing shot in which he happens to be on the wave. The board that he/they are on looks odd, as I remember it. I have seen another film showing paddleboarding in the 1930s or '40s, but I can't remember where I saw this, who had it, or anything else about it—which aggravates me. I only recall thinking at the time that this was a significant early view of the sport. And that's all I can remember.

Questions answered, but still questions: Was Duke stand up paddleboarding? Is it possible that SUP/SPS originated with the Waikiki beach boys, inspired by the gift of an Australian surf ski in the 1930s?

Controversial stuff—which could get a careless historian spitted and boiled in the Hawaiian Islands—but important in establishing a link in the evolution, because what the beach boys were doing in Waikiki from the 1950s on was absolutely an ancestor of what Laird Hamilton, Dave Kalama, Brian Keaulana, and Mel Puu were doing in the Hawaiian Islands and California from the 1990s into the twenty-first century.

They were all inspired by Duke. But where did Duke get the idea?

1950 and After: The Two Johns

As stand up paddling morphed from obscure Hawaiian side note to international sensation, SUP historians began looking for the roots of the sport.

A story titled "Upright" by Pohaku Beachboy Paddles and C4 Waterman founder Todd Bradley in a 1996 issue of *The Surfer's Journal* featured one of the earliest images of stand up paddling. Taken in the 1980s by Bobby Ah Choy, a member of one of Waikiki's most respected beach boy families, the photo shows the classic Diamond Head backdrop to surf riders in the foreground, but one of them is a silver-haired man with a supremely pleasurable smile on his face and a paddle in his hand—being driven along smoothly and swiftly by the sea on a large surfboard.

"Upright" begins with Todd Bradley talking with 65-year-old Waikiki beach boy Bobby Ah Choy: "I have asked him if we could talk about the origins of 'beachboy style' or 'stand-up' surfing," Bradley wrote.

As one of the growing number of surfers addicted to this hybrid sport of standing on an oversized surfboard and paddling, catching waves, and surfing with the aid of a lengthened canoe paddle, I wanted to hear something about its past from one of its originators. Many surfers mistakenly think stand-up surfing is a new sport, yet, like so many other water activities in Hawaii, there is concealed behind the new-fangled super-light boards, featherweight paddles, and snappy maneuvers a tradition that goes back a hundred years or more.

Bradley's personal experience witnessing beach boy surfing went back to the 1970s, when he was growing up on the beaches of Waikiki:

I remember Bobby, along with his brother, Leroy, and father, John, stand up paddling around Canoes with a pack of cigarettes wrapped in his sleeve and a Nikonos dangling from his neck, barking lessons at the tourists and taking photos of them as they stink-bugged past him. Sometimes, if he was tired or had had a festive night, he would set a stool atop his board and use his long canoe paddle to scoot around the lineup.

In the story, Bobby Ah Choy admitted that it was laziness and bad habits as much as anything else that inspired him and some of the beach boys to start stand up paddling, ". . . it enabled them to remain high and dry while taking snapshots of tourists—and also kept their cigarettes dry."

1950 and After: Jzap Takes the Baton from Duke

On April 29, 2010, the *Honolulu Advertiser* ran a story called "A Stand-up Guy," written by Paula Rath. The subtitle explained the story: "John Zapotocky, 91, recently got back on a paddleboard at Sand Island, after a four-year hiatus. His stand-up paddling was a familiar sight in Waikīkī for decades."

According to the article, Zapotocky had found his late 80s to be a little disabling, and after forty years of daily water time going back to the 1940s, two knee replacements kept him out of the water for four years, as he turned into his 90s.

Zapotocky was one of the earliest proponents of stand up paddling, so it was a big deal celebrated by many around Waikiki when "Zap" got back on his board at the age of 91 and paddled standing up once again.

One Waikiki regular quoted by the *Advertiser* was Glen Shea, 66, of Manoa, who called Zapotocky a pioneer of the sport. "Only two guys used to stand-up paddle: John and Pops Ah Choy," Shea said. "He used to be out there all by himself. He's been amazing. He always joked that he did stand-up because he didn't want to get his hair wet. He was out there almost every day. He would even carry his own board until fairly recently."

That observation was supported by no less a Hawaiian surf legend and stand up paddleboard advocate as Gerry Lopez, who "remembers seeing Zapotocky stand-up paddling in Waikīkī in the '60s, when Lopez was in high school," the *Advertiser* story claimed and quoted Lopez: "He's been doing it for, like, 70 years. He's a sweet, sweet person."

Zapotocky owes his longevity to a mostly vegetarian diet and a lot of exercise: "Movement is living and exercise is medicine," was Zapotocky's pull quote in the *Advertiser*. He went and proved that by paddling out sitting on his board, then standing, then paddling around in the ocean in his 90s, an age when most humans are long gone or bedridden.

Looking on the Internet, I found that the *Hawaiian Surf Series* local TV show did a feature on Zapotocky, and his narration from that show, printed word for word, fills in a big part of the puzzle:

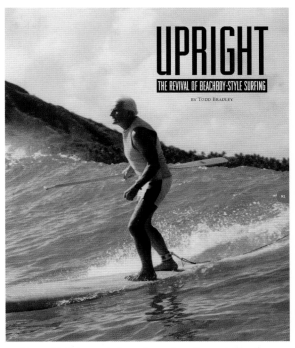

Todd Bradley's "Upright" article, with a photo of John Zapotocky taken by Bobby Ah Choy in the 1980s. Zapotocky and the Ah Choys are the missing links between Duke Kahanamoku and the modern sport of stand up paddleboarding
Spread courtesy of The Surfer's Journal
Photo courtesy of the Ah Choy family

Well, I was out there surfing one day and . . . and I see this gentleman coming in on a wave with a paddle. I says, "My God, that's something I should be doing!" So I asked some people:

"Well, that's Duke Kahanamoku!"

I said, "Well, who's he?" You know, I'm here from Pennsylvania, I never heard of him.

They said, "He's a world famous surfer and a swimmer and a Olympic star."

So I went and talked to Duke, and he said, "Well, get yourself a paddle and do it." I did that, and I've been doing it ever since. I've been surfing out here for

65 years and for 55 years I've been using the paddle. It changed my whole life. I've been stand up paddling ever since. They thought I was an oddball out there: "What is this guy doing out there with the paddle?"

I'd get in the way of the canoes and I got balled out a number of times. "Hey! Get that . . . board out of here!"

I remember all the Kahanamoku brothers. The old Outrigger Canoe Club. I joined the Outrigger Canoe Club—and at that time it was a fee of $50 to join and the dues were six dollars a month. The Outrigger Canoe Club—right next to the Royal Hawaiian.

SUP IN CHINA

Nicola Zanella is the editor of Italy's *Surf News*. He surfs the Mediterranean and Adriatic, but like that Marco Polo guy before him, Zanella has a fascination with China:

"You may know I speak Mandarin, lived in China and did some research about pre-contact surfing in China," Zanella said in an e-mail. "Found out interesting things, like surfing Buddha sculptures dating 1873 and tidal bore-riding deities venerated during the Song dynasty (960–1279). Stand up paddling is rooted in Chinese culture way deeper than wave riding." While traveling in China with photographer John Callahan, he found traces of stand up paddling along the Yulong and Lijiang Rivers in Guangxi Province, where they stand up and paddle for fishing, traveling, and all sorts of activities.

Once I started stand up padding, I didn't go back the other way. I used to surf out there with Bobby Ah Choy, and there was just two of us at the time, as I remember. But we did it every day because he was giving lessons. His dad, John Ah Choy? He used an oar. They both used oars and not canoe paddles.

I was using canoe paddles made in Mississippi— made out of ash. I brought it with me. Feather brand. Caviness Woodworking Company Incorporated. Calhoun City, Mississippi.

They didn't know I used it for surfing, and I used to order them by the dozen. Because the canoe paddle is made, you know, to sit down. You grab it down at the blade. Well, I was using it standing up, so I kept breaking them.

It took many years before stand up paddling came into play. I guess I did it for 20 years—or more— before it really came to play. Right now it's like a snowball. It's the finest exercise move. You can sit down, lay down. It's revolutionizing a way of life. You can take this paddle and you can exercise with it. You can twist and you can turn. You can go up and you can go down. You can go forward, you can go back. You don't need any barbells. Now people say, 'It's flat, there's no waves.' But with a stand up paddleboard you can go out and have a paddle. You can paddle down the Ala Wai. It's a source of exercise, people might not realize how valuable it is.

It's just unreal. They're having problems at Ala Moana, they're having traffic problems with stand up paddles. I think it's just wonderful. I think it's going to be all over the world—at hotels, lagoons—any place there's water, there's a place for stand up paddling. And I suggest you guys try it.

Zapotocky was 91 years old in 2010 when he made that exuberant prophecy. Counting backwards from 2010 minus 65, that means he started surfing in Hawaii in 1945 and started paddle surfing in 1955. If Duke started goofing around on that Australian kayak in 1939, that means he had sixteen years to discover that using a single-bladed paddle to catch waves on a normal surfboard was one way to go.

And because Duke's heart soared with the aloha of all the Hawaiian people, he passed on this paddle surfing standing up deal to the *haole* guy from Pennsylvania.

In the March 2011 issue of *Standup Journal,* Gerry Lopez added an epilogue to the "Jzap" story in a two-page story called *"Homage to the Grand Master of Our Sport. John Zapotocky. The Original Legend of Stand up Paddling."*

According to Lopez, Zapotocky stayed in Hawaii after the war and went to work for Dole as a mechanic in their state-of-the-art pineapple-processing plants. Sixty years later, Lopez was at a SUP contest called the Rainbow Sandals Battle of the Paddle at Doheny Beach, near Dana Point, California.

At the Battle of the Paddle event, 80-something Dr. Dorian Paskowitz (1921–2014) remembered spending time in Hawaii in the 1940s and '50s, and that John Zapotocky was the first person he saw regularly stand up paddling. That was confirmed by George Downing, one of the greatest Hawaiian surfers and shapers of the 1950s and 1960s, who also remembered Zapotocky standing up while paddling a surfboard around Waikiki: "[John's] engineering skills led him to design a special stand up board that he commissioned George Downing to build for him," Lopez wrote in *Standup Journal.* "As far as I know, that seems to be the first SUP board ever made. John told me that he still has the design plans for that board stashed away somewhere and would look for them."

Gerry Lopez and George Downing might as well be the burning bush(es), as far as Hawaiian surfing is concerned. If they claim it was some

haole guy with a funny name who took the baton from Duke in the first half of the twentieth century and paddled a lonely path with the Ah Choy family into the second half of the twentieth century, well, that is almost impossible to argue, as little to nothing that has happened on either side of Oahu has escaped the attention of Downing or Lopez in the past fifty years.

So Zapotocky (aka Jzap) is one of the missing links from Hawaii in the first half of the 1900s to Hawaii in the second half. Jzap learned from Duke Kahanamoku, and Duke may or may not have picked up stand up paddling from the Australians in the 1930s.

Chris Power is the editor of the UK's Carve Surfing *magazine. He sent this photo and explained: "The earliest Brit SUP'er was this guy, Charlie Force, who built a home-made hollow wooden surfboard in 1953 and paddled/surfed it in Newquay Bay. Charlie would sit down and use his paddle to get out the back, then ride the waves standing up. He's still alive, 80-something."*
Photo courtesy of Charlie Force/Orca Publications

1950 AND AFTER: SUP OHANA
The Ah Choy Account of Stand Up Paddling Evolution

According to the website for the John "Pops" Ah Choy Foundation, the patriarch of the Ah Choy family was born in 1920, the third eldest of thirteen children on the Big Island of Hawaii. He left school at twelve years old to work in the sugarcane fields. He married at eighteen and had three children: Suzanne Young, Bobby Ah Choy, and Leroy Ah Choy. The Ah Choy family moved to Oahu in 1943, where Pops found work at Pearl Harbor, then Hawaiian Electric, where he would work for thirty-seven years.

Another branch of the Ah Choy family was started when Pops married a second time and had three sons: Ricky, David, and Michael. The Ah Choy *ohana* lived at Waikiki, 2 blocks from Kuhio Beach, and Waikiki became a centerpoint for the play and work of many of the Ah Choys.

Pops began surfing during the war, in 1944, at Queens and Canoes. All of his children were in the ocean almost every day, but Bobby and Leroy became two of the most famous beach boys: surfing and canoeing, competing in the Molokai Canoe Races in the 1950s and 1960s, and making a living introducing endless swarms of tourists to the secrets of the sea.

Pops was *akamai* as the Hawaiians say—a clever man who let necessity mother inventions such as a surfboard trailer that could carry eight boards, early surfboard leashes, early skateboards, and a chair with suction cups for fishing from a surfboard. And all this invention and time in the water led to a branch of stand up paddling.

According to the John "Pops" Ah Choy Foundation website (http://johnpopsahchoy.webs.com/):

Later, Leroy and Bobby used this technique in their photo business of taking pictures of tourists surfing at Waikiki. Eventually Pops decided to use a canoe paddle, knee pads, and a Hawaiian Electric hard hat when surfing. He would keep his cigarettes in the hat so they wouldn't get wet, and would also smoke a cigarette or two between sets. When his knees began to bother him as he got older, instead of kneeling on the board he decided to stand up and paddle while surfing. That was in the late 1960s, which is how stand up [paddle] surfing began. Later my brothers, Leroy and Bobby, adopted the idea and used it once again for picture taking of tourists at Waikiki.

Mike Waltze is a Maui-based waterman who was one of the pioneers of sailboarding in the surf, a founder of Namotu Island in Fiji and now a convert to SUP. As this book was being written, Waltze was finishing a documentary on stand up paddling, *That First Glide*, that focuses on the contemporary state of the sport but also looks back at the origins.

Waltze said this:

That First Glide *touches on all the aspects of the sport, including wave riding, recreational paddling, and racing like Gerry Lopez's event, The Battle of the Paddle. The film also touches on the origins of the sport, mainly its ties to both outrigger paddling and surfing, both of which were brought to Hawaii from southern Polynesia many centuries ago by the Tahitians and made popular by the Hawaiians' resurgence of both sports since the early 1900s.*

In interviews with Brian Keaulana and Guy Pere, I learned about the Ah Choy family, (Pops, Leroy, and Bobby) who were known to do stand up [paddling] in Waikiki [during] the 1960s.

Pops Ah Choy died in 2014 at the age of 94. Leroy Ah Choy died in 1995 and Bobby Ah Choy passed away in May of 2007 at the age of 66. Michael Ah Choy is now 52 and serves as the director of the John "Pops" Ah Choy Foundation and also is contest director for the John "Pops" Ah Choy Surf Fest, which will celebrate its sixth event in 2015.

Michael speaks for the Ah Choy family and has problems with the way stand up paddleboarding history has been laid down: "What I have a problem with is the timeframe of some of the things that have been said about stand up paddling," Ah Choy said in a telephone interview in June 2011. "[I hear] these guys who say they saw John Zapotocky paddling a board standing up around Waikiki in the 1950s and the 1960s and the 1970s. Well I grew up on the beach at Waikiki and I talked to guys who have been down there since the 1950s. And none of them saw that. Now Gerry Lopez says Zapotocky was doing it at Tongs, which isn't Waikiki but around the corner at Diamond Head. Okay. But you go down to Waikiki and talk to Didi Robello and them and ask who was doing it, and they'll tell you."

The Waikiki beach boys were experts in all the ocean skills: swimming, lifesaving, surfing, tandem surfing, and paddling canoes. Many of them confirm what Michael Ah Choy says about his father stand up paddling in the late 1960s: "My dad first started paddling on his

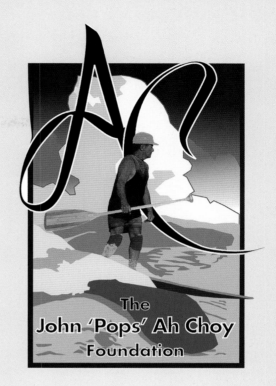

The John 'Pops' Ah Choy Foundation

knees with an inflated raft paddle, and then his knees started bothering him so he started using a canoe paddle that Leroy had given him and started paddling standing up. In 1993 or 1994, he started to use an oar because the reach was longer. I give him credit because that paddle was heavy and he would stay out a couple of hours—take his time coming around."

The Ah Choy legacy of stand up paddling, competition, and doing things differently is now celebrated every year at the "Pops" Ah Choy Surf Fest. The Ah Choy legacy is alive and well, and Michael just wants to be sure the historical record is straight as to the origins of stand up paddling: "To me there is no controversy, but I worry about someone in Ireland reading about stand up paddlesurfing, and if it's not the truth it's not the truth. The stories I am hearing these days are evolving and that's okay. Stories evolve, but the truth doesn't."

THE HAWAIIAN BATTLE OF THE PADDLE POSTER

This poster art for the Battle of the Paddle shows Duke Kahanamoku standing with a traditional hardwood plank surfboard and what appears to be a traditional outrigger paddle. The scene looks like Waikki in the early twentieth century, and if it was taken from a photograph, that throws off the "Australian surf ski in the 1930s" theory. When asked if it came from a photograph that would prove Duke was doing stand up on traditional Hawaiian equipment, the artist who created the illustration, Michael Cassidy, said it was a combination of histories, and he has his own ideas on the origin of stand up paddling:

The image is something I put together out of bits and pieces of things—not a real photograph. I used Duke's steering paddle just for the visual impact of it although he may have used a different paddle to SUP. As far as I know the earliest account of SUP is John Zapotocky's seeing Duke doing it. Would check with [longtime Hawaiian surfing pioneer] George Downing as to what he remembers. Gerry told me that George was under the impression that Zap was the originator until Zap said he saw Duke doing it which is what inspired the image we used for the poster.

It's a good thing to tread lightly when dealing with Hawaiian history. There might have been a direct influence from the surf ski . . . or maybe not. I would think Duke would have adopted a good idea wherever it came from.

A poster for the June 2010 Hawaiian Battle of the Paddle. Poster courtesy of Michael Cassidy, Pat Huber, and Rainbow Sandals

Making that conclusion without direct confirmation from the guys who were there is what might cause some criticism. . . . We just don't know for sure. A little mystery never hurts a good story. No one knows for sure except Duke anyway. . . .

Those beach boys did all kinds of things on surfboards: played polo on them, sailed 'em, fished, you name it. What can tweak some people in Hawaii is historians (or anyone for that matter) coming off like they know everything (whether or not it's correct). Humility goes a long way. . . .

Looking back is a little murky, but looking forward, what are the missing links from Duke to Zapotocky and the Ah Choys to Laird Hamilton and Dave Kalama and dem?

1960s to 1990s: Small Signs of SUP

From the Ah Choy family and Zapotocky at Waikiki in the 1960s to Laird Hamilton and Dave Kalama at Malibu and Maui in the 1990s and Brian Keaulana and the Makaha crowd circa 2003, there is a gap of more than forty years when stand up paddling was at best an obscure sport, practiced by Jzap and the Ah Choy family and not too many others.

What was happening with stand up paddling in the 1960s, 1970s and, 1980s? Anything? There are a few clues.

In the 1980s Malibu surfers Ray Kleiman and Morgan Runyon made a series of anarchic surf movies under the *Runman* title. These movies included surfing shot around Malibu but also on an Outer Hawaiian Island That Shall Remain Nameless.

In *Runman '69* there is a shot of a man standing up and paddling a big board down a narrow river to the ocean. This person's name is "Ambrose," according to Ray Kleiman, a former Malibu resident who grew up surfing Privates in Malibu (see below) but has lived on the Outer Hawaiian Island That Shall Remain Nameless for many years. Ray sent an e-mail for this Ambrose person, but it turned out his first name was Ambrose, and his last name was Curry.

Ambrose Curry's response was interesting:

Nice to hear from the mainstream. Haven't seen those photos in a while. I would be more likely to give you an accurate date after determining what board I was riding at the time Ray filmed.

I was paddling down the tidal estuary in Waipouli called Uhelekawawa [on the east side of that island].

. . . . _____'s rant should give you some idea of how pointless the search for the origins of stand up is. There is no history yet—it's all too new. We're too busy making history to recount it yet.

—*Sam George, in an e-mail on the origins of SUP, January 12, 2011*

This is adjacent to my house and enters the Waipouli Lagoon at the Bullshed Restaurant.

The first paddles I made were for surfboard paddling an 11'3" after becoming acquainted with "Pops" Ah Choy and his Waikiki niche. This was spring of 1976.

The first standing paddle board was finished in January 1977.

The second standing paddleboard was made in 1981 and was adapted to early, wood-boom sailboarding.

I have some photos of surfing small H____ alone in the late 70s. "Alone" is the key word as I refused to stay out in crowded conditions and vowed to not go out when the number out went past three. My greatest concern was the apparent inevitable conflict twixt what Thoreau called "the gross feeders in their larval state of consciousness."

In the Runman *movie, the following part of the sequence I have thrown the paddle over an oncoming closeout and caught the ensuing reform that goes and goes and goes and goes.*

The Waipouli area is old surfing and canoe-building grounds that dates back centuries to approximately 800 AD.

The contemporary surfing ethic has been overlooking this area for some time. The premier neighborhood

gets good seldom, and there is a strong outbound current.

The fall 2010 issue of *Standup Journal* has a photo of a sailboarder who got stuck in a no-wind situation and rode his board into the beach standing up, using his mast as a sort of paddle. The photo was taken at Clearwater Beach, Florida, in 1979, and the caption explains that there was no wind for the Windsurfer World Championships and competitors stuck a half-mile offshore had to get back as best they could.

So that was a fluky 1979 version of stand up paddling—a slippery sailboard covered in booms and sails paddled into a wave using a pole—but that same fall 2010 issue of *Standup Journal* named Laird Hamilton as Man of the Sport and laid down a foundation for Laird as the modern pioneer of stand up paddling and stand up paddle surfing.

1995: Laird and Dave and Dem: Modern SUP Emerges

Mike Waltze's narration for *That First Glide* does a good job of explaining how the stand up era of "the two Johns"—Zapotocky and Ah Choy—faded away, and then how SUP rose again on another Hawaiian island:

John Zapotocky and Pops Ahchoy were both humbly accepting the fact that their surfing days were behind them. Standup was soon to be left behind as a memory. You have to wonder why this style of surfing

Laird Hamilton and Dave Kalama (aka Too Short Crew) goofing around at Mudflats, near Maalaea on Maui, circa 1995. This sequence is considered to be close to ground zero for the new era of stand up paddleboarding. Look close, and you'll see they are using too-short outrigger canoe paddles. Soon after this, they weren't goofing around and got serious about paddles, boards, technique, and much bigger waves. Sequence: Sylvain Cazenave. Scanned page courtesy of *The Surfer's Journal*

and paddling, though viewed by thousands of people over decades, on one of the most popular surfing beaches in the world, never caught on. But the truth is, it never did.

By the late 1990s, the sport was nearly obsolete. It appeared that standup paddling would be gone forever from the only place it ever existed, in Waikiki.

But during the same time, by sheer coincidence, something happened on the island of Maui.

Shortboard windsurfing, tow in surfing, kite boarding and using footstraps and tiny boards on giant waves were all conceived on Maui's North Shore. For the past 30 years this island has been churning out some of the world's top ocean athletes, who are always pushing the limits on what type of craft can be ridden in adverse conditions.

Laird pioneered using a jet ski to catch large waves, and as you can see, his approach to big-wave riding on a tiny board is less conventional than the way most people approach riding large waves.

Dave Kalama is another extreme athlete on Maui who excels at anything in the water. One thing Laird had in common, was to ride big, 12-foot tandem boards on small waves in the summer as training for surfing giant waves in the winter.

A pull quote on a photo in the fall 2010 issue of *Standup Journal* shows Laird stand up paddling a river with his daughter Brody: "The tree of stand up paddling has many branches today and Laird is at the tree's trunk."

The story was written by Steve Sjuggerud, and he begins by listing all of the innovations and accomplishments Laird had racked up on his stand up paddleboard, while most of the rest of the surfing, kayaking, and paddling world were scratching their heads and thinking: "What in the world is that guy doing?"

In 2003 Laird stand up paddled into big waves at Jaws, a surf spot on Maui also known as Peahi.

In June 2006 Laird pedaled and paddled from London to Paris, riding his bike 148 kilometers in the rain from London to Dover in five and a half hours, then stand up paddled 48 kilometers (about 30 miles) from Dover to Le Touquet in six hours, then biked another 235 kilometers (146 miles) from Le Touquet to Paris in eight and a half hours.

In October 2006 Laird was joined by Don Wildman, Dave Kalama, and other friends from the "Malibu Mob" and the "Maui Mob" to pedal and paddle the Hawaiian Islands. Beginning at the bottom of the Big Island, Laird and friends rode their bikes across the Big Island, then Maui, then Molokai, Oahu, and Kauai, and also made hard, harrowing, windy, stormy stand up paddle passages across the different channels separating the islands.

Laird has appeared in dozens of surfing, sailboarding, and SUP movies, going back to the 1980s. He had a featured role in the big wave surfing documentary *Riding Giants* and is also featured in the recent best-selling book *The Wave* by Susan Casey. He is famous in the surfing, sailboarding, kitesurfing, paddling, and SUP worlds, but civilians know him from his appearance in nationwide television ads for American Express—and also his role as Troy alongside George Clooney in *The Descendants*. He hangs out with a lot of famous artists, musicians, and other celebrities, and he and his wife, Gabrielle Reece, are occasionally high profile.

Laird is arguably the most famous surfer since Duke Kahanamoku, and while that will inspire howls of derision in certain parts of Hawaii, it is true that when Laird starts doing something new, the rest of the surfing world takes notice. This was true for using boats and then personal watercraft to start "tow surfing" into giant waves in the early 1990s, something that was met with skepticism but is now an accepted facet of big wave surfing.

Looking at Laird in terms of surf history, he is to stand up paddle surfing what Tom Blake was to *olo* surfboards in the 1920s. Blake was a wanderer from Wisconsin who went west all the way to the Hawaiian Islands, when they were still the most isolated place on Earth. In Hawaii Blake discovered *olo* in the Bishop Museum—surf and paddleboards as long as 12' that had once been available only to Hawaiian royalty (*ali'i*), while commoners rode the shorter *alaia*, as they were doing in that 1906 Waikiki "actuality" by Robert Bonine.

Blake saw potential in those dusty artifacts hanging in the Bishop, and he modernized the *olo*, using aircraft technology to make big, sometimes hollow, floaty boards that paddled faster and could catch the "bluebirds" that came through on the biggest days at Waikiki.

Duke Kahanamoku rode *olo*. All surfers eventually rode some version of the *olo*. Come to think of it, riding beach boy style probably wouldn't have been possible in Waikiki until after Blake's big, hollow, floaty, modernized *olo*-derived boards came on the scene.

The Hawaiians definitely weren't standing up and paddling *alaia*.

What Tom Blake was to modernizing the Hawaiian *olo* board, Laird is to modernizing stand up paddleboarding. In the 1990s he rediscovered something Hawaiian that had mostly been discarded. Like Tom Blake, Hamilton tinkered with stand up paddling and modernized it through equipment and technique evolution. Blake caused some controversy in Hawaii in the 1920s and 1930s with his new big boards: Some local paddlers wouldn't compete against him and his newfangled boards in the annual race in the Ala Wai channel.

Likewise, Laird Hamilton has inspired some controversy with stand up paddling. But Tom Blake's *olo* revolutionized the surfboard, and stand up paddling is now a big sensation.

In January 2011 Laird Hamilton was on Maui with his family, enjoying a decent winter surf season that saw him on his stand up paddleboard more often than not. Toward the end of the month, Laird graciously interrupted his family, water, and quality time to do a telephone interview for this book.

He answered many questions, but the first one was: What inspired him to start standing up on a big board and paddling around? Was it Duke, the Ah Choy brothers, John Zapotocky, Ambrose Curry? What?

According to Laird, the very roots of modern stand up paddling were inspired by wanting to surf tandem with his first-born daughter:

I think the real spark of the whole thing really had to do with when I had my first daughter [Izabela]. She is 16 now, so this was. . . . 1995. I wanted to take her tandem surfing, so [Laird's father] Bill Hamilton built these 12' tandem boards. I wanted to get good at riding the board before I put my daughter on there.

I would kick out of waves at Hookipa, and the wind would be blowing and literally just blow me back to the lineup. I would stay standing, and I just remember thinking how I liked staying standing up and how I didn't want to have to get back down and paddle. I just wanted to stay in that position.

1995: Mucking About at Mudflats

In the 1990s Laird Hamilton and his friend Dave Kalama and others would ride big 12' boards at places like Hookipa on Maui and around Malibu and other places where the surf was small. In 1995 Dave and Laird were messing around at a place called Mudflats near Maalaea on the island of Maui, and they used paddles to catch waves on tandem surfboards.

Tom Blake at Waikiki Beach in 1929 with his quiver of olo-inspired paddleboards and surfboards. These boards are long, wide, and floaty, and the hollow ones would have been good for stand up paddling—if anyone was actually doing that in the Hawaiian Islands in the 1920s.

Photo courtesy of The Surfing Heritage Foundation

Circa 1936: Standing or Kneeling? And What's With the Gun? More SUP History Controversy

Oh great, what's this? As the first edition of this book was nearing deadline, Gary Lynch sent in this timeline buster that at first challenged the idea of Duke Kahanamoku on a surf ski in the late 1930s. Lynch is a Tom Blake scholar who wrote the book on the early-twentieth-century surfer/adventurer/designer: *Tom Blake, the Uncommon Journey of a Pioneering Waterman*. When asked to proof this history, Lynch sent this photo of two guys with Tom Blake paddleboards, holding paddles at the water's edge, who look like they are about to engage in stand up paddling. Lynch said:

These guys in Florida with the Robert Mitchell Blake boards have goods roped to their decks so it is obvious they would be standing up since the goods are in the way of prone paddling—plus they have paddles. Also one guy is wearing a handgun on his hip. You would not want to get that wet. It would have to be 1934 or later. Mitchell boards came out in 1934. If I had to guess, photo is probably 1936 or something like that. I guess SUP has been around in one fashion or another before stand up surfing even?

Swell, so that messes up the timeline. Who are these guys? What were they doing? And why is that guy wearing a gun on his hip? Alligators? Moonshiners? Revenuers?

This photo immediately went around to the stand up paddling community. Blane Chambers of Paddle Surf Hawaii answered remarkably early in the morning from Hawaii, and he based his thoughts on his own experience, and also the presence of that gun:

Not saying they weren't doing SUP, but looking at the paddles and boards and the rag where you would put your knees, looks to me like they were paddling on their knees, then sitting.

Any pics of them actually standing? I used to knee paddle a lot and their setups look perfect for

Were these guys SUP erectus, or SUP kneeling? Circa 1930.
Photo courtesy the Surfing Heritage Foundation

sit down and knee paddling.

Again, not saying they weren't SUP, but when I used to position all my gear, etc., it'd be exactly like that. For SUP that setup would make it hard and the paddles are short.

And the gun is more of a sign these aren't SUP setups. Those are surfboards of the time. Carrying a weapon on a tippy little board and all your gear . . . Gotta be sitting or knee-paddling. They'd be falling in all day otherwise.

Also, Blake was a builder and if he was doing SUP he would have instantly crafted a proper-length paddle. It's murder to paddle with a short paddle in the standing position. I know that. I used to do it. I never said I was smart.

Enough said, or maybe not. When Ventura surfer/cowboy/filmmaker/closet SUPisto Chris Malloy was shown the thinking on that photo, he had to chime in:

AH! This photo was stapled to the Malloy workshop wall for years! I knew exactly which one it was when you described it. Didn't need to see the picture. Keith and Dan [Malloy, Chris's water brothers] used the rigging technique as a blueprint for their Point Arguello to El Capitan [36–40+ miles] paddle over five years ago. The rig on the left is the inspiration. I went down to [top paddleboard shaper] Joe Bark's shipping container shaping bay in San Pedro and had him shape two, 12-foot Dale Hope–inspired surf/paddle boards. They were built so we could move quickly but also surf if there was surf. We put grommets on the bows and rigged dry bags like the one in this picture.

This should not screw up the timeline. On the 40-mile paddle Dan also brought a 40's era canoe paddle inspired by this picture. Turned out Dan on a 12' x 4" thick foam board could not hardly stand up paddle thing with that short paddle. Maybe too narrow and the bow weight threw him off?

I know Laird started with short paddles but he also had bigger, wider boards. Dan ended up paddling on his knees and then standing up once he caught a wave. I think the boards in the picture would have been near impossible to stand up paddle—even in flat water. I think they knee paddled or sat on them and paddled like a canoe. Maybe with their legs straddling their packs?

And here's the kicker. My dad and I built a 13-foot KookBox [derogatory name for a hollow paddleboard] replica and I used the same short 40's-era canoe paddle on a couple glassy days at C Street [in Ventura] in an attempt to stand up surf.

The boxed rails [square rails with no curve to them] made it almost impossible to turn and when sinking the tail to turn it would wobble out of control since it had no deep skeg [fin].

These look like Tom Blake–designed LA Ladder Company boards which were much smaller than the board we built. I know this because I went off of Blake's specs. I'm convinced they were at most knee-paddling these buggahs.

I'm not an expert on SUPs or Tom Blake or surfing so I humbly throw this in the mix as an opinion.

Laird Hamilton with Don Wildman hanging with Lady Liberty, alongside Tim Cummerford and Jason Winn in a Quickblade ad. Don King

In the January 2011 interview, Laird remembered the time:

You know, I don't really have any other memory of trying a paddle on a board until then. It all began with those big tandem boards and learning how to surf them and then wishing I could stay standing, and then Dave had those outrigger paddles at Maalaea. We went out and messed around because we were riding these real tiny little waves on those big boards, and it was kind of like, "Okay, you got some outrigger paddles . . ." and we caught some waves, and we were squatting down real low, and of course the paddles were way too short.

And that led to "Let's build some paddles specifically for it," which led to changing the board design. It just evolved.

A Sylvain Cazenave photograph of Hamilton and Kalama mucking around with boards and paddles appeared in the table of contents for *The Surfer's Journal* in 1996, and that photo is a decent landmark for the late-twentieth-century modernization of stand up paddleboarding.

That session was covered in *That First Glide*, with Laird and Dave explaining what went down that day at Mudflats in 1996:

Dave Kalama: *We were riding 12-foot boards regularly. I mean that was pretty much our standard-length surfboard. We were doing a shoot at Ma'alaea.*

Laird Hamilton: *You know, kicking out of little waves and standing there and some days the wind would just blow you back out.*

Dave: *I had a couple of canoe paddles in the back of my truck, from just having done a one-man.*

Laird: *So it was, "Okay Dave, get those paddles out. Let's try to paddle them."*

Dave: *So I went and grabbed them, just to screw around with, basically.*

Laird: *We'd already been windsurfing, kiting, towing. We'd done all these things where we were in standing position.*

Dave: *He was bent over and I was bent over paddling out, because the paddles were so short.*

Laird: *I mean, you're squatting down like . . . I call it the little Menehune paddle. You're down there, you know?*

Dave: *We just had fun and quite honestly, we laughed a lot.*

Laird: *So you get the idea that you can generate power and stay upright.*

Dave: *It wasn't anything revolutionary. It didn't dawn on us really at the time that oh we could change surfing. It was pretty innocent and simple. I think Laird enjoyed it enough that he went to Malama—one of the local paddle builders here on Maui—and had a proper paddle built.*

Brian Keaulana: *Laird was the first one I knew of that actually made a longer paddle.*

Laird: *I mean it only made sense, mathematically, if you're sitting and you have a little paddle, than if you're standing. And I mean really it's like a shovel. If you look at shovels you have a short-handled shovel and you're bent over and doing quick strokes, but when you dig a big hole you want a longer lever—more leverage—and then you're in a better position.*

Mike Waltze: *By the late '90s, Laird was surfing exclusively with a paddle. He was continuing to challenge himself in the surf, yet no one at the time really understood what he was doing.*

If Laird had seen Ambrose Curry stand up paddling around Kauai in the 1970/1980s, he didn't mention it, and in *Standup Journal* Laird confessed to being only vaguely aware of guys in Waikiki standing up and paddling around and riding waves standing up on big boards:

I'd never seen stand up paddle surfing before, per se. I saw a guy standing in Waikiki—Mr. Ah Choy. When I saw him, he wasn't surfing or riding waves and stuff. He was taking pictures of tourists. Gerry Lopez also talks about somebody in the 1950s that did it. . . .

In that January interview, Laird said he wishes he had seen someone doing it earlier:

I wish somebody was doing it in the 1980s because I would have started doing that as soon as I saw it. But it came when it came because . . . no wine before it's time. It happened when it was supposed to happen . . . at the perfect time at least for some of us just to keep our . . . enthusiasm for being in the water, you know?

So modern stand up paddling had its second (or third) genesis on Maui, around 1995, 1996. In that "Man of the Sport" article in *Standup Journal*, Laird explained how stand up paddling made the transition from Maui to Malibu: "But I really got into it later, coming here [to Malibu] . . . spending my summers in L.A. with my family, training in small waves."

1997: FROM MAUI TO MALIBU

Cameron Farrer is a resident of a west Malibu neighborhood that is home to more than a few celebrities and multimillion-dollar houses. Many of the streets end in cul-de-sacs with guarded gates that lead down to a semiprivate beach and surfing area with shifting, rolling waves that are just about perfect for wave riding on stand up paddleboards.

This area will be known throughout this book as Privates, because many of the contributors to this book would not contribute without that nondisclosure agreement (and because I like to go there every once in a while and would like to continue going there without fear of guilt or recriminations).

In the first decade of the twenty-first century, Privates has been a place of increasing tension between stand up paddlers and local surfers, many of whom feel a sense of entitlement to the waves there and resent the intrusion of SUP practitioners —aka "sweepers," "janitors," and "oarons"—sometimes with great vengeance and furious anger.

During the winter of 2006, vandals stole and torched six expensive stand up paddleboards on the beach, one of them belonging to the wife of Kenny G.

There has been a lot of trouble and strife at Privates, but the beach is significant to the history of stand up paddling because it was one of the original laboratories, going back to 1997. That was the year 6'3" Laird Hamilton married 6'4" volleyball player/model/TV personality Gabrielle Reece, and all 12'7" of them moved into a home in Latigo Canyon in Malibu to begin a biseasonal lifestyle: spring, summer, and fall in Malibu, then fall, winter, and spring on Maui (now Kauai).

Cameron Farrer has lived at Privates since 1995, and he witnessed the transition from Laird noodling around on a tandem board in the late

Witness to SUP history Cameron Farrer spinning a helicopter on his 9'9" Bob Pearson in September 2009. Courtesy of Cameron Farrer

Jeremy Portfilio at the 2008 Surftech SUP contest at Steamer Lane, Santa Cruz, with a trophy for sweeping the stand up paddle division. Photo courtesy of Surftech

1990s to the invasion of stand up paddlers ten years later. Cameron detailed his thoughts in a series of e-mails for this book, and for that we would like to thank him:

Laird and Gabby moved into their house up one of the canyons around 1997 and that is the summer I think Laird started windsurfing at Leo and surfing the Malibu point breaks. He rode a 12-foot Billy Hamilton with orange Hawaiian-print rails. That was the only board I ever saw him surf (prone paddling). People were stoked to see a world class waterman in the lineup and were blown away at his skill level. Laird set up shop at [Bally Fitness founder] Don Wildman's beach compound and kept every

water toy imaginable there: sailboards, kiteboards, foils, Jet Skis, etc. He was only around Malibu for the summers and was back to Kauai (and Maui when Jaws was on).

I would guess it was the summer of 1999 when he appeared in the lineup standing upright on the 12-foot Hamilton with a paddle in his hand. No one had seen it before, but we were instantly amazed at how many waves could be caught and the distance those waves could be ridden. Within a year (by 2000), [local surfer/citizens] Drew Aiello, Dave Anawalt, Wayne Rowland and I started doing stand up on tandem boards with crude, flat paddles. There was tremendous skepticism not only with shortboarders but also with the die-hard longboarders. Not many traditional surfers were as eager to attempt this new approach to riding waves. It wasn't long, however, before some of these critics—seeing how much fun we were having—were asking about board dimensions and where to get a paddle.

Over several years, the sport grew as surfers began to realize the ability to SUP small waves and have fun on days that most surfers would consider unrideable. The reality is, the greatest attribute of the paddle in waves is its versatility; it is a brake and gas pedal all in one, allowing for perfect trimming on imperfect faces or accelerating around folding sections. Unfortunately, with the growth of the sport came controversy in the lineup. This was a result of too many waves taken by SUP riders and their disrespect for surfers, in addition to non-surfers on SUPs paddling into the surf, trying to catch waves and creating a hazardous situation for everyone.

Skylar Peak, the 2014 mayor of Malibu who appears in this book as the stand up paddling instructor, grew up surfing Privates and was there when Laird first showed up:

FYI, Laird was riding them there before [some of the current opposition] were surfing there.

He started out always surfing on these 12' Hamilton boards. He would prone it up from his buddies' house south of the pier, catch one or two waves on the way up and work his way up to the point . . . and then he showed up with a paddle one day. It was definitely annoying to people who were on the 12' boards even when they were just paddle surfing because Laird could get into waves so early.

It was actually kind of funny watching everyone grovel with him surfing on his 12' boards. He didn't give a fuck and would smile. When he brought out the oar though, people then looked at him as a different breed. That must have been about 10 years ago. Classic.

2001: Loch and Laird

Loch Eggers is a 44-year-old waterman who has lived on Maui going back to 1998. He described his upbringing:

I was born and raised around Diamond Head, Oahu. Spent my childhood and young adult life learning water sports at the Outrigger Canoe Club. Moved to Hanalei Bay, Kauai in the early '90s and learned how to ride large point surf at Hanalei and canoe paddle with the Hanalei Canoe Club. Moved to Maui in 1998 to mooch out of my mom's fridge and see if I could get a Jimi Hendrix Rainbow Bridge experience. I guess the acid trip has lasted this long and I found myself standing up on a surfboard with a paddle in my hand. What's next?

Loch became a part of the Maui Mob, a loose affiliation of surfers, kiteboarders, sailboarders, and all-around water people who got into the tropical waters of Maui any which way they could. Eggers appeared with Laird and Dave Kalama in the stand up paddling segment of the video *All Aboard the Crazy Train* in 2005. In that movie, Laird and Loch and Dave stand up paddle surf a decent-sized day at Jaws (Peahi), and it was that segment that introduced many to this *acqua cosa nova*.

Eggers is now a dedicated stand up paddler who is regularly seen riding his 9'8" Naish gun in any surf from 1 to 10 feet plus. But that is now and this was then, and Loch's memories of SUP go back to the winter of 2001, when he would see Laird in the early morning at Anthony's Coffee in Paia with his big boards in the back of his truck:

I would always ask him if I could give it try. He started to get pissed at me because I was asking too much and not doing. So the early winter of 2002 we were all down in front of Dave Kalama's dad's house at Baldwin [on the north shore of Maui] having a beach day and Laird had the 12-foot, 45-pound Ron House boards with aluminum-shaft paddles. Talk about stone age.

I told Laird that I wanted to give it a try. He looked at me with that expression he gives to people like, "You are finally waking the @#%% up!" So I paddled 30 yards off the beach and went out for 10 minutes and proceeded to fall on my face 30 times. I came in with both legs cramping and my arms cramping, snot running down my face with a huge smile. It felt like I just got into a grappling match with a female Russian shot putter. I was in love with SUP right after that experience.

In communicating about this book in December of 2014, Laird's wife Gabrielle said:

In essence Dave [Kalama] took another few years to adopt standup paddling and it was in fact Loch who was riding waves and doing downwinders. Also on the California side Jeff Sweet was an early adopter with Laird to SUP. Jeff never gets mentioned but he was initially paddling and then started surfing.

Loch Eggers had this to say about that:

There was a lot of R & D that went on. Laird must have bought $50K in boards and paddles in the first two years. The relationship was kind of like a Steve Jobs meets Woz and they go SUPping.

It was not experimenting on my part. It was more like getting a free board and a free ride to the beach with a free meal when Laird and I were hanging out. Mahalo Laird and Gabby for keeping me fed and housing me. It was more about having fun than experimenting when Laird and I were paddling. And this is how I want to keep it: FUN!!!!!!"

1996 and After: Paddles Evolve

From around 1996 through Y2K, Laird was living that biseasonal lifestyle—Malibu in the summer, Maui in the winter—and he was using stand up paddling as part of his training routine. He went through a lot of paddles made of fiberglass and wood. For paddles he looked as close as Malama Chun, a Maui guy who made wooden outrigger paddles, and as far as a paddle maker in Oregon.

In the 2014 Gear Guide published by *SUP the Mag,* the editors interviewed fourteen SUP pioneers and asked them what SUP's most important innovation was. Laird Hamilton said:

The single most important thing was making a paddle specifically for stand up. Duke Kahanamoku and the Beach Boys in Waikiki used canoe and kayak paddles and probably thought it was fun. But they didn't recognize the significance of the technique enough to take it further, to take the time to perfect it. People have paddled standing up for centuries. But the sport began when we had (Malama) Chun make those first paddles.

Dave Kalama confirmed that in *SUP the Mag:* ". . . the paddles that Malama made us on Maui. It allowed us to stand up. Without the paddle there'd be no standup."

According to the website for Malama Custom Paddles:

Malama was born in Puʻunene, Maui and raised in the plantation town of Hailiʻimaile on Maui. His mother was Hawaiian and his father Korean. He attended Kamehameha School on Oahu and then returned to Maui after graduation.

Malama is not much of an e-mailer, but his *wahine,* Karen Chun, is a computer wiz. As the first edition of this book was being finished, Karen pried some syllables out of her husband about his early work on SUP paddles with Laird:

Q: Had you ever seen stand up paddleboarding before Laird came to you?

A: *Nope. I heard of it before in the old days in Waikiki, but I had never seen anybody doing it.*

Q: What kind of paddles was Laird using when he first came to you?

A: *First paddle I built for him was basically one long canoe paddle without any fiberglass for strength in the shaft—which he promptly smacked in half. So I went to [surfboard/SUP shaper] Jimmy Lewis to learn* how to fiberglass the shaft, but by then Laird was likely using carbon.

The first few paddles that I glassed the shaft, like, for Loch [Eggers] and them guys, they still would break them so that's when I started wrapping double in the middle, and now they don't break them. Since I added the extra 6 ounces in the middle, it seems like it's holding. I'm a paddle maker, not a stand up surfer, so I depend on input from the stand up surfers so I can build the paddle they want.

Q: What did you learn from making paddles for a new use like that, for a guy that big?

A: *Just that I gotta strengthen the shaft in the middle. The surfers use their paddles to lean on in the wave . . . the extreme stand up surfers need extra strength in their paddles. For the extreme SUP like Laird, Loch, and Kent Apo, I had to strengthen the shaft.*

Q: What year did your working relationship start, and how long did it last?

A: *Forget, but not very long. Mostly I make for the others. Laird has his own line of paddles.*

Dave Chun is not related to Malama Chun, except that he also makes paddles for outrigger canoes and SUP. In that 2014 Gear Guide, David Chun said:

The paddle was no evolutionary jump. It was just an outrigger paddle made longer. I've had good friends who knew I was a paddle guy but who never asked me about canoes or kayaks. But suddenly they're coming to me, asking, "What is this standup thing?" People are intrigued. Not just by doing it, but by the concept.

When asked by e-mail to expand on his quote from the *SUP the Mag Gear Guide*, Dave Chun laid down some history and gave all praise to Laird Hamilton, by way of Gerry Lopez:

The Oregon guy is me. Gerry Lopez, who is also a Bend, Oregon, resident, gave Laird the Kialoa Paddles contact.

Malcolm Gladwell makes reference in his book Outliers *that it requires 10 years or 10,000 hours of work experience to achieve mastery at a task. When Laird gave Kialoa the call in 2003, I had been earning my living as a paddle builder for 12 years. And with my 7-day-a-week, 10-hour-a-day work schedule, I had my 10,000 hours.*

I was at a place in my career where I was ready for the next challenge.

I remember asking Laird, "Why don't you just get a paddle from the guy who built you the last one?" He told me, "I broke all of them."

I refer to Laird's phone call as "the gift." I have nothing but gratitude for simply being in the right place at the right time.

In that 2014 *Gear Guide*, Scott Bass stated how important the Internet was in the early evolution of SUP, and how that led him to paddles by David Chun:

The popularity of standup paddling and the growth of the Internet are directly linked. Back in 2002 people were really just starting to get hardwired and it helped to connect the tiny SUP community. There was nowhere to get a paddle. A Google search showed me this guy up in Oregon (Dave Chun) who was making canoe paddles and I emailed him asking if he could make me an 82-inch model. And then when guys like Blane Chambers started posting new board designs—it was where you went for information. The significance of the Internet to SUP history shouldn't be overlooked.

Laird broke a lot of paddles and went through a lot of makers and materials until he connected with (Olympic paddler and now president of Quickblade) Jim Terrell and Quickblade paddles, which are made of carbon fiber.

In the first years Laird was riding a tandem board made by his father that was only 24" wide, a torturous width now considered only by professional stand up paddleboard racers.

In the January phone interview, Laird said this:

There were benefits to learning on those narrow boards with bad paddles—obviously that was a lot harder. I can remember in the beginning if you could go out for twenty minutes without your arches locking up, and not turning into Gumby, that was amazing.

And then it was thirty minutes. And then it was, "Now I can go for an hour straight, standing up the whole time." And then it was like two hours.

To stand up and paddle around and then catch a wave and ride as hard as you can on the wave, using your legs: That's quadruple the amount of leg effort you are ever going to put into conventional prone surfing.

2001: The Millennium Wave

During the summer of 2001, Laird traveled to the island of Tahiti as part of a crew shooting a movie for the French clothing company Oxbow. Laird went down with tow boards and foilboards and other boards, but his SUP wasn't yet part of his regular quiver:

I was stand up paddling at the time, but I had so much that I brought to Tahiti that I didn't bring my stand up gear. Bringing a 12-footer . . . I'm gun-shy to travel with those things because they are so big.

In August 2001 Laird Hamilton used his SUP-toned legs to tow surf a dangerous Tahitian left reef break called Teahupoo. Laird towed into a wave that day that surpassed anything that had ever been attempted before, and a photo sequence of the ride made the cover of *Surfer* magazine blurbed "Oh my God!"

Laird's "Millennium Wave" fired a starter's gun for a lot of extreme big wave riding. In the movie *Riding Giants*, surf historian Matt Warshaw

examined Laird's outrageous passage through that Teahupoo wave and asked: "What could be heavier than that?" Extreme surfers have been answering that question ever since, from Tahiti to Mavericks to South Africa to west Australia to Peru.

Was it stand up paddling in the summer that gave Laird the leg strength to make that wave? "I think everything leads up to the success or failure of whatever endeavor you do," Laird said, "but did it have that kind of effect already? Possibly."

September 12, 2002: Laird Goes Public at Malibu

One year and a few months after the Millennium Wave, Laird was in California in September 2002. A year and a day after the attack on the Twin Towers in New York City, a big southern hemisphere swell was sweeping into Southern California and lighting up the point break at Surfrider Beach, Malibu.

Laird went very public with the *cosa nuova* this day, paddling out at First Point Malibu using a paddle flying an American flag.

Some surfers out this day objected to Laird's "grandstanding" and accused him of using his advantage to drop in on prone paddlers. But everyone drops in on everyone at Malibu—the place is chaos on a big day when surfers are in a feeding frenzy (see chapter 6).

Laird goes public on this new thing, paddling out at First Point Malibu on September 12, 2002, and riding some bomb waves, a year and a day after the attack on the Twin Towers. At the time, most observers wondered: "What is Laird doing?!? What is that thing?" So pretty much everything that has happened in SUP has happened since 9/12/2002.
Photo by Bill Parr
Image courtesy Jason Rouse, Janice Burns, and Mia Dinelly

Monthly
Malibu
MAGAZINE

MALIBU · PACIFIC PALISADES
SANTA MONICA · TOPANGA

NOVEMBER 2002   VOLUME 1   ISSUE 8

SUN & SURF | FASHION | HOME | MUSIC | HEALTH | DINING | EVENTS | READING

Mickey Munoz has been surfing Malibu going back to the 1950s, but he now lives in Capistrano Beach, in a beach house and work space surrounded by sixty years of flotsam and jetsam. Munoz will travel all the way to Los Angeles for a big south swell, and in an e-mail for this book, he said that what he saw that day was unprecedented:

I saw Laird at Malibu on one of the biggest days in years. He was riding what looked like an old tandem board that must have weighed 40 pounds plus. In all my years riding Malibu I had never seen this before: Laird took off standing and paddling between First and Second Point and rode standing that big board through the pier. He did it twice that day! I was so excited after seeing that, I went home that night and cut a kayak paddle down and epoxied a handle on it.

Mickey Munoz has been shaping surfboards as long as he has been surfing, going back to a time when boards were carved out of redwood, balsa, and other hard and softwoods. He has shaped thousands of surfboards over fifty years and is one of the experienced shapers working with Surftech to produce their molded surfboards.

One of Surftech's most popular surfboards has been a 12-footer for beginners, offensive linemen, and tandem surfers, shaped by Munoz, which they made available in both Softop and Tuflite epoxy construction beginning in 1999.

Mickey Munoz with a weird growth on his head, at Huntington Beach. Photo courtesy of Surftech

This has been one of the best boards available to people who want to try stand up paddling, including Mickey Munoz:

The next day I took my 12' Surftech out and tried my first stand up paddle surfing. The surf was still big, but I managed to catch one wave before I was over it. It was not easy, and I decided it would be better to learn to paddle inside the [Dana Point] harbor before trying to surf. That was 8+ or so years ago.

Mickey Munoz stepping outside of his Capo Beach skunk works, holding a 12'6" stand up paddleboard prototype he made in the summer of 2008. Ben Marcus

Mickey Munoz sliding right on an 11' Laird Surftech Softop on the south side of Huntington Pier. Mickey teamed up with Hawaiian Kala Alexander in pumping surf. Photo courtesy of Surftech

I didn't think it was "lame," just a lot harder than I thought it would be. Once I started to figure it out I could see the directions it might take. That's when I fully committed to SUP.

In that 2006 "Upright" article by Todd Bradley in *The Surfer's Journal*, Sam George wrote a sidebar called "Meanwhile, in California," in which he pointed to Laird at Malibu for that big south swell:

Consider Laird's coming-out party. September 12, 2002. Southern-hemi, six- to eight-foot Malibu. Six-foot, two-inch Hamilton out on his 12-footer, standing for the entire session, wielding a custom paddle with an American flag affixed to the crosspiece. Shot the Malibu Pier—twice. Subtle.

Sam George was an early SUP practitioner, having first picked up the paddle after seeing footage of Laird Hamilton surfing Malibu on September 12, 2002. Riding his 11'6" Terry Martin tandem, followed by a Surftech Mickey Munoz 12' Ultraglide, George left first tracks at a number of Californian breaks. "Aside from Laird, I was the only stand up surfer between Cardiff and Capitola for at least a year," says George. "And the typical response was more curiosity than concern—back then nobody had any idea that an entirely new form of surfing was coming up over the horizon."

2002 and After: Scott Bass on SUP in San Diego County

Scott Bass is the founder of the annual Sacred Craft surfboard show, and he was a writer and online editor for *Surfer* magazine from 1996 to 2008. Scott was an early proponent of stand up paddling when it really wasn't considered cool for a traditional surfer to be so. When asked for his thoughts on the early days of SUP in California, Bass responded:

I can only comment on what I experienced, as there is a lot of flag waving regarding 21st century stand up paddle surfing (SPS) history.

My experience and knowledge resides solely in the San Diego area and most specifically in the North County San Diego area.

I first experienced live, in-person SPS at Cardiff Reef in the summer of 2002. The surfer was stoic, regal, noble, and calm. The surfer's name was Rick Thomas—a San Diegan with family ties in Hawaii, who resides in the South Bay of San Diego (Chula Vista area). Intrigued, I immediately befriended Rick and he took me out for my first SPS session that same day.

Rick picked up SPS from old time beach boys in Hawaii where he has Ohana (mother). He did not learn it from Laird, and San Diego's lineage to SPS, in my opinion, comes directly from Rick Thomas via the beach boys in Hawaii. Granted, I did see footage of Laird (Old Glory in hand) in one of [San Clemente surfer/shaper/raconteur] Herbie Fletcher's movies doing SPS on Fourth of July at Malibu.

Nevertheless, San Diego's SPS history comes directly from Rick Thomas—he was and is the guy. Rick Thomas's SPS paddle was the first to touch San Diego waters. I'm quite confident in that statement. He is extremely humble and sincere, not a personal promoter at all, and would probably downplay this statement. Rick Thomas pioneered SPS (with me his first disciple in 2002) at Cardiff Reef, La Jolla Shores, and Sunset Cliffs.

Not surprisingly, each of these areas [was] germinated and subcultures of SPS grew quickly in the San Diego waters at these spots. By 2003 simultaneous subcultures of SPS were in full bloom. The first San Diego pioneers were generally established local surfers at each of these spots, myself at Cardiff, Mitch Hagio (from Mitch's Surf Shop) at La Jolla Shores, and hardened Sunset Cliffs locals such as Chris Riesing. This was all before the mags, or hype, and it was still considered harmless, and/or nobody said anything negative to us because they couldn't.

Cardiff is where is at all started, the Mecca, for better or for worse, of SPS in San Diego, with Rick Thomas and myself the only guys doing it. The following year I sold [local surfer] Tom English my red Munoz 12' board and he was hooked. For at least two years, maybe three, it was just the three of us at Cardiff.

It was all very new to us, and we ordered our first wooden paddles through whitewater guys in Oregon and Vancouver, BC. I still have two of them, in the yard, rotting away. I should probably put them in the garage.

Kialoa had one stock SPS paddle. It was aluminum and heavy, but I ordered one of those as well. Anything out of wood or carbon had to be done custom (or so we thought—as Todd was already on it), and I ordered a wood/carbon custom from a guy named Brian Forester out of BC or Maine or someplace. He would only do customs, but his e-mails to me suggested they were getting big interest from Hawaii. Hawaii was definitely ahead of the curve, as paddle culture is what Hawaii is all about.

In 2002, Rick and I originally rode the Mickey Munoz Surftech 11' or 12' surfboards, or the Surftech Softop lifeguard boards were my first 11' or 12' boards.

This was before Mickey Munoz even did SPS because I remember telling him about it, that his boards were the only ones on the market that would do the trick, and of course MM was generally stoked and intrigued, the Munoz twinkle was evident in his eyes. So we had the wood laminate or the blue or the red MM model. Classic.

Eventually custom boards entered our mindset. [Surf shop owner] Bruce Jones actually had some big-guy big-brudda Hawaiian Makaha longboards— boards for 300-pound bruddas, in his surf shop—on the rack. Rick bought one of those and it was a real change for the better: smaller (10'6"), narrower (26.5"), and flatter rocker. The Munoz boards pushed water—they had banana rocker.

Around 2003 I called my shaper, John Kies (Encinitas Surfboards), and had him build me a custom SPS board. It was 11' long and 25" wide, which is extremely narrow. But I remember telling him: Man, this thing is wide! We had no clue, only MM Surftech numbers as a basis point (11" × 27.25"), and the Bruce Jones was narrower, so we decided to push the width down to 25". I was stuck on 11' long.

I still think that longer is better. I'm into stylish big board surfing—it is aesthetically pleasing and in my opinion, it is the proper dance partner for SPS. When I want to rip and tear, well, let's just say I have other surfboards for that style of dance. Eventually the guys at Hobie (Gary Larson and Mark Johnson) were making us boards. And [San Clemente shaper/designer] Ron House. They have their own story, I'll let them tell it. We started getting boards from everybody: [San Diego shapers] Gary Linden, Stu Kenson, and Rusty Preisendorfer. Rusty made a fabulous quad [four fin] that I took to Australia for the first-ever SPS event at Noosa.

Todd Bradley, Dave Parmenter, Dave's wife Claudia Parmenter, Brian Keaulana, Brian's tandem partner Kathy Terada, and other Makaha folks (along with some other Aussies) had an adventure at Double Island Point that year. I'm sure it was the first time SPS went down up there as well. (This may have been 2007 or 2008.)

As a side note, in a Malibu Surfing Association contest (2004) at 1st Point Malibu, in the final, I paddled out on a Munoz SPS board. I lay down with the paddle between me and the board, so as to evade comment from the PA. Outside I stood up and caught one nice clean 3' set wave. The PA guy was just all over me. I rode this wave for a long time, and he broke out the official MSA rule book and read verbatim the rules over the PA as I rode all the way through. I was DQ'd [disqualified], but the irony of Malibu/Dora rules and contests was not lost on many. Animosity toward SPS was quickly poking its head out of the sand.

By 2005 the SPS explosion was starting. Sub-cultures in California (Malibu, Doheny, San Onofre, Cardiff, La Jolla Shores) and Hawaii started intermingling via the Internet. The Cardiff crew would cruise up to Dog Patch at San Onofre and hang with [Orange County Mafia members] Ron House, Jeff Alter, Hobie Jr., Chuck Patterson and many others. The Dog Patch scene [at San Onofre] quickly outgrew the Cardiff scene in size: South Orange County was booming, but that is not my story.

Todd, Dave, Brian would roll through occasionally, and we would devour insight they would give us.

By 2006, it was the beginning of the end, in my opinion. Not trying to be salty, and I know I sound really, really old when I say this (not to mention cliché), but those first few years, when everything was new, and no one else was doing it, well, it was really cool.

Sam has a pretty good saying—I'm butchering it, but it's something along the lines of, "You could paddle past people and it was a look of astonishment rather than animosity."

2003 and After: West Side of the Story—SUP Comes to Makaha

The west side of Oahu is a corner of the island that remains proudly, locally Hawaiian. Makaha is the main surf spot on the west side, and starting in the 1940s, Makaha was one of the first places Hawaiian and mainland surfers began challenging big surf and fine-tuning the specialized "guns" needed to paddle into moving mountains of water and ride them to the end.

On any given day at Makaha, there are more kinds of wave-riding craft than anywhere else in the world: Skimboarders sliding off the beach into the shore break sometimes have to avoid bodysurfers and hand-planers riding that final burst of wave energy onto the sand. At Makaha you will see big Hawaiian braddahs bellyboarding traditional

wooden *paipo* boards. There are also dozens of more modern bodyboarders on their plastic slabs, doing belly spinners outside and risking their necks in the shore break.

When the wind is bad for surfing, sailboarders and kitesurfers rule the bounding main. But when the surf and wind conditions are right, at Makaha you will see every possible combination and configuration of shortboard, longboard, hybrid, and tanker: guys sliding traditional, finless *alaia*, fish, shortboards, hybrids, longboards, tankers, and tandem from 3' to 14' long. On top of all that are the outrigger canoes with one to six paddlers. The original Polynesian wave-riding craft are still enjoying the most supreme pleasure at Makaha; just stay out da way.

Anything goes at Makaha, and it often goes big, so it makes sense that the traditional Hawaiian act of standing up on a big board and paddling it with a canoe paddle caught on at Makaha. The revolution on that side of Oahu was led by a native son: Brian Keaulana.

The son of Buffalo Keaulana, a great Hawaiian bodysurfer/canoeist/surfer/waterman who was one of the leaders of surfing in the 1940s, '50s, and '60s, Brian Keaulana is an all-around waterman who innovated the use of personal watercraft in ocean rescue and has made a comfortable career for himself doing stunts and water safety for Hollywood TV and movie productions—that's Brian driving the PWC that Adam Sandler jumps onto in *50 First Dates*.

During the 1980s and '90s, Keaulana was often pictured in *Surfer* magazine riding waves at Makaha sitting on a lounge chair, standing on a ladder, and doing *all kine lolo* stuffs. At some point he took up a paddle, but if he was clowning around at first, he wen' get serious pretty quick.

In a bit of historic irony, SUP got a second boost by way of Tahiti—the place where Captain

The backwash-strafed Makaha shore break is famous/infamous for launching wave riders into the air. French competitor Antoine Delpero gets launched in the Oxbow Stand Up Paddle Expression session November 5, 2010, at Makaha Beach, Hawaii. Shutterstock

Cook and his crew first saw "the most supreme pleasure"—because Tahiti is where Brian Keaulana experienced his "SUPiphany" on the cusp of 2002/2003.

In *That First Glide* the narrator claims that as of the first years of Y2K, "Dave Kalama and Laird Hamilton were pretty much alone with this new sport on Maui, and for years they had trouble convincing their friends to give it a try."

In the documentary Keaulana states—like a lot of surfers and watermen—he wasn't all that keen on SUP, at first: "Laird was talking about how great this thing is, the exercise and all that and I'm like 'Yeah Laird, great. Another toy. Another kite.

Another windsurfer. Another foil board. Some other toy, yeah right.'"

Laird tow surfed into a very famous wave at Teahupoo in Tahiti in August of 2001, but he was a regular visitor to surf and tow surf Teahupoo, to kite surf, to sailboard, to *manger beaucoup de poisson cru*. But also just to enjoy a group of spectacularly beautiful Polynesian islands with a special blend of *aloha Française*, and where water skills, surfing, paddling, are everything. After the Millennium Wave in 2001, Laird was a bit of a legend in Tahiti and he flew down often, bringing his entourage of equipment: "When I would go back I started bringing my standup paddleboards too," Laird said in *That First Glide*, "and it's such a huge paddling culture."

Laird planted the seed of SUP among the Tahitians, and then Brian Keaulana traveled to Tahiti to train the local Tahitian water patrol members the most modern techniques in water rescue and the use of personal watercraft.

Keaulana remembered his "SUPiphany" in *That First Glide*:

While I was in Tahiti training the Tahitian water patrol boys, I was also with Poto [Tahitian surfer Vetea David], hanging out and training. And Poto was just paddling with Laird and he made one of those long canoe paddles, but out of hau. So for my birthday, he made me one. So I was like, "Ahhh what the hell, okay. It's flat, there's no waves, it's just a huge lagoon." So I paddled and we paddled for an hour or so, maybe more. But when I came back: wow, talk about a workout. You just . . . your core is burning and everything, and I was just amazed about the least amount of time we spent on the water, and the type of workout we had.

On Tahiti, Keaulana experienced "the most supreme pleasure" of stand up paddling, and he returned to Hawaii and brought his enthusiasm to one of the world's best test tracks for any watercraft: Makaha.

In *That First Glide*, narrator Mike Waltze and Brian Keaulana explain how stand up paddling caught fire on the west side of Oahu, at Makaha:

Waltze: *Home to Brian is the west side of Oahu, where Hawaiian tradition is engraved in the lifestyle here. And paddling is a big part of that tradition.*

Keaulana: *Any body of water, wherever you come from, you have a tradition, sometime it's an old tradition, sometime it's a new tradition. When we started the whole SUP standing up, basically I think it was just Laird and Dave [Kalama] and just us. That was it. And then slowly in Makaha guys like Bruce Desoto, Bunky Bakutis grabbed a tandem board and started paddling around and copying blades and stuff. And then I think Dad [Buffalo Keaulana] started the first SUP contest right here in Makaha.*

Waltze: *The Buffalo contest [Buffalo's Big Board Surfing Classic] at Makaha has always been a combination of all these different sports. It's just a festival of board riding. And enjoying the break and enjoying the ocean and adding stand up to that realm was a clear, easy fit from the beginning.*

Todd Bradley: *Brian had this wood paddle and at the time I was designing carbon outrigger paddles, being an outrigger racer, and I said "Oh, I'll make this out of carbon for us." . . . but I think the tipping point was really when the boards changed.*

Keaulana: *I asked Dave Parmenter to shape me one, you know, 10 foot smaller board . . . high performance board and from then on everything just kind of escalated.*

Dave Kalama: *The Makaha gang: Dave Parmenter, Brian, Todd Bradley, you know, all the local Makaha guys. Mel Puu. They were probably the original driving force behind the shorter boards that we're riding today.*

Waltze: *It was around 2004 when the Makaha boys took the 12-foot boards down to 10 feet.*

Getting back to that 2006 article on beach boy–style surfing in *The Surfer's Journal*, Todd Bradley also addressed the Makaha Effect and the nouveau/retro conflict in stand up paddleboarding/surfing in the first five years of the twenty-first century:

Many surfers mistakenly lump beachboy surfing into the "retro" trend, perhaps because of its Waikiki

Grandson of Buffalo Keaulana and a native son of Makaha, Noland Keaulana was born in 1989, which means he hit his teenage years just as stand up paddling was becoming repopularized in the Hawaiian Islands. This is Noland in home grounds at Makaha, competing in the Oxbow Stand Up Paddle Expression session in November 2010. Mana Photo/Shutterstock

roots and because it employs modified longboards. But for me and guys like Brian Keaulana, Dave Parmenter, Bruce DeSoto, Laird Hamilton, Dave Kalama, Archie Kalepa and other watermen, stand up surfing has progressed so far with new board designs and paddles that it now offers the same futuristic frontiers as tow-in surfing when it first started to take off. While the resurgence in stand-up surfing began as a fun method

to achieve core strength training or kill a lazy afternoon of small surf, a collection of all-around watermen focused their energies upon it and soon realized the sky was the limit.

In the article, Bradley pointed to a number of firsts in the evolution of beach boy–style surfing that came from the Hawaiian Islands, specifically, the west side of Oahu, at Makaha:

2003: *Brian Keaulana's first "short" stand-up board was a 10' × 28" × 4" multifin which Bradley called "the first quantum leap in the high-performance school of the stand-up resurgence," which allowed Keaulana to "attack 10- to 12-foot Makaha Bowl surf from behind the peak."*

2004: *Maui waterman and lifeguard Archie Kalepa was an unofficial entrant in the 2004 Quiksilver Molokai to Oahu paddleboard race. Stand up paddling a 12-foot EPS [expanded polystyrene]/epoxy board, Kalepa finished in six hours where the overall winner Jamie Mitchell finished in 4:56:03. (In the 2010 race, Dave Kalama finished first on a stand up at 4:54:15, while Women's SUP division winner Andrea Moller did it in 6:00:00. Jamie Mitchell won the overall paddleboarding with a time of 4:52:52—a difference of two minutes between prone and stand up.*

[In the latest 2014 running of Molokai-2-Oahu, the first 12 finishers were on SUP, with Connor Baxter in the Men's Unlimited Overall SUP class winning it all with a time of 4:08:08. Australian Matt Poole was the top paddleboarder, finishing 13th overall with a time of 4:52:02].

2004: *With its popularity at Makaha beach, Brian Keaulana decided to add "Beachboy Surfing" in 2004 as an event in the world-recognized "Buffalo Big Board Contest." The response was overwhelming with over 49 participants entering the division, which included many of Hawaii's elite watermen and past world champion surfers.*

In the "Oral History" article in the 2014 *SUP the Mag Gear Guide*, Todd Bradley said: "First Buffalo's Big Board Contest at Makaha in 2004, when the first beach boy surfing event was staged. Most everyone was riding tandem boards, but Brian Keaulana was on a 10-foot Parmenter and blew us all away with his high-performance surfing."

2005: *Stand up divisions are added to the 2005 Hennessey International Championships—a 10-mile*

downwind race from Hawaii Kai to Waikiki. Bonga Perkins won the stand up paddle male division with a time of 1:22:38.1 and he was followed by Todd Bradley, Brian Keaulana and Dave Parmenter. Jamie Mitchell on a prone paddleboard was fastest overall, with a time of 1:11:28.0.*

2005: *A team stand up division is added to the Quiksilver Molokai to Oahu race. This race brought together a field of nine paddle teams and was won by Todd Roberts and Brian Keaulana, who finished 10th overall in the Stand up Paddleboard field with a time of 5:18. Second place was the team of Archie Kalepa and Dave Parmenter less than three minutes behind.*

2006: *At the 2006 Da Hui Fourth of July Sunset to Waimea race, one-fifth of all entrants were stand up paddlers.*

By 2003 Brian Keaulana and his Makaha friends Mel Puu, Todd Bradley, and Dave Parmenter came up with their own name for stand up paddling—which they, with Hawaiian pride, referred to as "beach boy–style surfing"—and they moved it fast-forward when Todd Bradley started the first company to make custom paddles, Pohaku.

Where Laird Hamilton, Dave Kalama, and Loch Eggers on Maui and the Makaha guys and anyone else noodling around with stand up had been using kayak paddles or outrigger paddles made of plastic or wood, now Pohaku was producing purpose-built shafts and blades made of carbon fiber.

A huge stroke ahead for mankind.

2006: C4 Waterman

In November 2006 Keaulana, Parmenter, and Bradley formed C4 Waterman—Four Core = Balance, Endurance, Strength, Tradition—to apply modern design and manufacturing techniques to make stand up paddleboards for wave riders and racers, but also to satisfy the growing interest for

Feet planted and eyes focused on the future of a growing sport, Wingnut Weaver demoing a Surftech Laird board at the 2006 Outdoor Retailer Show. Photo courtesy of Surftech

inlanders who wanted to cruise lakes and bays and ride whitewater on rivers.

While Surftech and other surfboard manufacturers were producing stand up paddleboards, C4 Waterman was the first company to make *only* stand up paddleboards. They had their big unveiling at the January 2007 Action Sports Retailer show in San Diego and the Outdoor Retailer show in Salt Lake City, Utah, in August 2007.

2004 and After: Who Made the First Commercial Stand Up Paddleboard?

In cool guy terminology, stand up paddling began to "blow up" around 2003, 2004. All of the competition and innovation and marketing and exploding that happened between 2004 and 2015 could easily fill an entire book, because there are at least three magazines and countless websites dedicated to it all.

But the book I wrote before this one was a history of skateboarding, and one of the stories in there had to do with answering the question: Who made the first commercial skateboard? Skateboarding went commercial around 1959, but it's unclear whether it was Skee Skate or Roller Derby or Chicago or Greg Noll or some other person or company who first began producing skateboards for sale.

Stand up paddleboard history is much newer than that, so it's important to at least establish which person or company was the first to design, manufacture, and sell a board for stand up paddling.

About 2006, Sam George was getting into SUP using a Mickey Munoz UltraGlide, a board made for prone surfing at 12' × 26.8" wide × 4.6" thick. At the same time, George mentioned San Clemente shaper Ron House "cranking out Laird's personal sleds, considered by us neophytes to be too huge for mortal men (12' 4" × 30" × 5" × !!)."

Surftech had success selling their 12' Mickey Munoz hardboards and Softops to a world that was beginning to clue in to this new/old sensation. "The 12' was available around the time I saw Laird at Malibu," Munoz said in an e-mail.

Had I been smart enough to have looked in the future and made it 3" wider, I coulda been king! It did work out, though. It sold well, covered a lot of bases, and turned out to be a good rental board especially popular in Waikiki. The upside of that is, lots of big Hawaiians ride the Munoz 12-footer, so when I paddle up to them while surfing, ask them how they like the board and I introduce myself, they say, "Give him waves!!!"

I would have to check with Surftech on the question of a sales spurt when sups came into vogue. I do think it must have helped sales some. Surftechs are so durable that once the market has been saturated, sales would go a little flat until the next surge. The next surge was probably supping.

Laird Hamilton wanted to work with his friend Gerry Lopez to make the first purpose-built stand up paddleboards.

In *That First Glide*, Lopez remembered:

Laird asked me to build him a board. And I did it up in Maui. I got a 12'8" tandem blank from Clark. And I shaped it and we glassed it up there and the thing weighed . . . I don't know, the thing weighed like 50 pounds. The only one that could lift it was Laird.

And you know it didn't really interest me that much, and then when the board was done he came and got it and he goes, "This is great. Can you make 10 more just like it?" And I go, "Uggggh."

Lopez and Laird are long-term collaborators, but he almost needed roller skates to get from one end of a SUP blank to the other. So Laird had boards made by a Japanese shaper and glassed on Maui. You can see Laird riding the yellow/orange beast at Hookipa toward the end of the SUP section of *All Aboard the Crazy Train*.

Around 2004 Hamilton hooked up with Ron House, who gave his side of the SUP evolution in a couple of e-mails:

I first became aware of SUP when Laird [Hamilton], at [Gerry] Lopez's direction, called me and asked if I could shape these big, 12' boards, which I did. At first I thought it was a strange idea, but Laird wanted several for himself and his friends in Malibu, so I made them.

The original boards were between 25½" and 27". They also were heavy by design. It was really no big deal to shape the first boards as I had shaped lots of sailboards back in the day. They were Clark Foam until Grubby Clark shut down [December 5, 2005] and we went to EPS and epoxy. Boards became lighter with this construction and needed to be wider to compensate for more responsiveness and, therefore, less stability.

I didn't have an opinion on stand up paddling at the time, but after trying it I found, to my surprise, that I liked it a lot, especially riding waves. Many of my friends also got into it, so it looked like it would take off.

My friends and I, all longtime surfers, were having such a great time that we knew it would only be a matter of time until the obvious attraction of SUP became widespread.

I don't know if Laird was using other Surftech

conventional surfboards prior to Surftech producing his model. The first boards were usually 12', and I started making them in about 2004. When I shaped the first 12'1" Surftech proto[type], Laird wanted it 31" to make it beginner-friendly.

Since then everything has widened out a bit. A few years later the production boards came out, but it took a while to get them to the marketplace. I got involved with Laird in about 2004. . . .

Early on, as my friends and I got into surfing stand ups, we figured it was just a matter of time until the word got out and we wouldn't be going out with three or four guys anymore.

It is a bit surprising how quickly it went from "What do you call that?" to what has become a mainstream sport.

2005: Clark Foam's Blank Monday Inspires Use of EPS Foam

In the 2014 *SUP the Mag Gear Guide*, Ron House points to the 2005 closure of Clark Foam—the monopoly producer of polyurethane surfboard blanks—as a turning point for SUP, as the closure of Clark forced all board manufacturers to consider new materials and construction techniques:

In the beginning, we were all coming from a surfboard shaping background, but when Clark Foam closed in 2005 a lot of us shifted to EPS polystyrene foam and epoxy resin. We kind of had to. What we discovered was that the EPS/epoxy combination was not only much stronger especially where the paddle hits the rail, but boards lost about 10 pounds that day. Our modern standup board would not have been possible without making that switch.

That historical note on the closure of Clark Foam was supported by Dave Kalama in the 2014 Gear Guide: "And then when Clark Foam went out of business in 2005, Surftech was in position to provide epoxy composite production boards that

were accepted by the average buyer. Which lead to the industry as we know it today."

Duke Brouwer worked as the marketing director for Surftech as SUP evolved in the first decade of the twenty-first century. As this book was being written in the winter of 2014–2015, Brouwer was moving into a new role managing the Surftech retail store at the end of 41st Avenue in Santa Cruz.

Brouwer was at Surftech when SUP was bubbling, and he remembered the genesis of their stand up line like this:

At Surftech we first became aware of stand up paddleboarding when guys were using our 12' Mickey Munoz to SUP. At first we had a hard time selling those boards, then suddenly we were running out of them.

We thought the surf side of SUP was interesting, considering how overcrowded most lineups are. We were most intrigued with SUP on lakes and rivers. A couple of us snuck out to Lexington Reservoir [between Santa Cruz and San Jose] to give it a go and had a blast.

Our general manager, John Griffith, began ripping on the 12' Munoz out behind his house. Prior to SUP, JG was commonly seen doing power gouges at Sewer Peak [Santa Cruz] on his 6'6". After he caught the bug he started doing the same turns on his SUP!

So at Surftech we were intrigued by the surf aspect of stand up, but also the possibilities for the inland, flatwater and river uses. When Laird came to us with the prototype stand up boards he had developed with Ron House, we got behind it. Laird's 12'1" Ron House board was the first production SUP and my recollection is they were first available mid- to late-2005.

Sam George also mentioned Hobie shaper Terry Martin and Arrow Surfboards founder Bob Pearson, who were experimenting with the length × width × height × thickness equation around

(above) Laird Hamilton in Utah surrounded by a quiver of stand up paddleboards. Photo courtesy of Surftech

(below) Deliverables for the 2006 Surftech line of stand up paddleboards. Photo courtesy of Surftech

2006. As of 2006, most traditional surfers looked down on SUP as an "old man's sport" practiced by the hopelessly nostalgic and/or by people who were too old and decrepit even to ride longboards, which are usually in the 8' to 12' range.

As of 2006 there seemed to be a thawing among some of the better young surfers, especially those who looked up to or were influenced by Laird Hamilton and/or Gerry Lopez. Top pro surfer Rob Machado was one of those youngsters getting into SUP. At 5'10" and 150 pounds dripping wet DOH (depending on hairdo), Machado was neither awkward nor heavy nor slow, but he was often seen zooming around Cardiff Reef in north San Diego County "on his corky, nine-foot Merrick monster fish," according to Sam George in *The Surfer's Journal*.

Likewise Chris Malloy, another California surfer who had distinguished himself at Pipeline in Hawaii and around the world. Sam George wrote in *The Surfer's Journal*: "This past winter [2005–2006] Chris Malloy could be seen from the overpass, standing stork-like amongst the prone on his bright yellow Fletcher Chouinard, streaking across gray ten-foot walls at the Ventura Overhead."

Malloy had this to say about that:

At the time, doing stand up was like, well, pleasing yourself: fun, but don't let your friends catch you doing

Even with a stand up paddle, offshore winds can cause a surfer to drop in late. Santa Cruz surfer/SUPista attorney Colin Brown negotiates wind, kelp, and cliffs at Steamer Lane, Santa Cruz. Photo courtesy of Surftech

it. I was on that same Indo trip where Gerry Lopez got converted. I'd done it a couple of times, but the surf was overhead, pumping and shallow. Laird was on the trip and he just goes, "Get out there with me!" I wobbled out and Tom Servais shot a photo of me on my second wave that ended up on the cover of Standup Journal. *I'm still getting shit from all my friends for being on the cover of that thing.*

During the winter of 2005–2006, I was invited to surf at Privates. It was there I saw Laird in action for the first time: paddling circles around everyone else while standing up, catching all the waves he could handle, and doing the circuit—line up, paddle, catch, ride, turn, kick out, and paddle back. It really was very unusual, but Laird did it with what I now recognize as finesse: staying dry, handling a big board with skill, catching plenty of waves, but not being a hog. Really, it was something completely different to see someone standing up and paddling a surfboard into waves, and stay standing. It was unique.

But Laird made it look pretty good. Anyone else would have been tarred and feathered most likely—especially at Privates, which is a bastion of old-school protective localism.

There were other times around Malibu, when I was driving along Corral Beach with a view out to sea, or eating, drinking, and being merry at Geoffrey's or Paradise Cove, and would see a lone figure, way outside the surf zone, poking around in the kelp beds. It was always Laird, communing with nature or maybe looking for white sharks to wrestle.

Who knows what that guy is up to, most of the time?

Laird was very visible around Malibu, and the reaction was good and bad. Some thought what he was doing was different and cool, while others started coming up with epithets for this new kind of surfing: "sweeper," "gondolier," "oaron," "janitor."

There was a lot of sniggering, mostly behind Laird's back, because the guy is way bigger than most surfers. He must have been aware of it all, but Laird seems to do things inspired by that quote from Albert Einstein: "Great spirits have always encountered violent opposition from mediocre minds."

2006: Blane Chambers and Paddle Surf Hawaii

Blane Chambers is an Oahu resident who founded another of the first stand up companies, Paddle Surf Hawaii. According to a profile on Chambers in *Standup Journal*, he was inspired to walk on the water not only by visions of Laird Hamilton but also by misty, watercolored memories of the Ah Choys at Waikiki.

As Chambers was quoted in *Standup Journal*:

I bought a 12' Munoz surfboard, and made a paddle out of a dowel and a scrap of plywood. I went out to a beach near Haleiwa. It was double overhead, choppy and windy. I got my ass kicked and thought, "This is not for me."

I heard that [Hawaiian surfers] Bonga Perkins, Kamaki Worthington and Vitor Marcal were doing stand up too. I talked to Bonga and told him I was struggling. He asked me, "How you standing?" I say, "Regular foot," and he says, "Keep your feet parallel, pointing forward . . . it's easier to paddle flat water."

The next day I was in the Anahulu Stream [Oahu] standing on the Munoz, my feet aching. I paddled on the river for months. I did a lot of knee paddling in the ocean. Paddling was so intense. I loved it. I lost 40 pounds in the first six months; doing it all the time. Unlike regular board surfing—which requires lots of waiting around between sets—stand up paddling involves you from the moment you're in the water.

Chambers began shaping his own surfboards in the summer of 2005, and with just a little experience he took on the Daddy Mack of all shaping jobs: making a stand up paddleboard. He used a 12'8" Clark foam blank that barely fit in his 13-foot-long garage.

In January 2006 Chambers ordered two stand up boards from Dave Parmenter, who had become the guy to see on Oahu for the quickly evolving, difficult-to-shape boards. Parmenter is as busy as a Beirut bricklayer, making boards for devotees around the world, so as Chambers waited for his Parmenters, he shaped boards out of EPS blanks and glassed them himself with epoxy resin, and that put the hook in:

For me, this was the turning point. The beginning of the obsession. I was like a mad scientist. I was shaping, glassing, and skipping the gloss coat in a rush to finish each. I was doing as many as I could and I was keeping notes on them. I always wanted to surf each new board by the next morning.

By April 2006 Blane Chambers had produced a number of prototype stand up paddleboards that were working well for him and attracting the attention of others. In July of that year, Chambers registered Paddle Surf Hawaii LLC, and another of the first SUP companies was born. Chambers worked with Dave Parmenter at first, but then Parmenter found his allegiances torn when his Makaha friends wanted to start C4 Waterman. Todd Bradley was already making his Pohaku paddles and selling enough of them to convince everyone else that SUP was a growing market.

Parmenter went with C4, but both companies—C4 and Paddle Surf Hawaii—had more business than they knew what to do with as stand up paddle surfing caught the world's attention from 2006 into 2007.

By October 2007 Paddle Surf Hawaii had moved into a tiny building in Wahiawa, in the Oahu highlands between Waikiki on the South

Shore and the North Shore of Oahu. Working from a space "too small to swing a cat in," Chambers and his new manager, Austin Yonehiro, sold hundreds of boards in the first year: no advertising, just word of mouth. The stand up craze got that insane.

2007: Media Attention from Without and Within

Through the first half of the first decade of the twenty-first century, stand up paddling got spotty, usually grudging, and sometimes derisive coverage in the surf, sailboarding, and kayak media, but it also sometimes got noticed by the civilian media.

According to *That First Glide*: "In 2007, *Outside Magazine* did a feature on Laird Hamilton. And in it, he stated that his secret for staying in shape was standup paddling. Many give credit to that statement for the explosion standup paddling has enjoyed around the world."

That same year, 2007, Clay Feeter took a leap of faith and morphed *Wind Tracks Journal* into a magazine also dedicated to this new sport of stand up paddling. He explained the transition in an emotional e-mail.

We produced this June 2007 thru press date of Dec. 20th, 2007 . . . and bro you canNOT even imagine the mind@#@#% I was going thru; almost daily I was changing my mind:

"Should we go MORE with SUP, or less with sup?"

"How much of a role should windsurfing be after all?"

"Can an American mag really cover several 'naturally powered stand up watersports'—our original mission statement—or do readers like to have a mag for just one sport?"

I constantly put feelers out there thru the next year, over the first 2–3 issues (and I still do today!), but it was a VERY stressful time to have just quit my "real job." I pulled $49k out of my retirement fund . . .

Kai Salas hanging five on the south shore of Oahu, under the Hawaiian sun. Photo courtesy of Surftech

But then eight months later the huge banking collapse would have reduced that account by half anyway, so strangely good timing.

Starting *Standup Journal* in 2007 indeed turned out to be good timing. Maybe a little shaky at first, but the new sport needed an outlet of its own, and Feeter provided that aided by a number of friends and colleagues, including Associate Publisher Steve Sjuggerud.

In December 2010 Sjuggerud chimed in with his thoughts on the most important landmarks and turning points of recent SUP history:

To me, this sport really started when Laird [Hamilton] got serious. That's when people started to legitimately want to surf waves well or travel long distances on SUPs. (I actually own the first Surftech prototype Laird board. . . . It's the actual board he used to cross the English Channel.)

The Laird issue of Standup Journal *mentions many of the main things that Laird did before anyone else . . . crossing the Hawaiian Islands by SUP, riding Jaws, tidal bores, the Grand Canyon . . . you name it, he did it: first and biggest. Also the article talks about the evolution of the paddle, and the evolution of Laird's boards, all of which are important.*

For history . . . Gerry Lopez probably knows [it] best. However, to me, what happened Before Laird (B.L.) . . . that stuff is just interesting footnotes to the sport we're doing today. Even what Laird did in 1995 with Dave Kalama . . . that's just an important background thing, because they were just goofing around.

(Sylvain [Cazenave] has great shots from then.) I'm not trying to discredit John Zap [Zapotocky], or any of the early guys from Waikiki. I just think there is a clear distinction, B.L. and A.L.

A few other important highlights:

• The Makaha boys were the first surf community to embrace stand up paddling. I think it was part of Buff's Big Board Classic [a classic Hawaiian surf event that goes back to the 1970s] early on. These boys were on it. They were ripping first. And they turned a lot of people onto it. Later, the Ku Ikaika Big Wave Challenge at Makaha [2008 was the first year] was the first legit big-wave SUP event. It delivered! Big props to the Makaha boys.

• Blane Chambers starting Paddle Surf Hawaii. These were the first legitimate performance boards. Out of the box, they were made to rip, not made to be cruisers or noseriders. Ikaika Kalama immediately ruling Pipeline on Blane's boards. Eye-opening stuff.

• Todd Bradley (and crew) selling the C4 Pohaku paddle online. The paddle was pretty decent, even by today's standards. It's not that much different from what we use today. More importantly . . . it was AVAILABLE. No shops carried any SUP gear. But now anyone could get one of these through the Internet. Thanks to Todd for pushing hard. The C4Waterman.com site was one of the first, if not

Five-time stand up division champion Tony Mueller rounds a buoy as the judges watch for foot faults during the 2010 Surftech Jay Moriarity Memorial Paddleboard Race. Photo courtesy of Surftech

the first, and so was the C4 Pohaku paddle. The important thing was, it was AVAILABLE. Also AVAILABLE from Todd/C4—the first SUP deck pads. Now, basically every board comes with a deck pad. Once again, thanks C4.

- The timely death of windsurfing . . . leading to an open distribution channel for SUP boards. Windsurfing entered a coma about the time SUP was cranking up. The top windsurfing companies (like Naish and Starboard) had already built a complicated network to deliver big windsurf boards from Thailand to your local shop. These companies fortunately made the decision to enter the SUP market, plugging SUPs into their distribution chain. Surf shops had no idea how to deal with SUPs, and they'd never heard of Starboard or Naish. Surf shops avoided SUPs completely. But for windsurf shops, it was no big deal . . . just another big board.

- The timely death of Clark Foam, leading to more options in blanks [polyurethane foam ready for shaping]. The death of Clark Foam [which controlled the polyurethane blank market from the 1960s to its abrupt closing in 2005] sped up the wide-board EPS/epoxy SUP surf revolution. Backyard surf shapers were forced to figure out other shaping methods. Many quickly started experimenting with epoxy and EPS blanks . . . with much wider blanks than the Clark Foam tandem board blank.

- The "invention" of the recessed carry handle in the center of the board. This democratized the sport. You no longer had to be Laird to wield a 12-foot, 40-pound board. Now you just stick your hand in the hole and walk away. Not sure who the first one to do this was, but the SUP world owes you a big thanks!

- Dan Gavere, [reformed kayakers] Charlie MacArthur, and Luke Hopkins taking their mad river kayaking skills and instantly committing full-time to stand up paddling. River SUP went from zero to insane just like that. A footnote . . . [Uli company founder] Jim Weir and his ULI [Corp.] inflatable boards made their crazy river adventures even more possible.

- The arrival of Standup Journal. I'm biased here, of course, but the glossy journal made the sport more legit. Dog-eared copies lined the dashboards of the sport's first pied pipers. . . . These guys showed it to their skeptical buddies in the parking lots of their favorite surf spots: "Look at what people are doing on these boards!" the pied pipers screamed. The mag made their case. And people picked up paddles. The mag was introduced before it was economical to have a stand up mag. But it didn't take long for the mag and the industry to find its footing.

- Starboard's Extremist boards . . . and Starboard's "Whopper." When most boards were 12' long, Starboard came out with two boards they called "The Extremists": these boards were impossibly short and wide by the standards of the day. They were 9'8" × 30" and 9'0" × 30". Today, those are the normal dimensions of surf SUPs. Those boards were pretty darn good too. They were a bit flat-rockered, but you could both rip from the tail and nose ride 'em. The Whopper was crazy. . . . Until the Whopper, the beginner board of choice was the 12' Laird. The Whopper was comically fat, at 10' long and 34" wide. But surprisingly it surfs fantastically for its size. Beginners could learn much easier. And rippers could rip without thinking about falling. It's fun for everyone—a great board to have in the garage. Soon every company had its own version of the Whopper. Out of the couple major companies, Starboard has the most advanced constructions and the widest variety of boards, coming out with many new models and constructions every year. Their latest, called Brushed Carbon, shaves maybe five pounds off a typical molded SUP.

2008: SUP Racing and the Battle of the Paddle

In the 2014 *SUP the Mag Gear Guide*, a number of pioneering stand up paddlers point not to materials or construction, but to an event as a turning point in the evolution of stand up paddling. Sparky Longley is the owner of Rainbow Sandals and one of the founders of the Battle of the Paddle:

The Battle of the Paddle has brought more attention to the competitive side of SUP and competition is always the driving force within any sport. The race through the surf has created a uniquely dynamic and original format that has been equally exciting, fun and competitive for the racers and spectators alike. Not only has this event helped spread the joy of SUP far and wide but it has also been a driving force within the industry in the innovation and development of specialized racing equipment including boards, paddles and accessories.

The history of SUP racing is detailed in chapter 9, but the competitive part of SUP began to bubble around 2007/2008, according to a post on www.tahoetopia.com:

The first Ta-Hoe Nalu race happened on August 8, 2007—a seven-mile paddle from Jake's on the Lake in Tahoe City to Captain Jon's restaurant in Tahoe Vista. Thirty-four competitors from San Diego, Santa Cruz and Baja, and approximately nine people from Lake Tahoe

Laird Hamilton with Santa Cruz shaper Bob Pearson, both far from the ocean in Utah during the summer of 2010.
Photo courtesy of Surftech

From Polynesia with aloha and now extending to the ends of the earth. Paddling Patagonia, Chile. Photo by João Touma and Tiago Melo; courtesy of Surftech

competed in what would become the first ever SUP race. Dave King, of Santa Cruz and Kim Wittman from Cabo San Lucas became the first ever SUP champions.

So the SUP race scene began around 2007 and has exploded in the seven years since. According to a post on www.supracer.com:

There were a lot of SUP races this year [2014]. We had over 400 listings on the Rogue Race Calendar. We sent 137 race results to the Results by Riviera archive. You couldn't go a week without your Facebook feed being flooded with photos of SUP races here, there and everywhere.

See chapter 9 for a detailed history of SUP racing: how it started, where it is now, and where it's going.

2009: SUP Yoga Combines the Ancient with the Modern

The practice and art of yoga has been traced as far back as 3000 BC—some say India, others say Egypt—while stand up paddling on surfboards is no older than AD 1900. Around 2009 the ancient practice of yoga combined with the fresh practice of stand up paddling to form a subgroup of both pursuits: SUP yoga, which is also known as yoga boarding or paddleboard yoga—and some people call it Flo Yo or SUP Yo.

Whatever you call it, since around 2009 more and more yoginis are discovering how practicing yoga outdoors, on the water on a shaky paddleboard, "adds value" to the practice of yoga. The vibration of a stand up paddleboard even on the most placid waters adds a muscle and balance workout that also offers a more supreme pleasure.

There is no reliable metric on the number of stand up paddlers in the world, but take a look out your window at the nearest lake or bay or beach, and you most likely will see stand up paddlers—solo, or in flocks. They may be fervently paddling—toning their bodies from foot arches to core muscles to frontal lobes—but more and more stand up paddlers are laying down the paddle for a few moments to sit and kneel and lie and arch on

their boards, practicing yoga asana for healthier bodies and healthier minds.

See chapter 8 for more information on SUP yoga—and some beguiling photos.

2015: The Most Supreme Pleasure

And now it's 2015, 11 years after Buffalo Keaulana's Big Board contest had a beach boy surfing division at Makaha, 13 years after Laird Hamilton paddled out on a big day at Malibu on a tandem board with an American flag, 20 years after Laird and Dave Kalama were mucking about on tandem

Laird near the Kauai River with early equipment, around 1999. The board is a 12' × 24" tandem board made by Billy Hamilton. The paddle is a kayak paddle. If Laird looks a bit quizzical, it's because he's probably trying to figure out how to make it all stronger, lighter, faster, better.
Photo courtesy Reece-Hamilton ohana

Down a lazy river . . . One of many places opening up to stand up paddleboards as the sport progresses from its infancy to the next level. Photo courtesy of Surftech

boards at Mudflats, 76 years after Duke Kahanamoku was filmed paddling an Australian surf ski into a wave at Waikiki, 148 years after Mark Twain admired the *gondoliere* of Venice, and 238 years after Captain Cook (or the *Resolution*'s surgeon) saw that man riding waves in Tahiti stand up paddleboarding, or SUP or stand up paddle surfing or SPS or beach boy–style surfing or sweeping or

oarons or whatever you want to call it or how you want to spell it has gone *lolo*.

From Malibu to Makaha to the Maldives to Mozambique, from Lake Michigan to the Mississippi to the Mediterranean, from Waikiki to Whistler, you'll see lovers and doers of the sport.

The origins of stand up paddling are vague and still debatable. This history is likely to cause a stink, suggesting as I do that the beach boy–style surfing was inspired by Duke Kahanamoku's riding an Australian surf ski in the late 1930s. Maybe Hawaiians were paddling big surfboards with oars or canoe paddles before then, maybe not. Sam George could be correct: The history of stand up paddling is too fresh to detail. This history is by no means definitive, and if anyone has an image of someone in Hawaii stand up paddling before Duke in 1939, please track me down and let me know.

Regardless of where stand up paddling came from, it's clear today that it's going up and out like Charlie in the Great Glass Elevator. What humans have known going back to at least 3000 BC in Peru, and probably much earlier than that, is there is something supremely pleasurable aesthetically, functionally, and physically about standing up on a board and moving quickly and smoothly across the waters.

Twelve Years After: Laird Hamilton Looks Back on All He Has Left in His Wake

On September 12, 2002, Laird Hamilton paddled out at Malibu on a 12' × 24" Billy Hamilton tandem board using a paddle with an American flag affixed to the top—a tribute to the fallen from 9/11. Laird shot the pier at Malibu on that day in 2002, but this was a time when only a few people had any idea what he was doing—standing up and paddling into waves using a paddle? Egad, that lad is mad!

Just about twelve years later, Hurricane Marie produced one of the biggest south swells in Malibu history. On two days in late August 2014, Laird made it out to the lineup on a 10' × 27.5" Surrator—a very high-tech board of his own design. On this giant day at Malibu, Laird and others shot

the Malibu Pier, but it was Laird's rides that went online and around the world, from the *Huffington Post* halfway around the world to the UK's *Daily Mail*, and back to any number of surf magazines, websites, and news shows.

If you think of Laird taking off past the flagpoles at Malibu in September of 2002 and kicking out on the other side of the pier in August of 2014, as he wailed from point to pier, he could not have known that he would be launching a big sensation in his wake—a multimillion-dollar industry that had spread from Alaska to Zimbabwe and spawned dozens of SUP companies, hundreds of different models of SUPs, and who knows how many boards sold? Tens of thousands? Hundreds of thousands? Millions of boards sold, in only thirteen years?

Was Laird trying to cause a big sensation? We asked him about that.

Q: First thing I want to do is give credit to Jeff Sweet. When I go to karaoke night at Café Habana in Malibu, he always gives me stinkeye because I wrote him out of SUP history in the first edition of this book. Jeff is an LA County sheriff and he carries a gun, so I want to set that part straight. Where does Jeff Sweet figure into this?

A: *Jeff was an early adopter. Where Loch Eggers was my partner in the early days on Maui, Sweet was that guy in Malibu. What do they say, "When there's two or more, there shall I be?"*

Jeff gets in the water almost every day. He was paddling a lot with me in the beginning and then he was trying it on a wave. And then all he wanted to do was ride waves.

Q: You had your 12' × 24" tandem board when you were experimenting around Malibu. So what did Sweet ride?

A: *In the beginning we had windsurfers and anything we could stand on, but pretty quickly I had*

According to Laird's wife, Gabby, this an early shot of Laird launching out of Maliko Gulch for a downwinder on Christmas Day 2003. The board was made by Ron House, and looks smaller than typical downwind gear of ten years later. The wahine *is Bella, the eldest daughter of Laird and Gabby, who was 8 when the photo was taken.*
Photo courtesy Reece-Hamilton ohana

my Bill Hamilton stand up boards—the tandem boards—and eventually the Ron Houses.

Q: Okay, thank you. Now I can go to karaoke night at Café Habana with a clean conscience. Tell me about the Malibu swell the end of this summer of 2014. Gerry Lopez saw photos of it and he said it didn't look real. So it was special?

A: *Yeah . . . I mean we got a lot of different mixed reviews. Some people said it was the biggest swell in forty years, some people said it was the biggest in twenty years. Some people say it was the biggest swell*

in thirty-five years. For me it would have to be the biggest swell from that direction with that consistency. Spending time at Malibu in twenty years, there might be some big south swells but they don't have the Hawaii juice unless you go to the Wedge a couple times a summer when it's really unloading. Those southern hemisphere swells are tamer. So to have something with that kind of velocity coming into Malibu. It was interesting also to see the effect it had on land, because there was a kind of an energy . . . There's an energy the ocean creates that spills over onto land, people's movements and . . .

Q: That is true. A big swell in the water kind of energizes the land. What board were you riding that day?

A: I have a board called a Surrator that I was surfing over two days. There was the beginning and the upcoming of the swell, but unfortunately I didn't get there until a little later that afternoon, and then the next day I was there almost the whole day, but it didn't seem like the second day was as energized as that first night. On the upcoming part of the swell is usually when there's the greatest push. And the next day was still pumping waves.

Q: What are the dimensions of the Surrator?

A: Oh, the Surrator is 10'2" by 27" or something like that.

Q: Twenty-seven inches wide, really?

A: Maybe twenty-seven and a half.

Q: Do you think SUP is a billion-dollar industry yet?

A: It's hard to say, but if it's not, it will be next year. It's definitely going in that direction.

Q: This summer I worked at Lake Sammamish in Seattle, at Issaquah Paddle Sports which used to be a kayak rental place, but now it's a SUP rental place. They had sixty-plus SUPs for rent and on a busy weekend they would all be out, with twenty people in line, fiending to go paddling. It was crazy, the effect SUP had on this one obscure corner of an obscure lake in east Seattle. What have you seen that surprises you about SUP? About how much it's grown, that quickly. Anything that has shocked you?

A: I don't know about shocked me, but if you really want to see the explosion of SUP, go down to the Battle of the Paddle. I know people are stand up paddling around the world: Lake Geneva. They're doing it on

the lakes and somebody sent me a picture of a guy with a turban doing SUP on a Laird paddleboard in Dubai. But you go to the Battle of the Paddle and there are a lot of humans there who are taking it seriously. Hundreds of contestants. Battle of the Paddle is a whole 'nother level.*

Q: Serious boards, serious technology, serious athletes. But are you surprised it has gotten this big, this fast?

A: In one way I could say yeah, I'm pretty aware of its . . . broad appeal. Let's put it that way. I could say "Yeah, I had a pretty good idea it was going to do that," but then I could say that I'm equally as enthralled by the level of the participation, exposure, diversity. The global aspect of it. You knew it was going to have an effect. But when you really look at stand up paddling . . . it's surfing. You know, surfing blew up and went around the world. Stand up paddling is a little easier to deal with because you don't need a wave to go out and have that sensation. So I would attribute that to surfing. There's nobody that wouldn't like it if they tried it. At the same time, it is remarkable.

Q: What is the most far-flung place SUP has taken you? A place you would never thought you would go.

A: Obviously the Colorado River. I never thought I would be paddling my board down the rapids. I've been to Europe, the Mediterranean, Indo. When I first started I never thought I would go to Teahupoo and pull in.

Q: Where do you think it's going? Do you think it will be in the Olympics before too long?

A: I think it will be hard not to. There's the international appeal. Wave riding stand up I think is too difficult. But I think the straight up racing around the course, I think that's an absolute discipline if I've ever seen one.

When shopping for stand up paddling accessories,
don't forget the importance of good sunhats.
Photo courtesy of Lili Foster

CHAPTER 2

BUYING
A BOARD & ACCESSORIES

In plain terms, a stand up paddleboard is a high-tech beer cooler, wrapped in a bulletproof, candy-coated shell. That's putting it simply and cryptically, but modern technology applied to traditional surfboard manufacturing is one of the things that has made stand up paddleboards so popular—they are surprisingly strong, light, tough and well made, in a bewildering variety of flavors.

Making Sense of the Lingo

There is a lot to choose from in the world of SUP, and this section is designed to help you understand important terms and make intelligent choices.

The **BOTTOM** is the area of the surfboard that contacts the water.

CARBON FIBER is a material used for composite laminates, fins, and paddles that is light and stronger than steel. Carbon fiber is a polymer created by heating another polymer several times to "rattle out" almost all of the hydrogen and nitrogen atoms—except carbon—to form a fiber that is thinner than a human hair; when these fibers are woven together, they are stronger than steel and much lighter. Carbon fiber is expensive to produce and used as a component of composite laminates in some stand up paddleboards and also for fins and paddles.

As it applies to SUP construction, a **COMPOSITE** is a combination of fiberglass, wood veneer, carbon fiber, or other material that forms a new material that is greater than its components.

The top of the board is called the **DECK**. Most stand up paddleboards come with some kind of adhesive patch to provide traction between the rider's feet and the deck of the board. Some traditional stand up paddleboards use paraffin-based surf wax for traction.

A **DING** is a crack, fracture, or hole in the exterior of the board that allows water to contact the foam core.

EXPANDED POLYSTYRENE (EPS) is a petroleum product that is one of the most common plastics and is used to manufacture, among other things, CD cases, yogurt cups, and disposable razors. EPS, which is large cell, is often used for beer coolers and packing materials. The cheap, very breakable surfboards Mom used to buy at the five-and-dime were polystyrene. Because of its large cells, polystyrene is difficult to hand shape, and for that and other reasons—such as its buoyancy—EPS is not as popular in surfboard manufacture as polyurethane foam. But in the world of SUP, expanded polystyrene has become the foam core of choice, because epoxy resin does not react well

Daniel Geft proclaims "I'm king of the world!" on the deck of a long-distance SUP cruiser.

with polyurethane foam cores. EPS foam is usually machine molded, then laminated with a variety of materials and techniques: wood veneers, carbon fiber, epoxy resin, and sandwich construction. EPS is lighter and more buoyant than polyurethane, and when wrapped in modern laminates, the result is a board that is light, floats well, and is many times more durable than traditional polyurethane foam and polyester resin boards.

EPOXY RESIN is a versatile thermoset plastic that bonds well to a variety of materials, which makes it perfect for the wide variety of materials used in laminating EPS cores: fiberglass, wood veneers, and carbon fiber. Compared to polyester resins, epoxy resins are stronger and more resistant to shrinkage

and fatigue. Epoxy is always used to laminate EPS cores, because polyester resin melts EPS.

EPOXY COMPOSITE CONSTRUCTION is the use of epoxy resin to bond together different materials, such as fiberglass, wood veneers, and carbon fiber.

FUSED CELL EXPANDED POLYSTYRENE (FEPS) is an improved alchemy of EPS that does not absorb water when exposed in a ding.

FIBERGLASS is a woven material made of extremely fine glass fibers. Fiberglass is used as a component in the lamination of stand up paddleboards, sometimes in a composite blend with other materials. Fiberglass is also used in the construction of paddles and fins but is not as strong or light as carbon fiber.

The **FIN BOX** houses the **FIN.** The majority of stand up paddleboards have removable fin systems, with the larger central fin slotting into a fin box that is placed by the manufacturer on the centerline of the board, near the tail. The center fin is usually fastened by a screw and nut that goes or passes through a tab on the back of the fin. If the board has more than one fin, the side fins are smaller and usually screw into slots offset to the side.

LENGTH is the dimension of a board from nose to tail. Stand up paddleboards can be as short as 7'6" (and getting shorter by the month!) to as long as 16' for racing boards. Beginners will want to look for boards in the 10' to 12' range.

The front end of the board is called the **NOSE.** The nose measurement is 12" back from the tip.

POLYESTER RESIN is used to laminate most traditional, hand-shaped, hand-laminated surfboards. It does not react well with polystyrene (EPS) foam, and it is also heavier and not as resistant to pressure and shatters.

POLYURETHANE FOAM (PU) is the material traditionally used to make cores for surfboards and prone paddleboards. Boards made from this

Kolaiah "Fuzzy" Jardine leaves no doubt as to the dimensions of his board. The 8'10" is length, the 32" is width, and 4.6" is thickness. Photo courtesy of Starboard

construction are usually hand shaped and laminated by hand with polyester resin and fiberglass. This technique is still responsible for the majority of surfboards made in the world. The majority of the stand up paddleboard industry has turned to molded EPS foam laminated with a variety of materials to make boards that are lighter, stronger, and more buoyant.

In the surfing world, a **POPOUT** is a derogatory term for a surfboard that is molded and laminated by machine, rather than custom-made by hand by experienced and long-suffering surfboard shapers. With the exception of custom-shaped boards for professionals and racers, most stand

up paddleboards are made of molded EPS foam cores and are laminated by machine, but these techniques are standard for the industry and not derogatory. Manufacturers of stand up paddleboards go through many hand-shaped prototypes to determine an equation of length, width, height, volume, rail shape, nose shape, and tail shape that works—sometimes after many evolutions of prototypes—and then make a mold that allows that same board to be manufactured exactly to

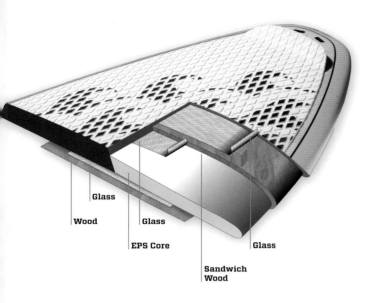

Glass

Wood   Glass

EPS Core

Glass

Sandwich
Wood

Sandwich wood board construction. Illustration courtesy of Naish

specifications. So an 11'6" Surftech or C4 Water-man or Naish you ride in California is the same Surftech or C4 Waterman or Naish 11'6" you rent in Thailand or Lake Michigan. Kind of like going to Starbucks and ordering a latte: No matter where you order it, you usually know what you are going to get.

The **RAILS** are the side edges of the board, which run from nose to tail. Rail shape is important for turning and speed. SUP rails are generally rounded although some racing boards use a squarer, "box-ier" rail. If you collide with another surfer or SUP rider, that is called "banging rails." If you do a turn wrong and the rail goes underwater, you are "dig-ging a rail." If you put your hand on the edge for stability through a difficult section, that is "grab-bing a rail."

SANDWICH CONSTRUCTION is a technique bor-rowed from the sailboard industry. A molded EPS

foam core is wrapped with a high-density sheet of foam and/or veneer and/or carbon fiber with the sheet reinforced with fiberglass and epoxy resin. This outer shell is made stronger and lighter and forms a better bond with the foam core through a process called "vacuum bagging": The board is placed in a bag, and the air is drawn out, which cre-ates an equal pressure that forms the bond evenly and withdraws extra material. Sandwich construc-tion creates a lighter board with an outer "sand-wich" shell that is much more resistant to dings and cracks and accidents than a hand-laminated, polyester resin and fiberglass shell. Better living through chemistry. Sandwich construction and vacuum bagging are expensive processes, usually done in Asian factories, but the boards produced are light and close to bulletproof.

The **SKEG** is a slightly antiquated term for fin. Still used by many.

The **TAIL** is the back end of the board. The tail measurement of a board is measured 1 foot from the tail of the board.

In general, the **THICKNESS** of a board is at its thickest point, as measured with calipers. Stand up paddleboards are thicker than traditional surfboards because they need to be more buoyant and stable.

THRUSTER is the surfing term for a three-fin setup: big fin in the middle and two smaller fins on the side.

TRACTION is what holds your feet to the board. Whether a stand up paddleboard is laminated with epoxy or polyester resin, the board is finished to be smooth as glass. The deck of a stand up paddle-board doesn't provide any friction between the surface and the bottoms of a paddler's feet, so traction is required: either wax or stick-on traction decks made of a variety of materials.

TRI-FIN is a three-fin setup usually used for per-formance wave riding. Also known as a "thruster," the tri-fin has one larger fin in the middle and two smaller stabilizing fins on the side.

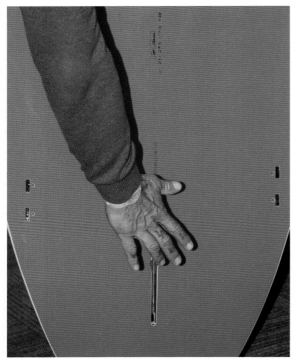

The tri-fin setup on a stand up paddleboard, a large adjustable slot for the middle fin and fixed side fins.

From the sailboarding world, **VOLUME** is a measurement (in liters) for the quantity of foam in a stand up paddleboard. For example, a Gerry Lopez 10' Surf Music SUP that is 10' long, 28" wide, and 4" thick has a volume of 134.2 liters. The volume gives some idea of how a board will float, but the distribution of the volume is also important. To work it out yourself, ½ (length × width × thickness) + (10 × every inch over 72") = a number in cubic inches, then divide by 61 to get liters.

WIDTH is the dimension of a board from rail to rail. Usually the widest point of the board is measured to determine the width of a stand up paddleboard. Most stand up paddleboards range from 27" to 34". More width generally means more stability and flotation, while less width translates to more speed and maneuverability.

Choosing a Board: Mitch Taylor of Becker Surf and Sport Guides Newcomers through the Reefs of Retail

In October 2010 surf journalist Marcus Sanders interviewed Laird Hamilton in the leading online surf media portal: www.surfline.com. In the interview, Laird explained how traditional prone paddle surfing wasn't cutting it with him anymore, and he was into pushing the limits of nontraditional forms of riding waves: stand up paddle surfing, foilboarding, and using personal watercraft to tow into giant waves.

SUP was still a controversial topic in the surfing world. As more and more people were taking stand up paddleboards into the surf zones, there was grumbling from Malibu to Makaha to the Maldives as longtime surfers complained about the ever-increasing waves of beginners blundering into the lineup on their oversized stand up paddleboards and causing havoc in surfing areas already crowded with too many surfers.

Laird understood the conflicts, but he reckoned the negatives of SUP were being far outweighed by the positives, and one of the positives was the boost that the production and sales of stand up paddleboards was having on surfboard manufacturers and retailers. "You're not going to stop it," Laird was quoted on Surfline.

You might try to deter it or steer away, but it's something that's helping all these industries; it's helping all these retail stores. A lot of these stores would be out of business; a lot of these shapers would be in the gutter. So you stimulate the surf industry at a time when it needs it in a genuine way with people

that are actually participating in the activity—not just buying the clothes and buying shirts and hats reflective of a lifestyle.

MITCH TAYLOR IS THE MANAGER OF Becker Surf and Sport in Malibu, California. A longtime surfer going back to the age of 7, Mitch looked askance at SUP and was a naysayer until he tried it himself. After some missteps using the wrong equipment, Mitch finally got his feet on the right-size board and his hands around the right-size paddle, and he was sold. Now he is a regular stand up paddler in the lineup from Surfrider to County Line, and he is often seen poking around out in the kelp beds, getting in his strokes and his exercise on days when the surf is flat.

Becker Surf and Sport's Mitch Taylor enjoying one of the big advantages of stand up paddling: elevation. Paddling over this wave, he is close to 10 feet above sea level, so he can see everything that's coming, has thirty seconds of early warning over prone surfers, and can get there twice as fast. He could take advantage, but he wants to remain welcome at the places he surfs, so Mitch takes his turn. But he always knows what is coming. Photo: Dan Tucker. Courtesy of Mitch Taylor

As a stand up paddler, Mitch Taylor is sold, and as a surf shop manager, he sees this new hybrid sport as a savior during the hard times of the economic downturn, hard times that have even poked through the bubble of prosperity that surrounds Malibu. "Yes, stand up paddleboard rentals and sales of equipment are keeping this shop alive,"

After a false start on the wrong equipment, it took about eight boards for Mitch Taylor to find the board he liked best for surfing, He loves his 9'6" Laird Pearson Arrow because he can turn it like his shortboard. Mitch cutting back at County Line. Photo: Dan Tucker. Courtesy Mitch Taylor

Mitch said. "Shops that aren't selling stand up boards and equipment—well, I don't see how they are making it."

Most surf shops are seasonal, but because Malibu is blessed with just about perfect weather year-around, the demand is pretty steady from June to December and back to June. "If it's a day when it's glassy and 75 degrees out, we'll sell anywhere from one to five stand up paddleboards," Mitch said. "Usually customers come in and say, 'We saw people out standing on boards and paddling. What is that? We'd like to try it.' I would say we average a sale of one board a day out of Becker's in Malibu, and some days we will sell as many as eight."

Consider that a new stand up paddleboard costs anywhere from $500 to $5,000+, and a paddle is anywhere from $100 to $400+. Add to that all the accessories, including surf leashes, board bags, paddle bags, wax, wetsuits, booties, rash guards, helmets, PFDs, sunglasses, repair kits, and board racks. SUP is keeping Becker's Malibu in business, during a time when surf shops, like all retail, are struggling from a down economy and competition from the Internet and elsewhere.

During the fall of 2010, Becker Surf and Sport had somehow managed to shoehorn about 600 feet of stand up paddleboards into the shop. The store carried fifty boards from a half dozen different manufacturers, ranging from as short as 8' to a 14-footer that required the Becker staff to remove ceiling panels so the board would fit in the store. "We carry Surftech, Pearson Arrows by Bob Pearson, Kings paddleboards by Dave Daum, Naish, and Lahui Kai race boards, as well as our own Becker brand," Mitch said.

Most boards are hand-shaped epoxy, which are very similar to a regular surfboard and ding as easily. We also have Surftechs, which are made from a sandwich construction. They are very light and strong and float better than hand-shaped epoxy.

The sandwich construction boards are by far our strongest material. I don't want to say they're bulletproof . . . you can still ding them. If you pile them onto the rocks, they are going to ding. But if you were on a regular epoxy hand-shaped board, the damage from the same hit would be much worse.

You can leave it on the beach. The sun is not going to destroy it. Like I said, they're pretty close to bulletproof. Not only are they lighter, but the buoyancy on them is much better than hand-shaped boards.

The first stand ups we sold were hand-shaped and glassed with epoxy, but after the sandwich construction boards came out, we could barely get rid of the old style because they weighed so much.

Becker Surf and Sport carries a variety of widths. "The narrowest boards are the 27" Lahui Kai race boards," Mitch said, "while most of the better wave-riding boards range from 8' to 10'6" long and are 29" to 31" wide. The widest boards are the 34" Naish, which will float anyone from offensive linemen to Grandma and her walker. And we do get a lot of very large people in here."

Becker's Malibu gets a lot of different kinds of people passing through, but the shop is atypical because it is within a bubble of 90265 prosperity due to its proximity to Malibu Colony and Malibu Road, home to the rich and famous. During the summer, some Malibu visitors think nothing of paying anywhere from $50,000 to $100,000+ a month to rent a home with an ocean view.

Malibu is one of the modern homes of SUP, so those million-dollar views are crossed every few minutes by stand up paddlers going to and fro, in and out of the kelp line, surfing, snorkeling, racing, cruising. A good percentage of the customers walking into Becker's are people of means living along the beach, and they think nothing of slapping down an American Express Black card and saying: "I'll take five of the best of everything for me and my entourage, bodyguards, and driver."

Instead of taking advantage of their very prosperous, often clueless high-end clientele for whom cost is not a concern, Mitch and the sales crew are now very experienced in dealing with first-time stand up paddlers, and they have a routine that gives their customers a safe, sane, and economically correct introduction to the sport.

Rent Before You Buy

Because people come in such a wide range of heights, weights, balance points, and physical abilities and disabilities, the stand up paddleboard industry is providing an ever-increasing quiver of possible SUP boards. It's a good idea for beginners to try a rental for a day or two so they can make an educated choice on what kind of board to purchase.

Out in the back of the Becker shop, there is a big, secure van with enough room for a half dozen stand up paddleboards, adjustable paddles, and other accessories for rent to beginners. At Becker Surf and Sport, the rental charge is $50 for a board and a paddle for twenty-four hours. "But if people try these boards and decide what they like and then come back to buy a board," Mitch says, "we put the expense of the rental toward the cost of

Pulling a rental board out of the van behind the shop, Mitch Taylor shows off both sides of the workhorse of the Becker beginner rental fleet: a 12'1" Laird, which will float just about everyone.

the board. So if they spend $150 renting boards, they get $150 off the cost of buying a complete rig. That seems to work for all involved." Many shops follow this same protocol, allowing people who are serious about buying a board to try out various styles without worrying that they're throwing money out to sea.

The shop keeps six boards in the van out back—all of them large and wide for beginners. "I have a 12'1" Laird as a demo, and that can handle just about anyone," Mitch says. "Although if we get a sumo wrestler in here, we have the 34" Naish boards we can use. And then we have a 10'6" demo and another 10'6" demo and an 11' demo and one more—I believe that is a 10'6" demo."

Width Matters

Stand up paddleboards range from 27" to 34" in width at the widest part of the board. The narrower boards look fast and cool, but Mitch Taylor knows that most beginners are unstable platforms, so they need stable platforms under their feet.

Width is your world of stability. A 5'3" woman who weighs 105 pounds will be able to stand on a 9' board that is 27" wide, but that board is going to be tippy and she is going to struggle. I would say 90 percent of boards on the market are in the user-friendly range, from 29" to 31" wide. The widest board we have is the 34" Naish. There are some really big guys who come in here who are too big even for the red Laird, which is 12'1" long and 31" wide. So when someone ducks under the door and fills the room and blocks out the sun, I steer them toward the 34" Naish, which will float just about anyone—even Shaq [Shaquille O'Neal].

Enter the Gefts

Michelle Geft is 5 feet, 4 inches tall and weighs 115 pounds. Noam Geft is 6 feet tall and weighs 185 pounds. Michelle is an experienced surfer and is comfortable in the water and with her feet on a board. Noam is an experienced kayaker and knows how to use a paddle.

Noam and Michelle walked into Becker Surf and Sport looking for his and hers boards they

Hand in hand and without fear, Noam and Michelle Geft boldly walk into Becker Surf and Sport in the Colony Plaza, Malibu, California.

Sizing up the Gefts: Michelle (medium), Noam (large), and their lovely lads, Daniel (toddler) and Evan (small).

"I'm *the surfer,* heeeee's *the kayaker,*" Michelle says, but Mitch Taylor does not discriminate about such things, because he knows that stand up paddling is an evolution for both disciplines. And a good place for the twain to meet.

could ride together. Noam has a bad back and can't do normal surfing and even kayaking had become uncomfortable. Michelle is a surfer who found kayaking uncomfortable and wanted to try stand up paddling as something she could do while Noam was kayaking. They both had seen people paddling around with their kids on stand up paddleboards and thought it might be fun for their whole family, which includes 7-year-old Evan and 2-year-old Daniel.

After many years of selling surfing and SUP equipment to strangers, Mitch Taylor has become as good as a carnival hustler at estimating height and weight, and he also knows that the equation of height and weight and experience equals the right-size boards for beginners.

Sizing up the Gefts for rental boards, Mitch said: "I would put him on a 12-footer and her on a 10'6". And 30" is a good standard width for most beginners, because width equals stability." After the Gefts have a chance to try out the boards, Mitch hopes they will return to buy boards, and at that point their final purchase will be made based on their experiences with the rental boards.

Starting Out on the Proper Board

Mitch Taylor speaks from experience when it comes to starting out on the proper board—something that is wide and stable and gives an unshaky introduction to stand up paddling:

I have surfed since I was 7 years old. Travis Stassart—who works in the shop here with me—started stand up paddling about six years ago and he was all enthusiastic: "Come on, you've gotta go with me, you'll love it!" About four years ago, I gave it a try. Because I weigh 20 pounds less than him, Travis thought I should be on a much smaller board. He was on a 12-footer and I was on a 10-footer, and this was when they first came out, so it wasn't 30 inches wide, it was

Mitch Taylor with his personal ride, a 9'6" × 28¾" × 4⅛" Pearson Arrow Laird: "This is probably the eighth board that I've owned. The performance of it for surfing is great, but it's also nice and stable for going for a paddle when it's flat."

27 inches. It was so wobbly that I could barely paddle. I couldn't even get my hand on the top of the paddle. And I'm thinking, "I don't know why anybody in their right mind would spend the money to do this." We went out four times and I had really bad experiences.

Then I went to a party at the beach and saw this guy who I know is from Chicago. He's 70 years old and probably 6'4" and 270 pounds. He walks down to the water with one of Laird's big boards, gets on it and strokes out to sea like he's been doing it his whole life.

I'm watching this and thinking, "I've surfed since I was a kid and I can't do it." So when he came back in I got on that board, and that's when I figured it out: "Now I get why people like this so much." It was so stable and so easy to do. I rode that board for six months. Just paddling. All I did was paddle that board every day for six months until I felt good about turning and moving. I didn't go into the surf until I knew what I was doing.

CHOOSING A BOARD SIZE

PADDLER'S WEIGHT	PADDLING ABILITY	
	Advanced Ability Good surfer, athletic, wants a board geared toward paddle surfing.	**Novice** New to the sport, little or no surfing experience, wants a board that paddles easily.
120–150 pounds	Length: 9' – 10'6" Width: 26' – 26½" Thickness: 3¾" – 3⅞"	Length: 10'6" – 11' Width: 27" – 27½" Thickness: 3⅞" – 4¼"
160–190 pounds	Length: 9'6" – 10'6" Width: 27" – 28" Thickness: 4" – 4¼"	Length: 11' Width: 28" – 29" Thickness: 4⅜" – 4⅝"
200–230 pounds	Length: 10' – 11' Width: 28" – 28½" Thickness: 4" – 4¾"	Length: 11' – 11'6" Width: 29½" – 30½" Thickness: 4¾"
240–270 pounds	Length: 11' – 11'6" Width: 29½" – 31½" Thickness: 4⅞" – 5"	Length: 11'6" – 12' Width: 32" – 33" Thickness: 4⅞" – 5"
280+ pounds	Length: 12' Width: 32" Thickness: 5"	Length: 12" Width: 33" Thickness: 5"

Narrowing Your Choices

There are a lot of choices available in buying a stand up paddleboard. The boards can be divided into several categories, and there are divisions within those categories: Beginner boards, wave riding, flatwater cruising, flatwater racing, downwind paddling, river/whitewater paddling, long-distance touring, and short- and long-distance racing.

Most of the people who rent boards from Becker Surf and Sport learn in the ocean, but when they come back in to return the boards and buy their own equipment, one of the first questions Mitch asks (after "Did you have fun?") is, "Where will you be using your stand up paddleboard?"

Because many of his customers are people visiting Malibu (there are a lot of snowbirds who come to Malibu in the winter for blue skies and 70-degree weather), one of the souvenirs they will be taking home is a stand up paddleboard and paddle, and the knowledge that this new thing they

CHOOSING A PLACE TO START PADDLING

The customers who rent boards around Malibu usually take them into the ocean at any number of beaches from Santa Monica to Surfrider to Zuma Beach to County Line. There aren't many freshwater lakes and rivers in the Malibu area. The exception to that is the Malibu Lagoon, which is where Malibu Creek pools up before flowing into the sea between Malibu Colony and the Malibu Pier. This would be a good place for flatwater paddling, in theory, but in reality it's a place where you really don't want to fall, because the water is brackish and notoriously polluted. Mitch Taylor strongly suggests that beginners avoid paddling Malibu Lagoon since beginners fall often, even in flat water. It's something to think about no matter where you live. If the quality of the water is such that you don't want to be immersed in it, find a different place to start paddling.

SO MANY SUPS, SO LITTLE TIME
A FEW BOARDS OUT OF MANY BOARDS FROM ONE COMPANY OUT OF MANY COMPANIES

Surftech was one of the first companies to produce stand up paddleboards around 2004. Eleven years later they are just one of many, many companies producing stand up paddleboards. Looking through the issues of several stand up paddle magazines in February of 2015, these were some of the prominent SUP manufacturers: 404, Advanced Elements, Amundson, BIC Sport, BOGA, Boardworks, BOTE, Coreban, Doyle, Easy Rider, Fanatic, F-ONE, Hala, Hippo Stick, Hobie, Ian Balding, Indigo, Infinity, Lakeshore Paddleboard Company, Naish, NRS, OAM SUP, Ocean Lineage, Odyssey SUP, Pau Hana Surf Supply, Riviera Paddlesurf, Rogue, Sea Eagle, Sevylor SUP, SIC, South Tahoe Standup Paddle, Stand on Liquid, Starboard, Surftech, Tahoe SUP, Three Brothers Boards, WaveJet, and Zulu.

That's to name only a few SUP companies, and not close to all of them. There are many more, small and large, in garages and factories, around the world.

Surftech has been innovating with SUP design and materials for more than ten years, and their 2015 lineup offers forty-eight different boards in five classifications: Racing, Downwind, Touring, All Around, and Surf.

These eight boards give an idea of the range of length, width, height, and design of modern stand up paddleboards, which have become very refined to fit a wide variety of uses at sea and inland, cruising and racing, surfing and doing asanas, going with the wind or staying out of it.

Beginner SUP
10'6" Blacktip

The SUP market has become extremely competitive from low to high, which is a headache for the competing companies but a bonus for the buyer. Many first-time SUPistas will go to Costco and spend $600 for a Wavestorm Stand Up Paddle Board Bundle, which gets them a 10'6" soft foam Wavestorm paddleboard which can hold up to 300 pounds, a paddle, and a leash. Wavestorms aren't the coolest boards out there, but they are a good bargain for people

Photo courtesy Surftech

who want to find their feet inexpensively, and then move up to a fancier board.

Surftech's Blacktip technology is used for surfboards and SUP, and their 10'6" Blacktip is 33" wide and 4.2" thick, with a volume of 185.5 liters and weighing 29.5 pounds. Blacktip construction is soft and safe but still durable—perfect boards for beginning SUPistas. The 2015 MSRP is $880 and comes with a Surftech adjustable aluminum paddle. So maybe not as inexpensive as a Wavestorm, but better construction and a board that will last a long time.

Surf
9'1" Caddi

Surftech was and is a surfboard company first, but moved into the SUP market early—and watched it explode. In the past they had produced a lot of great wave-riding SUPs from the likes of Laird Hamilton, Mickey Munoz, Gerry Lopez, and Robert August.

For 2015 they have only one surf SUP. The Caddi is designed by Channel Islands, one of the most

Photo courtesy Surftech

influential surfboard companies in the world. This Caddi is 9'1" × 29.5" × 4.4" with a volume of 136.6 liters—but there are also a 9'7" and a 10'1" model. The Caddi can be used for touring and cruising, but with added rocker and a thinned-out tail, it is also built to be ridden on waves from small to medium. This is a SUP that is meant to be surfed.

All Around
11'6" Universal

The Universal boards are stable and durable and very, very popular with many of the beach boy concessions and resorts around Hawaii—Disney's Aulani resort has a fleet of Universals because they can take a pounding and keep on rebounding. This Universal is 11'6" × 32" × 3" with a volume of 238 liters, but they also have a 10'6" and a 12'0" model.

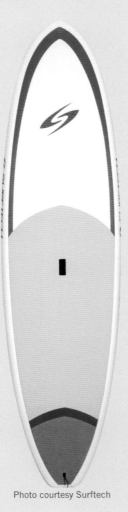

Photo courtesy Surftech

10'6" Margaritaville

Inspired by Jimmy Buffett—an avid surfer and paddler and frequent visitor to Surftech because he stores his boards there—the Margaritaville is 10'6" × 32.3" × 4.4" with a volume of 166.8 liters. This board is a Parrothead version of Surftech's Generator model. It's meant for easy cruising on inland waterways and bayous from Sag Harbor to Florida and anywhere in the world paddlers need a stable platform.

Photo courtesy Surftech

Yoga
10'6" Yogaversal

At 10'6" × 32" × 5" with a volume of 206 liters, the Yogaversal is an adaptation of the Universal, made for SUP yoga. The width and thickness provide the solid platform that yoginis need to bust their asanas out in open water.

Photo courtesy Surftech

Racing
14' Dominator

A mean machine, built for speed and built to win. The Dominator is the Ferrari of the Surftech line, and a dominant board in races from Molokai to Oahu to Orange County—and anywhere SUPs are racing. At 14' × 28" by 7" thick, the Domina-tor has a volume of 285 liters but weighs a shocking 28 pounds—a result of Surftech's Pro Elite construction.

Photo courtesy Surftech

Downwinder

14' Downwinder

Downwinder boards are made for places like Maliko Gulch on Maui, where paddlers launch in the relative calm of the small, protected bay, paddle out of the mouth of it, turn left, hook into the trade winds, and haul okole along the Maui coast for many miles—paddling with the wind, catching swells, dodging bumps, and having a blast, all the way to Kanaha Park.

Maliko Gulch and Maui are the spiritual home of downwinders, but stand up paddlers can get their downwind kicks anywhere there is a consistent wind blowing laterally along the shore—like the northwest winds that rake most of the California coast year-around, the Columbia Gorge in Oregon, and Lake Garda in Italy. All of these places and many others have perfect conditions for downwind runs, but the proper board is essential for downwinding. Or you are going to fall and flail and not have a good time.

Surftech's Downwinder is 14' × 28" × 6.8", which makes it a narrow, thick mean machine for riding swells and pushing through bumps. The board weighs only 28 pounds but the price is a hefty $2,499. The Downwinder is a serious board for adventurers who want to do the Maliko run, or maybe paddle from Molokai to Oahu with the wind.

Photo courtesy Surftech

Touring
12'6" Flowmaster

Touring boards are on the border of racers and downwinders—big, floaty boards meant to provide a stable platform for long-distance paddling. The blurbage on www.surftech.com reads: "Designed for the outdoor adventurer or entry-level racer, the 12'6" Flowmaster has a modest waterline which translates into maximum glide with minimal effort."

Photo courtesy Surftech

So Many SUPs, So Little Time = Try Before You Buy

Remember, this is just eight boards out of a line of forty-eight from one year—2015—from one company that has been evolving SUP going back to 2004.

There are many, many other SUP companies out there—some specializing in lake boards, some making inflatables, some specializing in boards for surfing, for cruising, for yoga, for flatwater cruising, flatwater racing, downwinders.

Add it all up, and the possibilities and choices can be bewildering. Shop around, do your homework, try as many boards as you can.

At the Surftech Hawaii shop, the employees encourage eager buyers to Try Before They Buy. These boards range in price from $1,000 to $2,500, and they don't want anyone walking away displeased.

Michelle checks out the deck of a 12'6" × 27" Jamie Mitchell racing board. Sexy, but not a board for beginners.

started doing in California will be just as much fun on the Missouri River, Lake Michigan, the Severn River, or the Black Sea. "I ask if they are going to be using the board in a lake or on flat water, or will they be using it in the surf," Mitch says. "That's the first dividing line, because then I steer them toward a single fin or multifin setup." Once Mitch determines how much the paddlers weigh and where they will be using the boards, he begins the whittling process to sort the hundreds of possible permutations into the right board for each particular paddler.

One Fin, Two Fin, Three Fin More

Since 1981 most surfboards have used a three-fin or "thruster" setup—one larger fin in the middle and two small stabilizers on the side—while some longboarders still use a single fin. A stand up paddleboard made for wave riding will most likely come with a tri-fin/thruster setup, as it gives the rider the option to use just one large fin, two fins, or all three.

For people who are taking their boards to flatwater locations—which include gentle rivers, lakes, reservoirs, fjords, bays, estuaries, and other bodies of water where waves don't break and strong currents don't flow—Mitch Taylor suggests buying a board made for flatwater cruising, which usually has a single-fin setup.

However, for people who want to use their boards for different types of water ranging from flatwater cruising to wave riding, Mitch usually suggests a tri-fin setup, just to have the option of using one fin, two larger side fins with no middle fin, or three fins.

Mitch, in the Valley of the Models, shows off a Tahoe stand up paddleboard, which is the Escalade of flatwater cruisers. At 14' long, 29" wide, and 5" thick, the entire Geft family could hop on this thing and make it to Catalina in a couple of hours.

BETTER TO BREAK A FIN THAN A FIN BOX

Some stand up paddleboards can't really be flicked back over the whitewater like a short-board when you get near shore, and sometimes they have to be ridden straight in toward the beach, where the water gets shallower and rocks and sandbars await. I have broken several fins out of my 12'1" Laird because of this. It always seems to happen at First Point Malibu, usually the result of riding the board while standing up or kneeling into too-shallow water and not getting off quick enough.

Part of the reason I break fins is because I can be clumsy and awkward, or maybe I'm feeling like a pansy that day, and I don't want to get wet and cold by jumping into the water. It's also partly because there is no sandbar at Malibu, and the rocks tear up human feet like piranha, which also makes me reluctant to jump off in time (see the Footwear section). For whatever reason, more than a few times my fins have been sacrificed.

Fortunately, one of the design ingenuities of stand up paddleboards is that the fins are designed to break out before the fin box that contains them. Almost all stand up paddleboard fins are part of a box system in which the fin slides into a plastic slot that is permanently set in the board by the manufacturer. The big middle fin fastens with a screw and nut in the back, and there is a small metal bar that slides in a groove and keeps the front of the fin in the box.

When a fin makes contact with rocks or sand, that little metal bar and the screw and nut in the back are supposed to break first. This renders the fin unusable, so you have to buy another one (they vary in cost from free when found on the beach to $10 to $60 or more). But buying fins is better and cheaper than repairing a blown-out fin box, an expensive repair that means your board is never quite the same again. Although it's rare to break the fin box, it is possible, so be careful.

Mitch Taylor shows the bottom of a three-fin "thruster" stand up paddleboard and explains how it can be used with one fin or three.

The Scoop on Paddles

When Laird Hamilton first began messing around on his father's 24" tandem boards, he broke a lot of paddles that were built for other purposes. He broke plastic paddles, he broke wood paddles, he broke 'em all. Laird is a big guy who was often out in treacherous conditions, and he usually broke paddles while "bracing"—holding the paddle against the current or wave or forward motion to slow down or turn.

Laird approached paddle makers like Malama in the Hawaiian Islands and others on the mainland looking for the combination of weight and strength he desired for stand up paddling, and so began the evolution of stand up paddles that has created the current inventory.

These days stand up paddles are available in many combinations of materials, lengths, weights, shaft shapes, blade shapes, and other variables. There are straight shafts and elbowed shafts, fixed length and adjustable, and paddles made of aluminum, wood, fiberglass, and carbon fiber. As a stand up paddler becomes more experienced, picking the right paddle becomes more

Michelle Geft is 5', 4" tall. The rule for sizing stand up paddles is they should be 6" to 10" taller than the paddler. Because Michelle is 64", she needs a paddle that is about 70" to 74".

Noam checks out the staple of the Becker rental paddle quiver, a Quickblade adjustable paddle

WHO MAKES THE PADDLES?

Stand up paddles began to go commercial around 2004, when Todd Bradley began selling purpose-built Pohaku Beachboy Paddles. During the winter of 2010–2011, C4 Waterman/Pohaku, Werner, Surftech, Quickblade, Coreban, Amundson/Aquaglide, Kialoa, Art in Surf, Sawyer, Kelp Farmer, Garrett McNamara, Whiskeyjack Paddles, and Mitchell were among the companies selling paddles for stand up paddling, using everything from wood to aluminum to Kevlar.

As of May 2015, Kialoa had a range of eight paddles priced from $149 for an Aloha recreational paddle to $479 for a Hula Race.

The Quickblade website explains that founder Jim Terrell is a four-time Olympic canoeist who began making his own canoe paddles in 1989. He began to transition into SUP paddles, and now Quickblade offers a range of five paddles from the Micro Fly All Fiberglass ($179) to the V-Drive All Carbon ($499).

Quickblade makes a bold statement on its website, and it shows a guy using a SUP paddle propped on a gas can to jack up a Land Rover with a busted tire, somewhere in the middle of nowhere. Clever, but not too far from the truth, according to Mitch Taylor: "I usually encourage people to use Quickblade paddles because they seem to be the best out there."

important, as those variables change depending on the experience and tastes of the paddler and how the paddle will be used: wave riding, cruising, running whitewater, or racing.

Because space is tight at Becker's Malibu, and because of that bubble of prosperity, Mitch Taylor stocks mostly carbon fiber paddles:

I normally carry both carbon fiber and fiberglass paddles, but right now we have only carbon fiber paddles. The reality is that 90 percent of the people in Malibu want the best. And most people who really end up getting into stand up paddling are stoked they spent the extra money on a high-end paddle.

A top-of-the-line Quickblade carbon fiber fixed paddle costs $339, and adjustable is $350. If anything happens to it, they'll fix it. I mean, if it's definitely your fault (like you beat up a white shark with it), and it was mistreated, then they'll replace the parts and it's going to cost you a little bit. But the reality is not a lot of other companies will do stuff like that. Pretty much everyone who's winning contests or paddle races are using Quickblade paddles.

For strength and weight, carbon fiber paddles are the way to go, according to Mitch, although they also come with a caveat: "I will say this, they are made of carbon fiber, so the last thing you want

GLOSSARY OF PADDLE TERMS

With thanks to Duke Brouwer, Karen Chun, Dave Kalama, Charles MacArthur, Todd Roberts, Mike Sandusky, Gary Stone, Jim and Elizabeth Terrell of Quickblade, and various online sources.

ADJUSTABLE PADDLE: According to a post on www.standuppaddlesurf.net, the first adjustable stand up paddle was produced by C4 Waterman in January 2008. The paddle had an aluminum shaft, fiberglass blade, a drain plug in the blade for letting out water, and an orb-shaped grip and was adjustable from 60" to 82". As noted on the website: "This adjustable paddle solves the length issue. If I want to knee paddle, just twist, turn and now it's 60" long. Time to stand up to get back out, now it's 77". Time to go in and paddle for a while, now it's 80". This thing has endless possibilities."

Jim Terrell of Quickblade adds: "For the record, we started making our first adjustable SUP paddles and two- and three-piece travel paddles in about 2007 but never advertised it. They were for custom orders, etc."

Whoever was on it first, since then, most of the major companies have produced adjustable stand up paddles made of a variety of materials. Some paddlers use adjustables for kneeling and standing, but the adjustable paddle is meant to accommodate different heights.

BALL GRIP: As opposed to a T-grip, a round ball at the top of the shaft that some paddlers prefer.

BENT SHAFT PADDLE: A paddle in which the shaft has a slight angle. According to the now defunct www.paddle-board.net: "The advantages of the bent shaft include a more natural hand position which gives more shaft contact for a lighter grip and better control and a natural wrist alignment which can reduce repetitive stress injuries and reduce fatigue. The bend in the shaft also increases the catch phase of the stroke (the catch is the beginning of the stroke which is where the majority of the power lies) by allowing a farther reach."

The FAQ for Pohaku Beachboy Paddles states: "If you haven't used an elbowed stand up paddle, I urge you to try one. Most people prefer it. The blade is angled forward from the shaft, so the more effective front part of the stroke lasts longer. It also prevents lifting water at stroke's end. Elbow paddles deliver more of your effort to the water. You'll go farther, faster, and with less effort. A straight-shaft paddle wastes effort lifting water at the end of the stroke; an elbowed paddle doesn't."

Todd Bradley of Pohaku adds: "This type of double-bend paddle is more efficient with outrigger canoe paddles, but because of the length of the SUP shaft, this type of paddle can be awkward."

BLADE: The wide, flat end of a paddle. Most blades are measured in square inches. According to the Quickblade website, "bigger, stronger paddlers generally prefer larger blades, while smaller paddlers lean toward smaller blades." Quickblade offers blade options from 90 to 110 square inches.

Most, but not all, paddle blades are measured in square inches. According to Karen Chun, official spokeswoman for Malama of Maui, "Malama measures blades in width and shape . . . never in square inches."

DIHEDRAL: According to Jim Terrell of Quickblade, a dihedral is "a distinct 'spine' or V on the power face of the blade that aids in the stability of the blade during the stroke."

FACE: The side of a paddle blade that is pushing against the water.

FRONT: The side of the blade opposite the face/power face. According to Charles MacArthur, "This is referred to as the 'back face' in river parlance."

GRIP: The molded top end of the paddle where the top hand fits and grips the paddle. Paddles can have T-grips or ball grips.

GRIP TRACTION: Stand up paddles can get slippery—especially from hands that recently applied sunscreen. Some paddlers don't mind a bare shaft, while others will use surf wax on the shaft to create traction and others will wrap it in grip tape. Try all three ways and see what suits you.

KEEL: C4 Waterman defines the keel as "a keel-shaped blade neck on the power face of the blade. This helps to steer the paddle straight for less paddle wander when taking hard strokes for the waves. This will also help steer the paddle and help minimize rail banging."

PALM GRIP: Mike Sandusky of Surf Ontario says, "Add the palm grip, which is more rounded than the T-grip but not like the ball. I think paddle companies distinguish between these two grips; however, they are close."

POWER FACE: The face of a paddle blade that pushes against the water.

SHAFT: The handle area between the grip and the blade. Shafts can be oval or round and/or bent and come in different diameters because human hands come in different sizes.

SHAFT STIFFNESS INDEX (SSI): A Quickblade innovation that measures the bridge distance (in inches) the shaft bends ¾" under a load of 165 pounds. The higher the SSI number, the stiffer the shaft.

STRAIGHT-SHAFT PADDLE: A paddle in which the shaft leads directly into the blade in a straight line, with no bending. "There is always an angle between the blade and the shaft," Karen Chun of Malama Paddles says, "just no bend in the shaft itself."

SWING WEIGHT: According to the www.wernerpaddles.com website (with a slight edit): "Swing weight is the dynamic weight you lift during a stroke. A paddle with a good swing weight will reduce fatigue, be well balanced, and have lightweight blades. In contrast, a paddle with heavy blades will offer an undesirable swing weight and may fatigue a [paddler] quickly. Be aware that published weights do not indicate swing weight. Two paddles may publish the same weight yet have very different swing weights. One may have weight savings in the blades with a good swing weight, while another has all the weight savings in the shaft with a less desirable swing weight. A simple test is to hold a paddle horizontal with one hand and tip it from side to side. It should be light and balanced. Compare several paddles and note the difference in swing weights. You're smart, you do the math. On any outing it doesn't take long for a few ounces to quickly add into pounds."

T-BAR: Same as T-grip.

T-GRIP: The majority of stand up paddles use a grip that has short arms extending a few inches to either side of the shaft. This allows a nonslip grip to the shaft and more efficient power to the blade and the stroke.

THROAT: The area on a paddle shaft that fans out into the wider blade.

TWO- AND THREE-PIECE PADDLE: Some companies make paddles that can be taken apart for ease of transportation.

Noam is 6' tall, so he adds 10" to his paddle to make it 82".

is them slapping you in the face. That happened to me in Hawaii, and it took about four good chunks out of the side of my face. I could imagine they would work pretty well to fight off a shark because they are pretty darned sharp."

Wave riders will want a paddle with a smaller blade that provides short bursts of speed. White-water river runners want a paddle with a wider blade for stability and turning. Long-distance cruisers and racers want paddles with wide blades that give maximum distance per stroke.

A beginner's needs are not as refined, so most shops like Becker Surf and Sport have available a supply of sturdy, adjustable stand up paddles. The

adjustable Quickblade paddles that Becker rents start with the Junior, a 90-square-inch blade with a shaft that adjusts from 70" to 78". The Standard has a 100-square-inch blade that adjusts from 76" to 84", and the Tall Boy has a 110-square-inch blade that adjusts from 80" to 88".

The sizing rule for stand up paddles is they should be 6 to 10 inches taller than the paddler. The test Mitch uses is to have people stand with their arms straight up. Their hand should just reach the top of the handle and curl over the T-bar/grip.

Stand Up Paddling Accessories

If you think your investment in stand up paddling ends after purchasing your board and a paddle, think again. A wide range of accessories, some necessary, some less so, are available to make your stand up paddling experience more enjoyable.

Leashes

Whether you are riding waves, running whitewater, or just paddling around in a local reservoir, attaching your board to your leg—or a PFD—with what surfers call a leg rope or leash is a good idea. Accidents will happen, and you can become separated from your board faster than you can say, "Call the Coast Guard!" Swimming with a paddle in your hands is awkward at best, so in most circumstances, it is safest to be able to retrieve the board by reeling in the leash and getting your hands back on it, then your feet.

Like french fries and hairstyles and country roads, SUP leashes come in two main varieties—straight and curly.

Mitch Taylor is a surfer, so he uses straight leashes designed for the wear and stresses of big surf:

I use XM or a DaKine big wave leash because I've found that a regular 10-foot leash for a surfboard just

STRAIGHT OR CURLY LEASHES?

I use a straight, long XM leash on my 12'1" Laird, but I often feel I should probably switch to a curly leash, because that frickin' straight leash gets caught on everything: the roof of my car when I'm taking the board off, around boat docks when I'm launching from the Santa Cruz Yacht Harbor, around rocks when I'm taking the board up and down the cliffs to the water. Worst of all, the straight leash will sometimes snag on kelp when I'm turning around to paddle into bomb waves at Malibu, and missing a wave on a SUP at Malibu is unforgivable. I should probably switch to a curly leash because they coil up and keep to themselves better and are less likely to snag on kelp, or cleats, or anything else.

One thing that has kept me from switching to a curly leash is that for a while I used my straight leash as a backup safety measure when transporting my SUP on the roof of my Corolla wagon.

That theory went out the window while driving Highway 1 near Half Moon Bay. The bungee cords failed, and the redundant backup leash

Straight or curly? Either way, leashes are a good idea because they keep you attached to your board.

did, too. The board flew off to the side of the road, but not before practically giving me a heart attack. A 12'1" flying through the air on Highway 1 could do tremendous damage.

I now transport my 12'1" inside a Ford van, so I no longer need the long leash as a backup tie-down. One of these days I'll get a curly leash and see if I like that any better.

doesn't hold up. Stand up paddleboards are big and heavy and create a lot of drag in the water, and that stress will pop one end or the other of a regular leash. So I use heavy-duty leashes even in circumstances that aren't heavy duty.

Whether you use a straight or curly leash, you should always have one. Accidents don't just happen to the inexperienced. Mitch knows of an

experienced local stand up paddler who was riding big waves at a Malibu spot without a leash:

This guy surfs great, but everybody falls at some point. He falls off his board, loses it, and swims to the beach, thinking it will be washing around in the shore break. But it's nowhere to be seen. He walks down the beach looking for it, goes up high in the cliffs, and can't see it anywhere. He gets a Jet Ski and does a search,

EVERYTHING'S OKAY UNTIL IT ISN'T, PART 1
Men vs. Shark: Why a Sturdy Paddle Is a Good Idea

On Sunday, July 23, 2007, the Tommy Zahn Memorial Paddleboard Race turned into a battle of life and death as two competitors fought off an aggressive 12-foot shark with their bare hands and one sturdy stand up paddle.

The race is dedicated to one of the all-time great Los Angeles County watermen. Zahn was awarded the L.A. County medal of valor in 1984, and he is a legend among local lifeguards and surfers.

In the 2007 race, there were forty-five paddlers in six prone and stand up classes, including men's and women's stand up. They left the Zuma Beach lifeguard tower at 9 a.m. for a 10-mile downwind race (considered middle distance by experienced paddlers).

One of the stand up paddlers was Vic Calandra, who was a 47-year-old investment banker for the Winter Group at the time, and previously was a board member and treasurer of SurfAid International. Paddling a Joe Bark racing stand up paddleboard using a carbon fiber paddle, Calandra rounded Point Dume and aimed straight for Malibu. About halfway, he was a contender for the bronze: "I was vying for third with a stand up paddler," Calandra said. He tells the story like this:

There were two guys in front of me, and I was about even with another guy who was farther out. We were clicking along at a good pace and had passed Paradise Cove and got past Corral Beach, and we were almost to the incline where Malibu Road starts. I was about a mile and a quarter offshore, and the other guy was about 300 yards farther outside. The ocean was completely glassy.

Suddenly I heard something cut the water. That is not unusual because you see and hear all kinds of marine life when you are paddling.

Usually it's a seal or sea lion or a dolphin or sometimes a fish breaking the surface, but "shark" is always in the back of your mind. This had a different noise, so I stopped paddling and turned around and saw something big in the water about 30 feet behind me. It had a different kind of surface track, and I thought it might be a dolphin, but the fin kept coming out of the water until it was 18 to 24 inches high.

Calandra was essentially alone, more than a mile offshore, and he had no doubt that he was being tracked by a very large shark.

I veered quickly to the right because I have a steering mechanism on the board, but the fin tracked with me for another 50 to 100 yards and closed in to 10 feet. That is when the melee began. Four or five times the shark approached me from behind or the side. It looked like a small submarine, the way the water was running off its back on both sides of the fin. I slapped at the water with my paddle just as the shark turned on its side. I got a full look at its belly, its mouth, its head and eyes. The shark was about 2 feet under the water, but I was about 6 feet above the surface, and I saw all of it. I would say it was 12 feet long, but it was the girth of the shark that really impressed me. It was just huge.

Calandra and the shark engaged in a deadly little dance, with Calandra dropping to his knees for balance so he wouldn't fall in, then standing up to see where the shark was and so he could slap at it with his paddle. He did this for several minutes until other paddlers came within range.

Joey Everett is now a Los Angeles County fire captain, but at the time he was a 37-year-old L.A. County lifeguard stationed at Zuma Beach. He was prone-paddling an 18-foot

Great white sharks are big, but so are massive paddleboards, and it might have been the presence of two of those boards, plus punches and paddle strikes, that persuaded the shark to swim away and stalk again some other day. Vic Calandra (right) with his 16' Joe Bark stand up paddleboard a few days after the incident. Joey Everett, who helped Vic fend off the shark, is on the left.
Ben Marcus

Unlimited Class paddleboard that day and was about six back in the pack when his race was transformed into a different kind of battle.

Vic was outside of me, and I could hear him yelling for help. I didn't know what was wrong at first, but when I was about 100 yards away, I saw a fin. I kept paddling, and when I was about 50 yards away, I saw the shark swimming aggressively, and when I was about 25 yards away, I saw the shark bumping the tail of Vic's board.

Faced with the fight-or-flight option, Everett's lifeguard training took over, and he did the ocean equivalent of charging a machine gun nest:

What it says in the [lifeguard training] manual is to hit a shark on the head and the nose.

So I went by the book, figuring if we could get the shark off Vic's tail we might have a chance. What happened next was like a bar fight. I paddled up and over the shark with my board and started swinging. I was screaming at the shark and bumping it with my board and hitting it on the nose, but I had no idea if that was scaring the shark or making it more aggressive.

Everett believes it was Calandra's paddle striking the water, and not striking the shark, that actually scared the shark off. The shark submerged, and the two paddlers looked for an escape route. The *Aquarius* charter boat was out to sea and a little too far off, so Calandra and Everett hopscotched to a closer, smaller fishing boat, watching each other's backs in case the shark decided to make a second charge: "We got to the boat, and Joey pulled his board in and got on the radio and called Baywatch," Calandra said. "I have no idea why I stayed in the water. I was kind of in a daze by that time, and I knew there were other paddlers who had gone past me. Joey stayed in the boat to organize the lifeguards, and I took off to catch the other paddlers and warn them. I figured Baywatch would come up to me along the way, but they didn't, so I finished the race."

Along the way, Calandra saw some girls in kayaks meandering along in the kelp beds, and he told them to get to the beach right away. Everett also got back in the water and escorted some of the female competitors, and got a free dinner that night from one of them.

Calandra got to the beach shaken and stirred. He had no doubt that the only reason he was alive was because a lifeguard with proper training came to the rescue: "The only reason this thing didn't strike me was because Joey was there to fight it off. I had seen this guy around but didn't really know him. I have no doubt he saved my life."

This battle between prehistoric animal and modern men was the talk of the Malibu coast in the days following. Some local residents pointed fingers at the *Aquarius*, the commercial fishing boat that essentially chums as it moves along, with bait being thrown overboard along with the refuse of cleaned fish. Others noted that the Monterey Bay Aquarium shark pen, which appears off the coast at Paradise Cove every summer, might have had something to do with it: "Maybe one escaped from there and was pissed," said paddleboard competitor Bill Kalmenson.

The truth is out there: White sharks exist along the Malibu coast, and Everett and Calandra were neither the first nor the last to encounter them. But they will certainly go down in local legend as the two men who fought off a big shark with bare fists and a sturdy stand up paddle—and won.

Author's note: L.A. County presents a medal of valor "to lifeguard personnel under the conditions that they have exhibited courage above and beyond the call of duty and risked their own lives by placing themselves under extreme personal risks." Hard to imagine anything more valorous than paddling toward a big white shark, a mile out to sea, and punching its lights out. But that is exactly what Joey Everett did, and in 2008, he was awarded the medal of valor.

When discussing the use of leashes, Mitch demonstrates that he prefers long and strong.

but nothing. *This is an expensive board, close to $2,000. He alerts the sheriff and local lifeguards, and they look for it. They were around in the helicopter, and they even looked for it from the air, but no go.*

A day or two later, it washed up on the beach at El Porto—miles to the southeast, relatively unharmed. So I guess the moral to that story is: wear a leash.

Life Jackets (PFDs)

The US Coast Guard and other watery law enforcement agencies are still trying to figure out how to regulate stand up paddleboards. Are these things surfboards? Kayaks? Small boats?

Regulations vary from beach to city to county to state, but in many places, stand up paddlers launching from yacht harbors or public piers or other public-built locations might be required to wear life jackets, also known as personal flotation devices, or PFDs.

Mitch Taylor doesn't insist that renters and beginners wear PFDs, but he certainly suggests it, as he is aware of many stories when lives have been saved, or could have been saved, by wearing a PFD. Even beginners—or should we say, especially beginners—who are going less than 100 feet off the beach in the safest lake in the middle of the country on a sunny day in the middle of summer would be wise to wear a PFD.

EVERYTHING'S OKAY UNTIL IT ISN'T, PART 2
Why Leashes Are a Good Idea

Around Malibu, the Santa Ana is a seasonal wind that blows from the land to the sea. Raymond Chandler described the effect of these winds on the landed populace in his 1938 short noir fiction *Red Wind*:

It was one of those hot dry Santa Anas that come down through the mountain passes and curl your hair and make your nerves jump and your skin itch. On nights like that every booze party ends in a fight. Meek little wives feel the edge of the carving knife and study their husbands' necks. Anything can happen.

These winds are common in the fall and winter, and they become a hazard to homeowners, firefighters, and mariners, as the winds are super-powered as they funnel through the canyons and blow with great vengeance and furious anger, almost strong enough to move waves backward.

This violent, troublesome wind is not unique to Malibu. Around the world, from the Abrohols of Brazil to the Zephyr wind of Greece, there are a lot of local, seasonal winds that can be a sailor's delight—or nightmare: Austru, Bayamo, Cape Doctor, Chinook, Elephanta, Haboob, Leste, Maestro, Mistral, Nashi, Nor'easter, Norther, Pali, Papagayo, Sharki, Sirocco, Vardar.

Many of these winds are seasonal like the Santa Ana, which blow from land to sea and can be big trouble to mariners, stand up paddlers included. That's why it is a good idea to always be connected to your SUP by a leash, use the buddy system, have an understanding of local conditions, and just generally treat the ocean—or any large body of water—with respect.

Big wave surfer Roger Erickson was famous for a Casey Stengel–quality maxim, when he described the dangers of big wave riding in one sentence: "Everything's okay until it isn't."

A case in point was brought up by Mitch Taylor, regarding the son of a celebrity who has a home in Malibu and is also an avid "SUPlebrity."

The celebrity's 18-year-old son went out by himself on a stand up paddleboard during a visit to Malibu. He was blown out to sea and nearly drowned or died of exposure during a winter Santa Ana wind—because anything can happen.

The full story of the incident was related by Marshall Coben, a resident of Malibu Colony and a former president of television at Paramount Pictures who is now a dedicated stand up paddler.

This was a few years ago—I think it was 2006/2007. We bought two 12-foot Laird boards right when they came out—directly from Laird. My friend's 18-year-old son came out from NYC and was in town for Christmas. This was a year when we had sixteen straight days of offshore winds. Most people think of Santa Anas as a fall phenomenon, but they can blow just as hard in December and January.

My friend's son and I were going out pretty regularly from off the beach at the Colony when the wind would lay down, and we would just head up to Malibu Road and back. One day we planned to go, but the wind was so strong I guess we just blew it off. We didn't even call each other to discuss. It was obvious that you couldn't go near the ocean that day. I kept my kids inside because the palm fronds were flying everywhere. It was really

HAPPY HOLLOW DAYS FROM THE MALIBU

2009 Christmas Greetings: Ben Marcus
2007 Fire Swell photo: Bill Parr

dangerous outside. Me and the kids got a bit of cabin fever I guess around midday and decided to run across the street to have a look at the ocean.

When we got there, we saw tire tracks heading down the beach. We looked and saw red lights blinking down at the other end of the Colony. I put my 2-year-old on a boogie board and dragged him by the leash as fast as I could, with my 5-year-old daughter running as fast as she could behind. When we got there my friend's son was sitting on the steps of his house crying, with his girlfriend holding him. The lifeguard was finishing writing his report and seeing me arrive decided he could go. A neighbor was telling the kid he should thank the lifeguard, but instead the kid said to the neighbor: "You knew I was out there! Why didn't you help me?" . . .

I took the kid inside and called his dad.

The author's 2009 Christmas card, featuring fierce Santa Ana winds that caused the October 2007 canyon fire in Malibu. The Santa Ana winds blow from land out to sea. They groom and sharpen waves and can be a surfer's delight. But when a stand up paddler gets caught in them, he or she will soon be out of sight. And if the lifeguard isn't on duty . . . Photo courtesy of Bill Parr

The story behind the incident is that he decided to go stand up paddling without me that day, not knowing the danger of the wind. He said he hopped on one of the 12-foot Lairds wearing a 3/2 wetsuit but no leash. He had a really easy time that day, paddling for a while before he finally fell and looked back and realized he had been blown really far out to sea.

The board flipped on him when he fell, and when the kid was turning the board around to climb back on, a gust of Santa Ana wind caught it and blew it up into the air, flipping it out to sea—a 12-foot Laird board, picked up like a palm frond! The kid swam after the board and caught it, only to have the same thing happen again. He was holding onto the board and clinging to a lobster buoy at the same time. His house was so far away it was like a dot in his field of vision, and he was clinging to the buoy waiting for help.

He waited in his 3/2 wetsuit shivering for about forty-five minutes with the wind blowing a gale in his face. He was so cold and tired he was starting to consider the option of sinking below the surface as better than what he was facing at that moment. He was sure that his neighbor—who was an avid kayaker and thirty-year Colony resident—had seen him go out and would be on the way to get him. It never happened.

Across the Colony road and down about twenty houses another friend was house-bound like the rest of us. For some reason he was up on his third floor, a place he hadn't been for months, and he looked out over the rooftops across the street with binoculars. He had recently been reading a harrowing account of a shipwreck, and he was feeling weird about the sea at that moment. All extremely uncharacteristic for him. He's not an ocean guy.

He had seen the kid paddle out by himself and knew what the wind was doing and knew something was wrong. He called 911, the fire department, and the sheriff until finally someone decided to give him the phone number for the L.A. County lifeguard shack at Third Point—just outside the Malibu Colony. None of those other phone calls produced help. Within minutes of that call to the lifeguard, a man on a red paddleboard was steaming up to the lobster buoy and reaching his hand out to the kid, while I was standing on the beach looking at those phantom tire tracks from the lifeguard truck and wondering WTF.

My neighbor was pretty shook up by this, as he says it must have been one in a million for him to be in a position to see this kid. Steve isn't an ocean guy, he's in the music business, and knows few of his neighbors. The third floor just isn't a place he goes. . . .

I wish I had a better moral to the story. But honestly, the best I can say is that I don't think the son has touched the water since. My friend replaced the board that never resurfaced, but I don't think he's used it more than once since then either.

Author's note: This cautionary title should be a warning to everyone to always be prepared for nature to do something unexpected and dangerous. Malibu is a benign place 95 percent of the year, until those devil winds come on and the whole place turns upside down. The same can be true for ocean currents, river currents, and treacherous winds around the world. Everything's okay until it isn't, and that is why stand up paddlers should use the buddy system whenever possible, let people know where they are and where they are going, and always keep a wary eye on the weather.

Nikki Gregg shooting Chile's Trancura River with Dan Gavere, both of them wearing personal flotation devices and helmets, with their leashes strapped to their PFDs. Photo courtesy of Starboard

People drown PDQ in the darnedest ways, in the "safest" of conditions, and wearing a PFD can be a BFD in the difference between life and death. If you feel goofy wearing one, just remember, many of the world's best big wave surfers wear a PFD on the giant days at Jaws and Mavericks and Cortes Bank. And the same is true for almost all whitewater runners in boats, on kayaks, or the new breed on stand up paddleboards.

So if it's cool enough for them, it should be cool enough for you.

There aren't any PFDs made specifically for stand up paddling yet, but in general, if you are using a stand up paddleboard on a flatwater lake or river, the PFD made for inland boating and kayaking should work well. The same goes for people stand up paddling in the ocean. Find a PFD made for ocean boating and kayaking, and you'll be right as rain.

Wetsuits

It is better to be warm and dry than wet and cold. Remember that in your arc from beginner to veteran.

Ideally, you will be learning to stand up paddle on a perfect summer day in the Maldives or Lake Michigan or somewhere in the Mediterranean, when the air and water are both 70 degrees. Or if not that, you are taking your first strokes inside a coral reef in Tahiti or along a pristine beach on the Adriatic Sea in the middle of summer: sunny and hot, warm water, no wind, idyllic.

That's not always the case, though, so some degree of protection from wind, wetness, and the elements can be necessary.

Wetsuits, which are usually made of foamed neoprene, come in a thousand different combinations of uses, styles, thicknesses, and so on. There are wetsuits for kayaking, surfing, sailboarding, sailing, wake boarding, and kitesurfing, and they can be long johns, short johns, full suits, spring suits, zipperless, front zip, back zip, full zip, three-quarter zip, hooded, no hoods. There are also detachable hoods, booties, gloves, and rash guards.

Skylar Peak, Christian Shubin, and Morgan Runyon, suited up in 4/3 wetsuits for a summer adventure in the brisk waters of northern California. Photo courtesy of Skylar Peak

SURF ONTARIO: THESE GUYS KNOW NEOPRENE

From the Bio section of the www.surfontario .com website: "Mike Sandusky grew up on a farm in southwestern Ontario, Canada, and turned his competitive swimming into body surfing on the Great Lakes, and then morphed into surfing. After earning a Commerce Degree at the University of Guelph (with a minor in *Franglais*), Sandusky went walkabout to 200 surf spots around the world, including Hawaii, Australia, New Zealand and Costa Rica. Wherever he may roam, the Great Lakes are home, and in 2002 Sandusky started Surf Ontario as a way to share his passion—and dispel the myth that you 'cannot ride waves on a lake.'"

That same year, Mike became aware of stand up paddling when he witnessed another blond, Nordic-looking guy by the name of Laird Hamilton doing stand up at Hookipa Beach on Maui.

Sandusky first tried stand up in 2007 in Lake Ontario on an 11'6" Amundson Aquaglide and experienced then what he sees others experience now: "Many surfers are hesitant to try SUP because they're stepping out of their comfort zone, and it's almost like learning to surf a wave all over again, but the instant you try, you're hooked just like surfing. That's how I felt the moment I first tried."

The Surf Ontario website became self-aware in 2005, and Sandusky introduced SUP into Surf Ontario in the summer 2008. "Now we're selling a variety of boards such as inflatables, racing, all-round, to surf-specific SUPs,"

Surf Ontario founder Mike Sandusky paddling Lake Ontario not in summer, wearing a hooded 6/5 Infiniti wetsuit by Xcel and doing his best to not fall. Photo by Grant Kennedy of Surf Ontario

Sandusky said. "The popularity of SUP has fostered growth in the surf business as more and more people are realizing they can surf and surf the SUPs on the lakes."

Because Mike and his friends surf year-round on the Great Lakes, they have wardrobes of wetsuits that are appropriate for everything: "On Lake Ontario, air temperatures can fluctuate from 86 to 90 degrees in the summer to 5 degrees Fahrenheit in the winter," Sandusky said. "Water temperatures fluctuate from ice water in the winter to 70 degrees in the summer."

Here is how Sandusky breaks down his wetsuits by season:

We have to be prepared SUPing and surfing in the winter months, and most stand up paddlers will wear a hooded 6/5/4 mm wetsuit with 5, 7 or 8 mm boots and 5 mm mitts. We recommend wearing the wetsuits as they maintain mobility, and if you fall in, there's no problem with hypothermia. If you're riding a wave, the wetsuit will handle the "wash cycle" well!

These winter suits are something else—you climb in through the neck and pull the hood and shoulders over your head and zip the front tight.

Around Lake Ontario they say, "No sign of ice? Conditions are nice!" This is late spring on Lake Wilcox. From left, all wearing 4/3s from Oneill, Tiki, MEC, and Quiksilver, are Benson Cowan, Jonathan Lansdell, Mike Rhiem, and Oliver Lansdell. Photo courtesy Mike Sandusky/Surf Ontario.com

By this time you are pretty much sweating and sealed from water getting in and anxious to get out in the frigid air and water to cool off.

Getting out of the suit is no easy chore either; you pretty much have to turn into a contortionist to take it off, but with practice it becomes easier. It took a few times with my wife's help to learn how to take it off before I could take it off myself.

One other note about wetsuits during the winter would be to always bring a jug of hot water in case you get FROZEN in your suit. If you're in and out of the water, ice begins to build up around your head, neck, shoulders and zipper, making it impossible to get out of your suit without a quick melt. Sometimes you have to drive home in your suit and thaw out before getting out of it.

In the springtime, the water is still extremely cold; however, the air is in the 70s, so we can get away with a 5/4 or 4/3 with 1 to 3 mm gloves and 5 mm booties. Split toe (boots with the big toe separate from the rest) booties tend to give

Grant Kennedy, Sonia Jaafar, and Mike Sandusky getting away from the shady turf of Toronto and catching some rays in the glassy waters of Lake Ontario. Photo courtesy of Michael Shin

better mobility for your feet on the board compared to round toe; however, you do sacrifice some warmth in the big toe. The wetsuit choice depends on if you're surfing the SUP or on flat water: On the flats you'll likely overheat in a thicker suit with warmer air temperatures. But if you're surfing and wiping out often in the cold water, you'll appreciate the thicker suit.

In the summertime when the air is hot and humid and the water is in the 60s and 70s, we go without a wetsuit, or a shorty if the surf is up.

In the fall, the water remains warm into the later months, but the air temperatures drop, so we generally use a 4/3 with a light 2 mm hood and 3 mm boots, 1 to 3 mm gloves, as the air will chill us off, but the water can remain in the upper 50s and 60s.

Wetsuits are miracles of modern material and design: incredibly warm, flexible, durable, and even stylish. They are quite a science, and the best wetsuit will depend on what you are going to be doing on your stand up paddleboard. The thickness of the wetsuit generally determines its warmth. Sometimes the body of the suit is a different thickness than the limbs; for example, a 6/5 wetsuit is 6 mm in the body and 5 mm in the limbs. You want to match the thickness to the conditions and water temperature you expect to be encountering most often. Beyond that, it's largely a matter of personal preference.

Drysuits

Gina Bradley is a SUP instructor on Long Island, New York, who spends part of her winter in Puerto Rico, so she has paddled in the widest range of conditions, from subtropical to subzero. Clothing options for Puerto Rico are easy: as little as possible, while being responsible for sun protection. When conditions are cold water and/or windy, the perfect garment doesn't yet exist. "There needs to be something invented for stand up paddling in the cooler temps for those who can't help but fall in occasionally," Bradley said. "Wetsuits are not ideal once you fall in, and they get so hot if you don't. They are not really made for the sport, but that seems to be what the surf shops are selling."

Winter in New York goes to freezing and way beyond, but Bradley believes she does have the ideal garment for that: "In the winter I use a Kokatat drysuit. They cost a fortune [$500–$900+]. I got a pro-model from Randy Henriksen of NY Kayak. It is sort of that cross between

Gina Bradley in her Kokatat drysuit. When it gets to freezing or colder around Long Island, she will be snug as a bug in a rug. Photo courtesy of Gina Bradley

the two. I just jump into it in my clothes, and if I fall in, I don't get wet. My husband, Scott Bradley, has a Bare one as well [$300–$900+]."

Ken Hoeve lives in Vail, Colorado, and rides his paddleboard in whitewater year-round. Wetsuits don't cut it in the mountains of Colorado in the winter when the water temperature is close to freezing and the air temperature is even colder:

The Colorado River in Glenwood runs year-round. In the winter it's not only freezing, but you also paddle with the possibility of swimming with mini icebergs that can weigh thousands of pounds. I prefer to wear a Kokatat Gore-Tex drysuit for its ability to make the coldest temps tolerable. Falling in is always a possibility when running whitewater, and you might get

Ken Hoeve running The Wall rapid on the Class III+ Shoshone stretch of the Colorado River in early spring.
Photo courtesy of Ken Hoeve

separated from your board, so wearing something that keeps you warm AND dry is critical. To be honest, I don't know why any stand up paddlers wear wetsuits. Cost, I guess. It must be, because nothing works better to keep you warm, dry, and comfortable than a drysuit. It is a must-have if you plan to paddle year-round in cold weather environments. Wetsuits are wet and cold. A drysuit is exactly that—dry.

Gina Bradley and Ken Hoeve swear by drysuits, but these technical suits can be twice to three times as expensive as wetsuits, and they can also heat up even more than a wetsuit. Drysuits are something beginning stand up paddlers should be aware of but not necessarily worrying about at first.

If you are learning to stand up paddle in a place where you need a drysuit, you are hard core.

Footwear

Ooky sea anemones, sharp broken bottles, venomous stingrays, coral, lava, rocks that are sharp, rocks that are slippery. From Bantham to Bora Bora, the underwater world is lined with unseen hazards that can damage your feet.

Learning to stand up paddle is a lot more fun when your feet are protected and you aren't worried about what dangerous things you might step on when you put your feet underwater.

Even when your feet are up on the board, they still are often the only part of your body exposed to the splashing water, which means they can be cold to the point of numbness. It's important that you can feel your feet for safe and enjoyable paddleboarding.

Wearing foot protection is a good idea not only for beginning stand up paddlers but also for veterans, to protect feet from frostbite or stonefish or the dozens of other critters that lurk beneath.

Mitch Taylor finds that many of the female beginners want to protect their pedicures, so persuading them to protect their investments with wetsuit booties is an easy sell:

The sand comes and goes around Malibu, but I usually recommend people wear booties, especially women. Men might not mind stepping in a gooey sea anemone or feeling something wiggle under their feet and swim away, but some women mind that very much.

Also, some women put a great deal of care into keeping their toes and toenails and feet healthy and undamaged, and booties can protect expensive pedicures. I tell guys that if they are hoping to spend time with their wives or their girlfriends in the water, they should be sure their wives and girlfriends are as safe and comfortable as possible. And so I usually recommend booties or some kind of foot protection.

Dane Jackson wearing NRS Desperado Booties while surfing a wave on a whitewater river. Photo courtesy of Dane Jackson

Also, some people who have not developed calloused "surfer feet" find the soles of their feet are not compatible with the sometimes abrasive adhesive traction pads, so foot protection makes the experience more comfortable.

Fortunately, the wetsuit and footwear industries have a wide variety of protective designs available: booties, reef walkers, aqua shoes, and sandals, shoes, and boots that are waterproofed for a variety of uses, none of them specifically for stand up paddling, but most of them adaptable. Some of these shoes are open with hard bottoms, others are closed. If you will be stand up paddling in warm water, you might want open-toed reef walkers that won't overheat your feet in the tropical sun.

Utah native Caroline Gleich—pronounced "glike"—out for a November paddle in 20-degree weather on Jackson Lake, Wyoming—pronounced "BRRRRRR." Caroline paddles from spring to fall, from Utah to California, so her footwear choices are as varied as the conditions and surfaces she encounters: "These are actually just my running shoes—they are Timberland trail running shoes. On this particular SUP session, I originally had on my neoprene booties, but they were cold and wet from another day, and my feet were freezing, so I went back to the car and put on running shoes and socks.

"For whitewater SUPing, I wear surf booties, neoprene with grip on the bottom. I also got a pair of Vibram FiveFingers for Christmas, and I'm looking forward to wearing those on the river with shorts. My rule is booties are okay with pants or a long wetsuit, but no surf booties with shorts (it doesn't look good). So FiveFingers or Tevas or whatever with shorts (sandals okay with shorts). Does that make sense?"
Photo: Caroline Gleich/GoPro

Around Malibu, wetsuit booties are popular because the water temperature is generally in the 60s. The Malibu beaches that are sandy can be home to stingrays, broken glass, and other nastiness. Many of the spots are lined with cobblestones covered in urchins and also small snails that can be as sharp as coral when they come in contact with soft human skin.

Sun Protection

You may find yourself cruising the Adriatic almost entirely exposed, looking like Borat in a mankini. Or you may find yourself covered from head to toe in neoprene, paddling around Juneau, listening to the bald eagles screech.

Regardless, if you are stand up paddling, you will be exposed to the sun. Whether it's just a bit of your face peeking out from the hood of your 6/5 fullsuit or all of you getting roasted in the tropical sun, you need to protect yourself from the harmful effects of the sun, which can range from sunburn to temporary blindness to skin cancer.

Stand up paddling is so fun, engaging, and time-consuming that it's easy to forget how much exposure you are getting. You really don't want to ruin your weekend, your vacation, or your life with sun damage. The options for sun protection can be as simple as wearing sunscreen of at least 15 SPF, a sun-proof T-shirt and/or rash guard, sunglasses, and/or a hat, or as involved as a full-body sun-protection suit. There isn't room here to discuss all the different kinds of sun protection out there, but I just want to offer a caveat: You are standing, you are turning every which way, and you are exposing almost every square inch of yourself to the sun, so cover up.

Helmets

Helmets are de rigueur for river runners, as mandatory as PFDs and Power Bars. Riding the ocean and flat water is not as inherently perilous to the human head as running rivers and shooting rapids, but some experienced stand up paddle surfers will wear helmets in big surf and crowded conditions because you remember what Roger Erickson said: "Everything's okay until it isn't."

Helmets for beginners are not mandatory, but it's always better to be safe than sorry. There are no helmets made specifically for stand up paddling—yet—but it makes sense to use surfing helmets for wave-riding or ocean stand up paddling and kayak helmets for rivers, rapids, and flat water.

Becker Surf and Sport in Malibu doesn't stock surfing helmets, but the store can order Gath helmets, which offer a wide range of head protection.

In the middle of a hot Long Island summer, Gina Bradley leads three friends wearing different levels of sun protection.
Photo courtesy of Oliver Peterson

Final Word

It takes courage to walk into a surf shop, kayak shop, sailboard shop, or specialty stand up paddleboard shop not knowing much about stand up paddleboards and equipment: epoxy, polyester, volume, thrusters, curly or straight leashes, recessed handles, carbon fiber, short john, spring suit, PFD, and so on. There is a lot to know, a lot of decisions to make, and a potential investment of as much as $5,000 to fully equip yourself with the right board, the right paddle, and all the correct accessories to

Cruising Tavarua Island, Fiji, under the blazing sun. At certain times of the year, Fiji is the sun's anvil, and a little exposure can go a long way. Ideally, these two slathered each other in sunscreen of at least 15 SPF before heading for the water. Photo courtesy of Scott Winer/www.tavarua.com

make your experience safe, comfortable, and enjoyable. Take your time, rent some boards, figure out what you want. Then lay your money down and make the purchase. It will be worth every penny.

Nikki Gregg paddling her board down a river in Chile and approaching rapids with caution, wearing a helmet and a PFD.

Photo courtesy of Starboard

Two 12'1"s for Michelle and Noam, and Skylar Peak's 10' stand up paddleboard—custom-shaped by Tim Ryan—on the beach near the Malibu Pier. Ready for a dry run-through on wet sand, before hitting the water.

CHAPTER 3

LEARNING
THE BASICS OF SUP

You are the world's best surfer or an Olympic kayaker or someone who sailboarded around the world, blindfolded, in forty days. Or you're the person who kiteboarded off Niagara Falls and made a perfect landing on *Maid of the Mist*.

Or you're not.

Regardless, you are going to struggle with stand up paddling at first: fall, get wet, get frustrated, utter oaths, want your money (or kayak) back, maybe wander into the surf zone, shipping lanes, or a feeding frenzy and have a brush with embarrassment and/or death, and wonder if it's worth it.

It's worth it, but there is a learning curve at first.

Stand up paddleboards for beginners are long and wide and awkward, and on top of that you are carrying a paddle.

Fully kitted out, you may find yourself carrying a 12'1" board under one arm or on your head, a 5' paddle in your other hand, encased in a full 5/4 mm wetsuit with booties, hood, and gloves, with a PFD on top of that. You could have a helmet on top of the hood, waterproof sunglasses around your neck, and a 12-foot-long leash—ideally not attached to your leg or PFD until you are at the water's edge.

But even if you are wearing just a bathing suit, stand up paddleboards are big and bulky. They don't weigh as much as you might think—one of the wonders of EPS and sandwich construction—but even with a recessed handle, they can be hard to carry and to get into the water. That's where it really gets tricky, making that transition from horizontal to vertical, and from wobbly faller to smooth, efficient cruiser. So it's best to get to know your equipment on dry land, where things are stable.

On the beach, you can start to get a feel for how to stand on a stand up paddleboard—or "walk on water." For surfers, standing with feet parallel is not a natural feeling, as they either stand with their right foot or left foot forward. Those who have never ridden waves but want to try stand up paddle surfing will need to know what is their natural stance—right leg forward (called "goofy") or left leg forward (called "regular")—so they will know which leg is back, because that is where wave riders strap their leashes.

Some stand up paddleboards come with a surfaced deck, so wax isn't needed. But if wax needs to be applied to the deck, the beach is where that can be done, as long as you keep sand and dirt out of the wax and off the deck of your board.

Preparing to stand up paddleboard doesn't take quite as much training and preparation as flying the Space Shuttle, but there is some getting acquainted involved, and it's best to do that on the shore.

Skylar, the Instructor

Noam and Michelle left Becker's Malibu with arm-fuls and handfuls of gear, but also the business card of Skylar Peak tucked safely away. A lifetime resident of Malibu, Skylar began surfing at age 4½, taught by his late father, Dusty. He began giving surf instruction at age 14, passed the Los Angeles County Lifeguard test at age 22, and still guards the northern section of L.A. County.

"I've been surf instructing on and off since I was 14," Skylar says. "I taught at Malibu Makos Summer Surf Camp for eight years, taught an elec-tive surfing class for Pepperdine University, and since then have taught private lessons for hun-dreds of adult and child students. I started my own mini grom [surfer slang for young surfer, derived from "gremlin"] camp in 2008 at the request of

Good times, bad times, Skylar Peak has had his share in the ten years he has been riding a stand up paddleboard. This is Skylar getting whacked (wiping out) at a secret spot in In-donesia in the summer of 2009. He surfaced unscathed and SUPed some more. DaveCollyer.com

some of the local parents but limit it to only six kids surfing the summer. The one-on-one attention is really what makes a difference for the groms."

Skylar has worked as a surf instructor for a variety of celebrities including Kevin Bacon, Mel Gibson, Kyra Sedgwick, Jonathan Davis from Korn, Leonor Varela, Orlando Bloom, and Mike D of the Beastie Boys, who is now a daily surfer and a quiet presence in the lineups around Malibu.

As the first edition of this book was being writ-ten, Skylar was working with actor Gerard Butler,

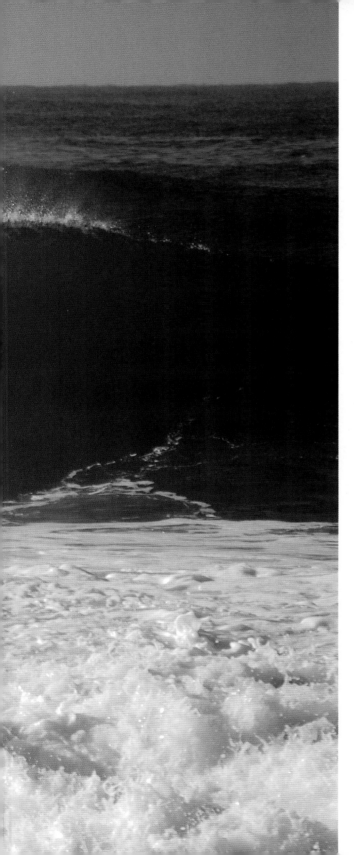

teaching him surfing, SUP, and ocean skills for a sequel to *300—Sparta Goes Hawaiian.* Or maybe it's *Gidget Goes to Sparta.* Or something.

Skylar also participated in Operation Amped, a mostly volunteer group that puts on surf events ranging in duration from one day to a week. Vets who've been wounded have the chance to get free of the constraints that illness or injury have imposed on them and get in the ocean. Many have never set foot on a surfboard. Many have never set foot in the ocean. Some can't even swim. But with the support of this grassroots effort, everyone has fun.

Skylar grew up surfing around Privates. This was the same place that Laird first used in the late 1990s as a laboratory for stand up paddleboarding. Skylar first became aware of this new thing when Laird began messing around on that 12' × 24" Bill Hamilton tandem surfboard. He witnessed Laird's equipment and technique become more and more sophisticated, until curiosity got the best of him. "At first I despised the sport!" Skylar says. "As the sport grew, people who never surfed were doing it, and that made for dangerous situations in the lineup. Beginner SUPers often do not understand etiquette in the ocean because they haven't grown up around it. I didn't really give much respect to SUPers at first, but I have to say Laird made it look pretty fun in the early days."

Skylar first began stand up paddling in the winter of 2003–2004: "The first time I did it was on a Bob Pearson tandem board I grabbed from Dave Anawalt, and another time I switched boards with Laird. Eventually, like many others, I scored a 12'

And this is Skylar getting shacked (riding in the tube) at one of his favorite winter spots, north of Malibu, riding an 8'11" Gerry Lopez "Little Darlin" in the winter of 2009.
Dennis Merryman

Skylar in the summer of 2010, rigged up and ready for anything, somewhere in the Sinkyone Wilderness south of Shelter Cove and north of Westport in northern California.
Photo courtesy of Skylar Peak

Munoz Glide because it was lighter and surfed better. That was my first stand up paddleboard."

Like a lot of surfers/kayakers/sailboarders/waterpeople before him, and many to come, Skylar got hooked on SUP: "A few years back we took some boards up north, had some fun in the beginning of winter, and then headed to Hawaii. All I have to say about that is, good times."

Skylar is now a believer: "I'm not an addict, but I love it as I do surfing and other water sports. It's the best thing that happened to surfing since the tri-fin."

Over the past ten years, Skylar has had some adventures on his stand up paddleboard, from Zuma to Australia. He has surfed some of the world's best waves in the Mentawai Islands, and during the winter, he will take a regular shortboard and a stand up paddleboard to the beaches of Ventura County, where he takes turns getting shacked (riding within the curling part of the wave) on both disciplines.

During the summer of 2010, Skylar and his friends Christian Shubin and Morgan Runyon drove to northern California and out to a secluded coastal town called Shelter Cove. They launched from the boat ramp there and started stroking south for a three-and-a-half-day adventure along the Sinkyone Wilderness: paddling as far as 3 miles offshore at times. "We botched that one," Skylar says. "We ignored the GPS and ended up way offshore, 5 miles past where we were supposed to camp that night."

They also had brushes with orca, elk, black bear, "hundreds of sketchy seals," sea caves, and other wonders and dangers by land and sea (see chapter 5).

But Skylar survived that adventure and made it back to Malibu, where he gets in the water almost every day, every which way he can:

I try to SUP four days a week. It depends on my real work schedule. I prefer being in the water regardless, but when it's good, I will take a day or two or three in a row off of work and head up north for some fun, larger waves. I find myself usually solo at the beach breaks where some surfers give me stinkeye. Then they watch me catch a few and are like, "Man, you are crazy!" Then they start checking out my boards and asking questions. I like the fact that I can have fun surfing on anything.

Skylar has been giving stand up paddleboard instruction for five years. He has had his accidents in the water and nearly been victimized by others. So it's in his interest and the interest of everyone in the water that beginners get proper instruction not just in how to handle themselves on their stand up paddleboards, but also on how to behave around others. "The hardest thing to teach for beginners is etiquette, because it's something that is learned through experience," Skylar says. "That instruction comes from time in the water."

On the Beach

Santa Monica/Venice, Sunset, Topanga, Surfrider, Privates, Zuma, and County Line: There are a number of beaches within a few miles of Malibu that are good for surf instruction. When teaching beginners how to surf, it is important to find a beach with gentle waves and a sandy bottom that offers some space away from other surfers, where newcomers can focus on the ocean and paddling a surfboard around the surfline, catching waves, and riding them.

Stand up paddling can be taught in just about any body of water—chlorine, fresh or salt, natural or artificial—but SUP instruction has its own requirements: open water, wind protection, no strong tides or currents, a lack of visible and invisible obstacles, preferably a sandy bottom, and as little cross-water traffic as possible.

"For some, the ocean is not the ideal place to learn SUP," Skylar says, because even on the calmest days, the ocean is still in motion: tides, currents, winds, and so on. "But when it's in your backyard, you're foolish not to take advantage of it."

The area of beach between First Point at Surfrider Beach and the Malibu Pier on a calm, no-surf day is a good place to learn SUP, especially for people like Noam and Michelle, who are familiar with the ocean already. They expect to mostly be paddling in the ocean, and, as such, they have an eye toward riding waves on their stand up paddleboards.

Malibu gets more swell action from the south in the summer than it does from the north in the winter, so on a calm, flat day in October, Noam and Michelle bring all their gear to the beach—including Michelle's mother to watch their kids, Daniel and Evan—and meet up with Skylar.

Skylar meets Michelle: "That's the ocean. Learn it. Know it. Live it." Michelle (who knows Fast Times at Ridgemont High *by heart): "Whoa."*

All surf instructors have smiled quietly to themselves as they watched beginners put on wetsuits inside out and backwards. Noam is no stranger to wetsuits, but the darn things have so many zippers and gaskets and other gizmos, they sometimes still require assistance. On this autumn day along the California Riviera, Noam is wearing a 3/2 full wetsuit, while Skylar is trunking it, and Michelle is bravely bikining it in 57-degree water.

Michelle has been surfing since 2007, so she knows she is a goofyfooter and knows how to strap a leash to the tail of the board.

And, she knows to strap the leash to her left/back leg when she is in her surfing stance. Noam is a kayaker and not as familiar with surf leashes, so Skylar shows him how to make a firm connection to the tail of the board.

Skylar makes sure that Noam and Michelle left Becker Surf and Sport with the right-size paddles. Reach up and curl your hand around the paddle, and it's A-OK. Skylar also agrees with the choice of boards: "The 12'1" Laird is probably the ideal board to learn on because of its stability and strength," Skylar says. "Boards for beginners take a pounding, but the Laird boards can take it."

① To start the lesson, Skylar accuses Noam and Michelle of being chickens of the sea. He draws a line in the sand and dares them to cross it. ② No, actually Skylar's line in the sand explains to Noam and Michelle that the best way to paddle out through breaking waves is straight through, perpendicular to the waves: Ideally, the board goes straight up and over the waves or through the broken whitewater. If you turn sideways at all, the board loses forward motion and stability, and the waves will hit the board from the side. The result could be an injurious or embarrassing wipeout.

Skylar lays down some preliminaries: "This is the side of the paddle that pushes against the water."

He also introduces them to the proper way to hold the paddle. Michelle has it wrong. Noam is closer to the proper grip.

The proper way to angle the paddle blade (left) and the improper way (right).

Skylar then gets down and explains that, for beginners, the safest thing is to get clear of the beach and the surfline by prone paddling with the paddle safely underneath you. Stand up paddleboards from 30" to 34" wide are awkward even for experienced surfers and paddleboarders.

It might be more comfortable to paddle on your knees to get clear of the surfline and shallow water along the shore before making the transition to your feet. "When you're on a board in the ocean," Skylar says, "you need to be comfortable paddling on your stomach and paddling on your knees, as well as paddling on your feet, because if you lose your paddle, how are you going to get back to the beach?"

① *When done with experience and finesse, the motion from prone or kneeling to standing up is done quickly and efficiently, with the paddle going from underneath you or on your side to in your hands and blade in the water and moving, as fast as possible. Surfers sometimes have to make this move with big waves coming at them—or a river runner has to recover from a fall and get vertical before the next rapids or waterfall—so with experience, all stand up paddlers will get this move down automatically. At first, the motion to your feet is a little awkward, especially with the paddle in your hand.*

② *The idea is to know where the "sweet spot" is on the board: the balance point where you want to be standing and paddling once you get to your feet. But that takes experience and familiarity with the board.*

③ *For surfers like Skylar and Michelle, getting to your feet and standing parallel goes against everything they normally do on a surfboard. In old Hawaii they called the parallel stance "bully style." But for stand up paddling, feet parallel around the middle of the board is the standard paddling stance.*

④ *When done with finesse, the move from prone or kneeling to standing is done with the goal of getting the paddle in the water as fast as possible. The paddle is another balance point to lean on, and forward motion is also your friend when it comes to balance = speed = stability. "The paddle becomes your leverage point that keeps you on your feet," Skylar says. "It's like hitting the gas on a motorcycle. If you keep paddling, you can paddle through a fall. By moving in a forward direction, it's more stable."*

⑤ *Around Malibu, it's common to see beginning stand up paddlers flailing around using a variety of incorrect grips on the paddle. It's not a baseball bat or a broom or an electric guitar. "It's also important to have the blade facing the right way," Skylar says. "It's amazing how many people will start to paddle with the blade going in the wrong direction. Sometimes the T-bar throws them off. Most stand up paddles have a logo on the blade, and that logo should be toward the front of the board."*

⑥ *The proper grip places your top hand around the T-bar or palm grip of the paddle and your lower hand about halfway down, maybe a little higher or lower. "If the paddle is too long, you can choke up on it," Skylar advises, "but you don't want your hands too close together. Your bottom hand is a pivot point. You don't want too tight of a grip on the lower hand." There is a sweet spot for holding the paddle, just as there is for standing on the board.*

⑦ The proper stroke can be described many ways. Skylar describes it like this: "You are driving the force from the top of the paddle into the ocean at the same time it's propelling you forward. That force is traveling all the way through your body. You are balancing and trying to stay vertical as you stroke." Some beginners think the ideal stroke is done with both arms locked rigid at the elbows. That is not correct. "Your top arm isn't always going to be straight," Skylar says. "You will drag your paddle if you do that."

The reason the forward stroke is such an efficient form of locomotion, and also an effective core-strengthening exercise, is that the power of the stroke comes from your legs and your upper body and is transferred through your arms to the paddle. "You are pulling yourself through the water with your arms, your chest, and your stomach muscles," Skylar tells his students. "Just as Laird does it to keep his legs strong for tow surfing in big waves, others do it to keep that core strength in their upper body. People will look at surfers and not see a ripped, yoked out dude. Well, Laird is an exception, but most surfers don't look like that. Being on the ocean is more about using energy and strength effectively and wasting less energy to move forward in one stroke."

⑧ The ideal stroke places the blade of the paddle in the water just in front of your toes, then brings it out of the water with the paddle level with your chest. You don't want to lean too far forward or back, because that affects balance and puts wobbles into the planing speed of the board. Skylar defers to the New Wave band Devo when finishing a stroke: "If you whip your paddle by turning your top hand when it comes out of the water—give it a little tweak—you will propel yourself farther."

⑨ *Skylar slipping into the "goofyfoot" stance, which is right foot forward: "Notice that the most important thing in this stance is to step* backwards *from your back foot. So when a goofy-foot person goes to the turning/ surfing stance, you should step backward with your left foot. A lot of beginners step forward with their front leg, and they lose their balance and fall forward."*

⑩ *Skylar surfing "regular foot," or left foot forward. Most beginning stand up paddlers should avoid the waves and the surf zone until they have their paddling, turning, and maneuvering skills down. Usually Skylar eases his students slowly into the lineup, but Michelle knows how to surf, and Noam is eager to join his wife sitting on top of the world, so Skylar moves ahead in the usual lesson plan.*

① *Skylar is a huge Three Stooges fan, and sometimes he will do the "poking in the eye" shtick, even in the middle of a lesson, when he should be serious. No, actually, what Skylar is communicating here is one of the cardinal rules of stand up: Don't look at your feet, look forward. "You need to maintain good peripheral vision, too," he says. "You want to know what is going on around you. When people lose their balance, they look down, and they fall down. Keep moving, and the board is more stable. And it's easier to keep the board moving if you are looking forward. Looking at your feet while stand up paddling is like walking down the street texting on your phone: You are going to fall into a manhole. So keep your paddle in the water and your eyes up."*

② *Indeed, eyes up and looking for whatever might be coming at you: surfers, stern-wheelers, sneaker waves, oil tankers, waterspouts, amorous sturgeon, killer whales, or other VLFs (Very Large Fins). Whatever. Situational awareness will keep you warm and dry and safe and unbitten. Don't look at your feet. Look at the water.*

③ *Look down, and you will lose your balance.*

④ *You will fall.*

⑤ *You will get wet.*

⑥ *And those around you will chortle at your awkwardness and misfortune. So don't look at your feet.*

① *Skylar encourages his students to know how to prone paddle a stand up paddleboard, because that is important in the transition from falling and getting wet to back to standing. Also, if you lose your paddle or get in trouble in the wind, you might have to prone paddle to get back to shore. "I'll tell beginners to never paddle farther offshore than they are willing to swim," Skylar says. The stroke for prone paddling is similar to freestyle swimming.*

② *Michelle has seen stand up paddlers cruising into waves at First Point Malibu and is eager to try it herself.*

③ *From her surfing experience, Michelle is most comfortable paddling in the prone position and getting to her feet that way, but having a paddle involved is something new. "The blade of the paddle rests nicely underneath your chest, with the shaft pointing up and in front of you," Skylar says. "If you are paddling like that going through waves, as soon as you release pressure, that paddle will get loose and knock you in the face. Keep pressure on the paddle."*

④ *Michelle's regular board for surfing is 9' × 24", and she doesn't have a paddle in her hand.*

⑤ *She gets a feeling for this new sensation on a 12'1" × 30" on the beach. It's a little awkward, making that move to her feet and grabbing the paddle.*

⑥ *Skylar suggests that Michelle knee paddle with the paddle in her hand, get clear of the surfline, get some speed going, then make the move to her feet. "When you are paddling on your knees," Skylar directs, "you don't want your top hand over the T-bar grip. Both hands can be around the middle of the paddle, fairly close together."*

⑦ *Michelle works out what to do with the paddle in that transition from paddling to standing. "Most people find it a lot easier to get to their feet once they learn how to paddle on their knees," Skylar says. "Paddle five or ten strokes on your stomach, get enough speed to get to your knees, paddle some more, get some speed and stability, then get to your feet."*

⑧ *Michelle finds it helps to be a yoga instructor in making that transition from knees to feet in a quick, relaxed motion. "A lot of adults, when they try to do things quickly, they get rigid and lose their balance," Skylar says. "It's important to be relaxed and remember you are dealing with the water. It's more of a fluid motion."*

⑨ *In her yoga lexicon, this move is called "getting to your feet."*

⑩ *Michelle is on her feet but too far back on the board and holding the paddle like Eddie Van Halen. Skylar directs her to move forward toward the recessed handle in the middle of the board, because the sweet spot is somewhere in that vicinity. "Your objective in doing this on the beach is learning how to go from your knees to your feet and end up in the right place without thinking about it, without looking down," Skylar says. "That needs to become second nature. And that's why you work on it on the beach."*

FROM PRONE TO STANDING UP

① *Now Michelle is up on her feet, and it's time to start paddling. It's easier to move forward on a stand up paddleboard when it's stuck in the sand, but Michelle correctly uses the paddle for balance, which will be the case when she is wobbling on the water. "The quicker you can get the paddle in the water and get a stroke, the easier it will be to keep your balance," Skylar says.*

STARTING TO PADDLE

② *Michelle has moved up closer to where the sweet spot will be when she is in the water, and Skylar moves into the most important aspect of stand up paddling: the forward stroke.*

③ The stroke is hard to practice on land and is best done in the water. Michelle and Noam are both eager to get out in the water, but Skylar wants to be sure he grounds his students in the fundamentals before he entrusts them to the deep and dark blue ocean.

④ What makes stand up paddleboarding such an effective form of locomotion, and also such an effective upper body/core workout . . .

⑤ . . . is that the forward stroke, done properly, is done with both arms firm but not locked and uses the upper body and core muscles to pull the paddle through the water. "Your legs are straight, and your waist becomes your pivot point," Skylar instructs. "All the pulling and power comes from your core."

① *"The ocean is always throwing something at you,"*
Skylar says . . .

② *. . . as he swerves out of the way of a kamikaze*
seagull.

③ *Michelle cannot bridle her enthusiasm and has already slid*
from the parallel paddling stance to the right foot back goofy-
foot stance for surfing.

④ *Now Michelle is surfing, but she has this huge pad-*
dle in her hand. What to do with that? Use the paddle
to catch the wave, then toss it aside, ride the rest of the
wave, and paddle back out and find the paddle? No.
"What is important to remember is you always want
two hands on your paddle," Skylar says. "When people
are surfing, some will grip the paddle with one hand,
but there is more chance of getting hurt with one hand
on the paddle than with two."

1 *Noam is closer in experience to most beginning stand up paddlers because he has not surfed much and is not comfortable paddling a board prone or kneeling. It is important to be comfortable on the board paddling prone, too. Looking up while paddling prone may irritate your neck, but you will develop stronger muscles the more you do it.*

2 *Noam is pushing his chest up off the board as he attempts to go from the prone position to his knees. This is easier to do while the board has momentum and is moving forward. It is best to do it after you have taken a good ten to fifteen strokes on your stomach.*

3 *While doing this, he maintains control of the paddle in front of his body on the board and keeps his focus in front of him.*

④ Noam quickly gets control of his paddle and gets the blade in the water.

⑤ Notice how his knees are not together; having them spread apart on the rails of the board allows for added stability and makes knee paddling easier.

⑥ Noam is gripping the shaft of the paddle with the kayak grip, which is wrong for stand up paddling. "Noam needs to reverse his top hand so it comes around the back of the shaft," Skylar points out. "Also, if his lower hand were closer to the blade, he would be paddling with more power." You want to get comfortable knee paddling as you do prone paddling. When SUP surfing in larger surf, even experienced stand up paddlers can be seen knee paddling their boards to get out through the waves quicker, as they are more stable on their knees.

⑦ *In windy conditions, even the most experienced stand up paddlers will take to their knees.*

⑧ *Skylar shows Noam how to adjust his grip on the paddle in the kneeling position—changing his kayak habit. Skylar demonstrates the proper grip and stroke, which is about three to five strokes on a side before alternating to the other side.*

① *Noam is ready to stand up from the kneeling position. Ideally, he should have his hands on his paddle as he is getting up, then grip the paddle to take it with him as he makes the move to his feet.*

② *Noam is getting up bowlegged, which only works if he does it fast. But the biggest problem here is that Noam is looking down at his feet and not where he is going.*

③ *This is not the proper way to take the paddle in hand, grabbing it by the blade and then moving it around.*

④ *Again, grabbing the paddle this way is awkward.*

⑤ *Noam's grip is wrong, but he corrects it quickly.*

⑥ *Now Noam has his hand over the T-grip and his bottom hand about halfway down the shaft.*

⑦ *This is Noam doing it right and making it look good: feet balanced over the sweet spot, head up and eyes looking forward, top hand on the T-bar, and bottom hand in the middle.*

⑧ *With his paddle in the water and moving forward, Noam is money: speed, stability, flow.*

⑨ *All three wonder what stance Noam will surf in when he is ready to ride waves. Skylar instructs Noam to step back with whatever foot feels natural.*

⑩ *Turns out that Noam is a regular foot, which means he surfs with his right leg back. Marriage between regular and goofy foots is illegal in some California coastal counties, but fortunately Los Angeles County has no law against it, so they proceed.*

① *"Stand up paddleboards are big, heavy, and bulky,"* Skylar explains. *"I even have trouble lugging the things around sometimes. So a dainty little gal like Michelle? There are tricks that help."*

② *But Michelle does not like to be underestimated: "I am woman!" she declares. "Mother of two! Yoga instructor! Surfer!"*

③ *Most stand up paddleboards come with recessed handles, which makes carrying something that big and bulky surprisingly easy. But for boards without a handle, Skylar shows how to carry a big board braced on your shoulder. "Just like you'd carry a piece of plywood," he says.*

④ *"This is how they did it old school,"* Skylar explains, *"when surfboards were made of hardwood and weighed 100 pounds plus. Either this or carry it on your head."*

① *The deck of a board can have an adhesive traction pad or wax. Skylar advises putting the deck to your head either way and using a towel if there is wax. "If you carry a waxed board deck up, the sun is going to liquefy your wax."*

② *Due to the weight of a SUP board, it is easier to start by picking it up from one end, either the nose or the tail.*

③ *Here Michelle picks up the board from the tail, then starts flipping it over to get the deck down.*

④ *Flip.*

⑤ *Flip.*

⑥ *And flip some more.*

⑦ *This is the way to get underneath a stand up paddleboard to get it on your head. Rest the nose in the sand, then carefully walk up underneath it, maintaining control of the board. There is a sweet spot for balance here, too.*

8 *Keep walking it up.*

9 *Once Michelle is a little past the middle of the board, she bends her knees, pushes up, and slowly lifts the board onto her head.*

10 *Here Michelle has properly picked up the board and balanced it on her head. Sometimes you may need to readjust the board while it is on your head. When doing so, move it a little at a time.*

① *Michelle asks, "Now what? I want to get wet!" Skylar says, "Hold on, not without your paddle. Let me show you how to carry your board with one arm so you can grab your paddle, too." Depending on whether you are left or right handed, it's probably going to be easiest to carry your board with your stronger arm. Skylar instructs Michelle to extend her arm along the rail: "You are going to cradle it."*

② *Once Michelle's arm is on the rail, Skylar instructs her to get the board positioned comfortably and balanced by using her opposite arm to maneuver the board.*

③ *Skylar hands Michelle her paddle, and she is on her own. On the beach at least.*

④ *Michelle needs to put her leash on and learn how to put the board down. Skylar instructs her to jam the paddle firmly into the sand. "Make sure you don't jam it into a rock," he says. "The paddles are strong, but they don't like hitting rocks."*

⑤ *Putting the board down is almost the reverse of picking it up. Michelle gets both hands on the board, slowly brings the nose down to the sand, and works her way back to the tail of the board.*

⑥ *She picks up the board . . .*

⑦ *. . . and turns it over.*

⑧ *With the board safely on the ground near the water's edge, Michelle unwraps her leash.*

① *Meanwhile, Noam is focusing on getting his leash on properly before picking up his board.*

② *He picks it up . . .*

③ *. . . and sets it on the side.*

④ *Noam moves forward . . .*

⑤ *. . . and grabs the handle.*

⑥ *Sometimes the boards aren't balanced evenly with the recessed handle, so there is some searching for the sweet spot with that as well.*

① *There is a third way to get a board into the water, something made possible by the toughness of stand up paddleboards. Skylar picks the board up by the tail and slides it nose first toward the water.*

② *"Sliding it nose first means the least amount of board is in the water," Skylar says. "The board is easy to push, and it's easier to control. You can also drag it in tail first, but I think pushing it nose first is best."*

③ *Skylar says, "Just make sure it goes perpendicular into any oncoming waves. You have probably ten seconds to get from the beach, onto your board, and out past the shore break."*

④ *"Let's say there are two waves X amount of distance apart; you have about ten seconds to get your board pointed straight out, get on your stomach or knees or feet, and start paddling."*

① *This is how a hot dog does it. Place the board in the water, jump on it, and start paddling. This can lead to disaster for even an experienced stand up paddler if the fin catches the sand or the bottom and is definitely not a good idea for a beginner.*

② *Skylar is feeling a little edgy from being on the beach, so he jumps out on the board and takes a few strokes.*

③ *Skylar does a jibe turn with one foot back.*

④ *He takes a few standard strokes on the left side, while applying pressure on the tail to propel the turn around.*

(5) *He turns back toward the beach . . .*

(6) *. . . and heads into shore.*

(7) *Skylar grabs the board by the tail . . .*

(8) *. . . then swings it around and pulls it to shore. That's the finesse way to go about it, but it's technique that is off in the distance for beginners.*

① *Another angle on Skylar's nose-first entry. This isn't the only way to get the board into the water, but it's not a bad idea for beginners with big boards.*

② *Instead of standing back a few paces and jumping on the board . . .*

③ *Skylar makes sure the fin is free and clear of rocks, sand, and other obstructions.*

④ *He takes to his knees and paddles out . . .*

⑤ *. . . then maintains balance while paddling over the small incoming waves.*

⑥ *Skylar rides down the back side of the wave.*

⑦ *Once over the wave, he takes a stroke or two to get beyond the break.*

⑧ *Now it's time to stand up. Skylar places his paddle across the deck of the board and places his hands shoulder width apart and pushes quick and smooth to his feet.*

⑨ *Once standing, Skylar begins to paddle.*

⑩ *He's off and stroking and getting some of that supreme pleasure.*

① *After launching through the waves, Skylar prepares to do a jibe turn and return to shore.*

② *With a jibe turn, it's important to step back into a surfing stance. This helps sink the tail where you can pivot by paddling forward on your front side.*

③ *After you are turned in the direction you want to go, slide your back foot back into your paddle stance. It's usually easier to move your feet on the board while your paddle is in the water. This helps with balance.*

④ *Take a strong stroke toward shore.*

⑤ *When you near shore, prepare to get off.*

⑥ *Skylar steps off onto the sand bottom, shooting the board out in front of him. Like the jibe turn, this is an advanced move. Skylar is very experienced and has this down to an art. It's best for beginners to go back to their knees and step off onto the sand.*

⑦ *Skylar lands on his feet.*

⑧ *Once you're off your board, pick it up by the tail . . .*

⑨ *. . . pull it around . . .*

⑩ *. . . and bring it on to the beach.*

① *Noam and Michelle have seen enough. Skylar's finesse and crazy jibes have driven them into a tizzy, and it's time to make that transition from landlubbers to experiencers of the most supreme pleasure.*

② *Michelle and Noam are just about to take the plunge and learn it, know it, live it. Noam uses the recessed handle, while Michelle emulates Skylar's nose-first slide.*

③ *Noam slides his board out into the water. With such gentle waves, getting out past the break is not really a problem. That's why it's always best to learn in a calm body of water—one less thing to worry about.*

④ *Noam is first to glide out onto his stomach.*

⑤ *He moves the paddle into position.*

⑥ *With the paddle properly placed under his chest, Noam begins to paddle out in the prone position.*

⑦ *Here Skylar encourages Michelle to move up a few inches on her board so the board isn't "pushing water" as she paddles. "If she is too far back, she won't paddle fast enough and will get frustrated," he points out. "Similarly, if she is too far forward, the nose will dive into the water: also known as pearling." Michelle knows how to paddle a regular surfboard, but this stand up is 3' longer and 6" wider than her surfboard, so it's awkward even for someone with experience. She has to find the sweet spot for paddling, too.*

⑧ *Once past the surfline, it's good to stop, look, and listen: What is the wind doing? What are the currents? What is the best way to go? Are there pods of cruising orca? Let's go check 'em out! Skylar shows the couple how to straddle their boards.*

① *One way to turn a board while sitting is to twirl your legs underneath: clockwise to go clockwise, counterclockwise to go the other direction. Here Skylar demonstrates for Noam and Michelle.*

② *Next, they get on their knees and practice taking a few strokes.*

③ *Michelle is quick to her feet as she says, "Wow, this is much easier than I thought." But she is a surfer and a yoga instructor after all. Skylar replies, "Don't blame it on your instructor when you get wet."*

④ Here, Michelle practices turning the board around by doing a reverse stroke. One of the important things to note here is how her eyes are up and not looking down at her board or paddle.

⑤ To do the reverse stroke, Michelle places the blade in the water behind her, then moves it from the tail of the board to the nose. The reverse of a normal stroke, and when done on the left side like this, has the effect of turning the board to the left (counterclockwise).

⑥ Turning.

⑦ *Still turning.*

⑧ *Now turned out toward sea, Michelle can do forward strokes to get where she wants to go.*

Skylar, Noam, and Michelle head out to the deep blue sea for a lesson in maneuvering their boards and surfing some waves.

CHAPTER 4

HOW TO
MANEUVER YOUR BOARD AND START SURFING

Posing around on the beach and practicing strokes and getting to your knees, then back on your feet and pretending to stand up paddleboard while scratching sand is all very fine, but at some point it is time to turn theory into practice and go into the water. Learning to stand up paddle is a function of time invested.

Do not be alarmed. Well, be a little alarmed at first, because no matter how good of a gymnast, beach boy, Class V kayaker, big wave surfer, gold medal downhill skier, OC1 [one-person outrigger canoe] champion, circus performer, or whatever you are, with stand up paddling, you are going to flail a bit at first. The fact is, walking on water isn't as easy as it looks.

Flail, fall, turn left when you want to turn right, go backward when you want to go forward, get blown out to sea or too close to shore, get in the way of shipping, interfere with ferry schedules, piss off surfers, fly fishermen, and yachtsmen, get dunked, get wet, discover that your $150 Maui Jim sunglasses don't float (twice!), lose other equipment, break equipment, sprain joints, get laughed at by landlubbers and spooked by shadows and shapes moving under and around you.

Beginning stand up paddlers will flail. It's part of the time-familiarity continuum. Learning how to stand up paddle is like learning how to do anything: No matter what your previous skills, becoming comfortable, then proficient, and finally good is a matter of sweat equity—or maybe "wet equity" is a better term.

But get up, stand up. Get back on the horse that threw you. The more time you spend paddling around in different conditions, the more stable and comfortable you will become, and at some point in your learning curve you will look around, see that you are cruising comfortably, enjoy the feel and the speed and the view, and have a "SUPiphany."

All of a sudden all of the expense and shopping and decision making and lugging around of equipment and making time and falling and flailing and getting dunked will be worth it, and you will be cruising on the new sensation that is sweeping the world.

Small Steps, Into the Ocean

For their dry run on shore and first steps into the water, instructor Skylar took Michelle and Noam on the west side of the Malibu Pier. That was a calm, windless day, but Malibu isn't always calm and windless, and when learning how to stand up paddleboard, the flatter the surface of the water, the less wind and bump and current, the faster you will progress.

Today Skylar is taking Michelle and Noam out into the ocean to really learn how to stand up paddle. There is a bit of swell rolling through Surfrider Beach at Malibu, and there is a pesky west wind that is ruffling an otherwise usually protected, placid stretch of beach.

But the Malibu Pier acts as a shield, which takes most of the wind bump out of the surface of the water, so by walking less than 100 yards to the east, through the pilings, under the pier, and to the east side, Skylar finds an area in the lee of the pier that is relatively windless and flat and a good location for Michelle and Noam to leave the beach, head out to sea, work on proper strokes, do some turns, and begin to put in the muscle equity and time that will lead to their proficiency. "By heading south of the pier," Skylar explains, "we're away from the other surfers, so we won't get in their way. And the wind will be pushing us away from the pier and not toward it, which can be dangerous."

GLOSSARY OF PADDLING STROKE TERMS

With thanks to Charles "Cmac" MacArthur for contributing to these definitions.

BACKPADDLE: An expression from kayaking, paddling backward to slow or reverse motion.

BRACING: A balance stroke, used to steady the board and steady yourself on the board. There are high braces and low braces.

CADENCE: The speed or tempo of paddling.

CATCH: The first part of a stroke, when the paddle blade enters the water. According to Dave Kalama from www.davidkalama.com: "Catch is about three things: reach, torso position, and timing."

DIPPING A RAIL: Once you become a competent and then an expert stand up paddler, you will find that most of your adjustments are very subtle. For example, kicking out of a wave usually just means putting a little foot pressure on the inside rail; even on a big board like a 12'1", that will slow you down and redirect the board enough to get over the back of the wave—as long as it's a small wave. Putting that pressure on the rail is called "dipping a rail."

This applies to flatwater paddling as well. If there is a wind or a current coming from the side, and it's pushing or tilting the board in a direction you don't want to go, you can tilt back by applying a bit of foot pressure on the rail that is in the direction you want to go, and the board will go in that direction, gradually or abruptly, based on foot pressure.

Charles MacArthur adds: Dipping the rail on the same side as the paddle stroke also helps counteract the natural turning of the board to the opposite side, an inherent problem of paddling on one side of the board. Dipping a rail and using a J stroke on the same side provides excellent steering under power. This helps when using shorter fins as well.

1. CATCH

The beginning of the stroke when the blade first enters the water

- Be sure to drive the blade deep into the water before pulling
- Extend out to a comfortable reach but don't try to over reach

3. EXIT

The end of the stroke when the blade is released from the water

- Take your paddle out at your feet, don't pull beyond your feet as this will allow you to start your next stroke sooner and the board / boat will not decelerate as much between strokes
- Be sure to exit by dropping your top hand downward and not by lifting the lower hand up. This is a more relaxing way to exit and will also help get the blade out of the water clean and fast.

2. POWER PHASE

The driving of the board forward past the submerged paddle blade

- Be sure to think about driving yourself past the paddle blade not pulling the blade through the water
- Use your upper body and shoulder rotation for power and use your arms as just extensions from the shoulders. Your body is much more powerful than your arms.
- Try to keep your top hand over your bottom hand during the pull to allow more strokes per side.
- The paddle is most efficient when it is vertical or has positive angle like at the beginning of the stroke.
- The power phase should finish at your feet (while standing) or at your hip while seated.
- Pulling back too far will only cause more deceleration between strokes

4. RECOVERY

The return of the blade back to the start of the stroke

- Point your thumb forward on the recovery to allow the blade to "feather" on the return. This will allow the blade to be in the most aerodynamic position on the recovery. This is particularly important when paddling into the wind.
- Relax your shoulders on the recovery to give your body a relaxed feeling in between strokes
- Don't rush the recovery as a nice smooth recovery will aid in the next stroke being more powerful.

Catch, power, exit, recovery: the four phases of the forward stroke. Diagram courtesy of Quickblade

DRAW STROKES: Used to pull the boat or board sideways; literally a lateral power stroke.

DUFFECK STROKE: Cmac says: The Duffeck was named for Milo Duffeck, a Czech paddler in the 1950s who invented a faster turning stroke for the 13-foot-long slalom kayaks of the day. The blade and shaft are placed in vertically next to the paddler's hip with the power face toward the nose of the boat. It is akin to grabbing a fence post and swinging around 180 degrees.

EDDY TURN: A river-running term in which you use the calm water in the eddy of a rock or obstruction to make a turn back upstream.

EXIT: The point at which the paddle leaves the water at the end of a power stroke. Depending on the paddler and the kind of stroke, this can be in front of the feet, even with the feet, or behind the feet. Some paddlers will twist the shaft to rotate the blade for less resistance as it leaves the water.

FEATHER: Turning the blade parallel to the current or wind to reduce resistance.

FORWARD STROKE: There are several parts to the forward stroke: the catch, the power, the exit, and the recovery. The ideal forward stroke is done with knees bent, bending slightly at the waist and pulling with the core muscles. The catch enters the water forward of your feet. The power stroke comes back in a straight line. The exit comes out of the water in the vicinity of your feet: slightly before, parallel, or slightly behind. The recovery is lifting the paddle out of the water and bringing it forward for the next catch.

There are two basic versions of the forward stroke: the Hawaiian and the Tahitian. The

Hawaiian is a longer stroke, while the power and recovery of the Tahitian stroke are shorter.

HAWAIIAN STROKE: Stand up paddle surfing carries DNA from both surfing and outrigger canoe paddling, and the traditional stroke for stand up paddling is the Hawaiian stroke. As defined by kanuculture.com, there are two forms of the Hawaiian stroke used in outrigger canoeing:

The "traditional" Hawaiian stroke was very long [from entry to exit] coupled with exaggerated body movement and lunging forward, so the ribs almost touch the canoe gunnel. All this contributed to a much slower potential stroke rate—as low as 45 strokes/minute. The stroke was slow, long and deliberate, with emphasis on the pull at the front and the push at the rear of the stroke, and the paddle exiting at the back of the paddler's seat . . . with little or no "feathering" of the blade.

The traditional Hawaiian stroke was replaced with a more upright technique, rotating around the spine, leaning shoulder forward, top arm back and entry achieved by dropping the shoulder to drive the paddle downward for the entry. The emphasis is now upon rotation of the body around the spine, careful paddle placement and keeping much of the emphasis of the stroke, the power phase, "up front," then during the "vertical" phase, pulling the blade out early at the hip. This allows the crew to maintain higher stroke rates and enables the wa`a to "run."

HIGH BRACE: Cmac says: Taken from kayaking, the high brace is a supportive "stroke" in which the shaft is horizontal, the blade face is placed flat on the surface of the water and is a leverage point from which paddlers right themselves by untipping their boats with their knees and hips. They literally rock the boat back upright. A stand up paddler does the same and rocks the board back up right with his or her feet and legs.

JIBE: Also known as a pivot turn, a fast 180-degree turn in which the paddler moves from a parallel stance to a surfing stance, puts pressure on the tail, and combines that with a hard stroke on one side of the board to bring the board around 180 degrees. Be sure your feet are on opposite sides of the center line when you do this.

Ekolu Kalama riding a 14' × 24" racing board, making a fast, backside jibe turn around a marker during the Jever SUP World Cup at Hamburg, Germany, in July 2009. Photo courtesy of Starboard

J STROKE: A J stroke allows you to paddle in a straight line while on one side of your board. It is accomplished at the end of a power stroke by twisting the grip and shaft with the top hand. Push the thumb forward for the twist. The paddle travels in a J-shaped arc away from the tail of the board. The power face is engaged through the twist and faces away from the tail of the board at the stroke completion and counteracts the natural turning effect of the power stroke.

LOW BRACE: A balancing stroke with the arms held close to the body and the back face of the paddle held against the flow of water for support.

MOTION TURN: As paraphrased from the Werner Paddles website: The motion turn involves moving forward with speed, taking a step or two back, and sinking the tail. While doing this, make a strong reverse stroke on the side of the board you want to turn. As the board spins, take a strong forward paddle on the opposite side while stepping forward. You will be going in the opposite direction.

PEEL OUT: Cmac says: A river boarding term, you paddle from the eddy into the oncoming current. This turns you downstream.

PIVOT TURN: See jibe.

POWER STROKE: The meat of the forward stroke. Once the blade is in the water, the power stroke pulls with your core muscles and your arms to sweep the paddle back to your feet and a little farther; the length of the power stroke depends on the proclivities of the paddler. The power stroke for the Tahitian stroke is shorter than the Hawaiian stroke.

The J stroke helps keep the board going straight.

RECOVER: The third and final part of a stroke, when the paddle leaves the water. Some paddlers bring the paddle out in front of their feet, some level with their feet, some behind their feet. Some paddlers feather the blade when it comes out of the water, twisting it 90 degrees as it leaves the water to lessen resistance.

REVERSE STROKE: Sweeping the paddle in reverse motion toward the front of the board, then around the front and along the other side. This is an effective way to turn the board.

The sweep stroke is good for steering the board at slow speeds.

RUDDER STROKE: Cmac says: The blade is behind the paddler in the water, vertical with the shaft angled diagonally to the water. It is like a fishtail, pushed from side to side to act as a rudder. A super-powerful turning stroke for surfing, it is more necessary when using small or no fins at all.

SKULLING BRACE: Cmac says: A brace in which the blade is manipulated out to the side of the board on the water surface as if buttering bread. The blade skims the water smoothly in an arc to create more lift and support for the paddler.

STATIONARY TURN: From the Werner Paddles website: This SUP turn tends to be the most stable. It involves using a long, powerful forward or backward stroke from a stationary position on the side of the stand up paddleboard. It is used to swing the board 180 degrees. Remember to keep your balance centered, and don't bend at the waist; this will cause the board to dip too far forward or backward, throwing off your balance and causing the board to stall.

SWEEP STROKE: Cmac says: This stroke is for turning the board, especially when still or at slow speeds. The paddle shaft is extended out to the side, with the blade vertical. The shaft is on a low diagonal to the water. The blade is submerged and levers the water to spin the board as much as 180 degrees forward or backward. The blade is pushed in an arc away from the board rail relative to the board for maximum spinning leverage.

TAHITIAN STROKE: A shorter stroke with a faster cadence than the Hawaiian stroke. As defined for outrigger canoeing by the kanu culture.com website: "The Tahitian—*va`a*—stroke is easily identifiable as having a high rating [70+ per minute] consisting of a quick, short, powerful stroke with minimal body movement, less emphasis on rotation, and the exit of the paddle around the level of the hip. The arms, shoulders and upper torso of the paddler play a major role in applying power to the stroke. Because the stroke is short, timing must be absolutely precise."

① *On the beach, on the east side of the Malibu Pier, everyone is trunking it, for some reason, on a chilly day in October. Michelle's body language says it all: "This is gonna be cold!" Skylar uses his paddle to stretch, but he reassures her: "It's only cold if you fall."*

② *Skylar busts out some lines from* Macbeth: *"But screw your courage to the sticking place, and we'll not fall!" With that, he picks up the tail of his board and leads Michelle and Noam out into the briny.*

③ *Now Michelle and Skylar take the lead, pushing through the broken whitewater and going into water deep enough to support their weight when they go to their knees.*

④ *Skylar hangs back and watches as his students do the right thing and take to their knees to get off the beach and past the surf zone.*

⑤ *Michelle and Noam are moving out of the broken whitewater and into blue water, making swift progress, so Skylar goes briefly to his knees.*

⑥ *Skylar is up and stroking, while Noam and Michelle keep to their knees as a small wave approaches.*

7 *If Michelle and Noam had gotten to their feet right away, this little wave probably would have thrown them, they would have fallen, and it would have been cold. But on their knees they go up and over without losing speed or stability. Skylar does it standing up.*

8 *Safely past the surf zone, Skylar tells Michelle and Noam they can make the move to their feet. The best way to do this is straight into the wind or any bump that is in the water. If wavelets are hitting the board from the side, stability is a problem. Even the widest paddleboard will lose all stability when being buffeted from the side. Sometimes it feels like an invisible hand reaches out and grabs your board—like Lucy pulling the football from Charlie Brown—and the paddler eats it. Take any wind or waves on the nose to maintain stability.*

9 *Noam makes the move first, a little awkwardly. If there were any waves coming, or if the wind were blowing or there was any bump in the water, he would probably have fallen from this position. "He's a little awkward, but his board is moving forward and stable," Skylar says. "That's the most important thing. Speed is stability."*

10 *Michelle and Noam get to their feet and are off and stroking: catch, power, exit, recovery. Catch, power, exit, recovery. Skylar looks back toward the beach for a moment, just to see where they are in relation to land.*

① *The "catch" is where the blade enters the water. People come in all shapes and sizes, so the location of the catch will vary. Here Skylar is doing a regular forward stroke so the catch is in front of his feet. Some people like to use a shorter, more rapid "Tahitian stroke," where the catch is closer to the feet.*

② *The "power" is the meat of the stroke. Skylar sweeps the paddle back and propels the board forward.*

③ *Still in the power phase. Ideally, Skylar is using all the muscles in his upper body to transfer energy through the shaft to the blade and into the water. Do it right once and you'll get the feel. It feels good.*

FORWARD STROKE

④ The "exit" is when you bring the paddle out of the water at the end of the power phase. Some paddlers feather the blade for less resistance so it comes out smooth. Like the catch, the location of the exit differs from person to person, and also the purpose of the stroke. Surfers and river runners trying to catch waves or get out of trouble will bring the exit up quick. Paddlers cruising on flat water might let the paddle stay in the water longer.

⑤ During the "recovery" phase, the paddler lifts the blade from the water and brings it forward for the next catch.

⑥ Then it starts all over again.

① *With the reverse stroke, the stand up paddler will start by doing the reverse of a forward stroke by entering the blade behind the feet and then pulling the blade forward to turn the nose to the right or left. Here Skylar is using the reverse stroke from a dead stop to start a 180-degree turn. He places the blade in the water behind his feet and sweeps it toward the front of the board.*

② *Sweeping the paddle from back to front, Skylar brings the nose of his board around from a dead stop.*

③ *As the board is turning and moving forward a bit from the reverse stroke, Skylar places the paddle on the other side and starts a forward stroke.*

④ *With the momentum from the reverse stroke combined with the forward stroke, Skylar has turned almost 180 degrees from a dead stop.*

⑤ *And now he is off in an entirely new direction.*

⑥ *Beginners will find themselves using the reverse stroke a lot—for balance, to turn, to redirect motion.*

① *Noam and Michelle both do decent sweeping turns, putting a little weight on their right rails and stroking on the right side to turn their boards to the right, then look for what's his name, who seems to have fallen behind.*

② *Ever notice how people who have been married for several years tend to paddle the same way?*

③ *The instructor, Skylar, is so proud of his students for doing a good turn that he decides to celebrate with a jibe turn wide to port.*

④ *A jibe turn is an advanced move. It requires taking your feet out of the parallel stance and standing in a surfer stance. Skylar is a goofyfooter, so he puts his left foot back to sink the tail and strokes on the right side to turn to the left. "Again, one of the most important things with the jibe turn is to step backward with your back foot," Skylar explains. "Keep your paddle in the water for leverage and balance and movement, because speed is stability."*

① *Noam and Michelle don't feel ready for all that jibe, so they do a standard turn. With their feet parallel, they put weight on the rail on the side they want to turn. Michelle has her paddle on that side and is backpaddling, sweeping her blade from back to front. "The problem with backpaddling is you slow yourself down, and that makes the board tip," Skylar says. "So when you backpaddle to turn 180 degrees, you have to counter that action with equal and opposite forward paddling on the other side, immediately following your backstroke for speed to complete the turn. This becomes even more important in the surfline when you are controlling your board to catch waves."*

② *Michelle and Noam have both backpaddled on the left side to start the turn to the left, and now they are forward paddling on the opposite side for speed to complete the turn. "When you backpaddle, you are pushing the board backward, and that makes the fins catch and turn the board," Skylar says. "So that starts the turn, then follow that with a forward stroke on the opposite side for speed and stability and to complete the turn."*

③ *Michelle and Noam, halfway through a wide, counterclockwise turn to the left. Michelle is turning tighter than Noam, so he backpaddles a bit on the left side to bring the nose around.*

④ *Feeling like a mother duck leading her ducklings, Skylar backpaddles as his students complete their turn and catch up.*

1 *Not wanting his students to be cut to ribbons by the barnacles and crags on the Malibu Pier pilings, Skylar directs Michelle to turn hard to port by reversing her stroke. "This is Michelle doing it exactly right," Skylar says. "She gets the turn started with a simple backstroke. Her eyes should be up, but she is making sure her paddle is in the right place."*

2 *Michelle strokes her paddle from back to front: the back-paddle.*

3 *She ends her first backpaddle stroke . . .*

4 *. . . and reaches back to start the second.*

⑤ *She strokes the paddle from back to front as her board turns to the left.*

⑥ *One backpaddle, two backpaddle, then a fast transition bringing the paddle across her body and putting it back in the water on the other side for a forward stroke to put some momentum into the turn and complete it.*

⑦ *Michelle starts the forward stroke, which will keep the board turning to the left.*

⑧ *From a standstill, Michelle has turned almost 180 degrees with two strong backpaddles and a couple of well-placed forward paddles.*

① *Skylar now shows Noam a textbook jibe turn. Well, almost textbook. "I shouldn't be looking at my feet," Skylar says. "I should be looking where I am going and want to turn."*

② *Skylar steps back with his back foot and strokes on the right side for stability as his balance shifts.*

③ *The tail is sinking, putting the board on a pivot point, and Skylar keeps his paddle in the water for leverage as he strokes the board around to his left.*

④ *The jibe turn generally doesn't require any backpaddling and is used as a quicker, forward-moving turn. You can do a jibe turn at any speed. "A quick three strokes and you're going in the opposite direction," Skylar says.*

⑤ *This is a "frontside" jibe turn, but it can also be done backside. "Give credit to Sam George for coining the term jibe turn," Skylar says. "I guess that is directly from his windsurfing in the 1980s—not that there's anything wrong with that."*

⑥ *Michelle and Skylar have turned 180 degrees, and now it's Noam's turn to do what is a fairly advanced maneuver.*

⑦ *Skylar says, "To be honest, I didn't think Noam was going to get the jibe turn down, but those big Laird boards are so stable and well designed, they make it easy for beginners to learn to keep their balance on their feet and control their boards while doing the more advanced maneuvers."*

⑧ *"It's hard to sink the tail on a board that big," Skylar says. So Noam's turn doesn't come around as fast as Skylar's jibe turn. But again, this is an advanced maneuver, and Noam is bringing it around gradually. Noam needs a little work on his jibe turns, but the truth is, two months after these photos were shot, Noam got all surf stoked, bought a 9'6", and was whipping these turns around from Malibu Road to Haleiwa like nobody's business.*

① *As seen from the pier, Skylar shows the proper stance and paddle position for a goofyfooter moving into a jibe turn.*

② *He steps back and gets a paddle in the water to shift his weight, sink the tail, and start propelling the turn.*

③ *By pressing down with his back foot, he puts weight on the tail and the inside rail to direct the turn and paddles on the opposite side to propel it.*

④ *As Skylar instructs, "One of the most important things when moving your feet on the board is to have your paddle in the water for balance."*

⑤ *Skylar completes the turn, then paddles forward for propulsion.*

The Surf Session

Surfin' is the only life, the only way for Michelle Geft. But for Noam, not so much. With three years of surfing experience behind her, Michelle began stand up paddling with an eye toward riding waves on the things. She had seen others doing it at Malibu, liked how it looked, and wanted to have a go herself, to see if she could apply her ocean and wave knowledge to this new technique.

Noam hadn't surfed much, because a bad lower back made the prone-paddling position uncomfortable—a fact true for him and also for a lot of older surfers who have gotten into stand up paddleboarding for the same reason.

Normally, Skylar encourages his students to spend many weeks paddling in flat water and getting their skills down before going into the surf, for their safety and the safety of others. But he was confident in Michelle's surfing experience and Noam's athleticism, so on a day in early November, Skylar paddled off the beach with Noam and Michelle and guided them into the surf zone, to lay down some fundamentals of safe, responsible stand up paddle surfing.

① *Skylar caught this wave with his feet parallel, but then stepped back with his left foot into the "goofyfoot" stance. Meanwhile, Michelle is out the back. Someone not accustomed to wielding a big board with a paddle should not be in the surf zone. Skylar is keeping his eye on both Michelle and Noam, so as not to break the unwritten law.*

② *Sliding right, with his eyes on the wave and both hands on the paddle, Skylar propels himself down the line while using the paddle for steering, propulsion, and stability.*

③ Skylar "cross-steps" up to the nose—moving forward a bit to gain speed.

④ Here, Skylar is almost riding "bully style," or parallel stance, a form and function combination that goes back to the beach boys of Waikiki, who would sometimes ride in parallel stance. This is an old-school style that stand up paddle surfing has brought back. It feels cool and looks good when done right.

⑤ Now he is "walking the nose," moving forward to the very front of the board to "hang five" or put five toes over the nose of the board.

⑥ What looks like a "helicopter"—a 360-degree turn done from the nose of the board—is actually Skylar starting another old-school move, something not seen much since the 1960s called a standing island pullout.

⑦ This is a standing island pullout with a twist, because if Skylar does it correctly, he will kick out of the wave and stay standing, rather than falling into the water. Notice how he bends his knees and leans on his paddle to gain leverage and keep his balance as the fins come out of the water, and the nose sinks.

⑧ This technique is advanced, but Skylar nails it. He is too far forward and burying the nose, but a small step back and feet parallel and he'll be stroking back out for more, or at least to check on the progress of his students. Where is Michelle, anyway?

① *Little Miss Surf Stoke couldn't curb her enthusiasm and went charging into a wave, doing a couple of things right and several things wrong. Her legs are parallel, she is holding the paddle correctly, but her angle across the wave is all wrong. Malibu is a right point break, which means the wave breaks to your right as you are paddling for it, toward the beach. Michelle should be heading to her right as well, but she's going left.*

② *She isn't going "straight off, Adolf," which means riding the wave perpendicular, straight toward the beach (another no-no). However, she is going "Wrong Way Corrigan." Also, Michelle should be moving into her surfing stance at this point. She has caught the wave early, no longer needs to paddle for speed, but her feet are still parallel, making it harder to turn or control the board. She should be turning at this point.*

③ *There is a left at Malibu at the top of the point during the summer. But Michelle is not at the top of the point, and this isn't summer. She is on the inside, over the rocks, in the fall, and she is going the wrong way. Sliding left.*

④ *"In this photo," Skylar says, "Michelle is trying to change her stance, but the most important thing when changing your stance is to have the paddle in the water for balance." She doesn't.*

⑤ *Here Michelle has stepped back with her left foot into the goofyfoot stance, but because she is going left, she is surfing "front side," or facing the wave, whereas if she were going to the right, she would have her back to the wave.*

⑥ *She is having some control issues, trying to womanhandle that 12'1" × 30" board and keep her hands on the paddle. If she were a style master, she would cross-step back to the tail, use the paddle to do a swooping turn to her right, and head for the pier. Can't argue with the smile, though.*

⑦ *But Michelle doesn't have that mastery yet on a stand up paddleboard, so she is a prisoner of all that width, length, stability, and speed. "But, hey, let's give it up for Michelle," Skylar says. "She is going the wrong way, but she has just paddled into her first wave on a stand up paddleboard and loving every minute of it."*

⑧ *Michelle finds herself sliding left, toward the beach and the rocks. Skylar says, "Michelle should have her top hand on the T-bar. She should always be ready to put her paddle in the water, and here she isn't ready. Michelle is used to riding a regular board, she isn't used to having a paddle in her hand, so I forgive her." Michelle is risking running her fin on the rocks and/or sand and breaking it out, or falling off and stepping into sharp stones, or taking out the photographer—who stopped clicking and got out of the way.*

① *Michelle has her pride, and she ain't no quitter, so she went back out there and started making some gains. Here she has stroked into a small wave that surfers call a "double up." Skylar says, "She took her hand off the paddle and yelled, 'What do I do now?' I replied, 'Have some fun and get your hand back on that paddle before the T-bar whacks you on the face.'"*

② *One wave has overtaken another slower wave, and they have combined their energies. Michelle is caught in the middle of the two waves. With more skill, she would paddle furiously to get out of that swell crevasse and drop down into the bottom wave. "It's working for her, though," Skylar says, "because as the wave doubles up, it sucks out more water and exposes rocks. So it's good she is passing out the back of this one."*

③ *Michelle didn't do a standing island pullout like Skylar. She kicked out normally, with her feet back on the tail and the wave passing under her. Now she employs some yoga skills to keep both feet on the board and her body out of the cold ocean. This is October, after all, and she is in a bikini.*

④ It's touch and go for a moment. Will she fall and get cold and wet?

⑤ No, she makes it to her knees, gets her paddle in the water, and gets some speed. "She didn't get wet, made it to her knees, she has her paddle in the water. She'll be back on her feet in no time," assures Skylar.

⑥ Up and paddling, Michelle uses a reverse stroke to turn the board 180 degrees and head back to the top of the lineup. This is how it goes when you are learning how to ride waves on a stand up: Trial and error, flailing, falling, but little by little you get better at it.

① *Skylar hovers in the background shouting directions as Michelle angles into a wave, going right this time. That's Noam on the shoulder, daring to drop in on his charging wife. This is a no-no, but anything goes between married couples. Seriously, though, do not drop in on people like this.*

② *Michelle is off balance here, but she has dropped back her left foot, is applying pressure to the inside rail with her right foot, and is paddling on the left side of the board to propel it to the right. A little bit right and a little bit wrong, but will it work?*

③ *Michelle catches the wave but stands too far back on the tail, losing her forward momentum and letting the wave pass underneath her. As she is shifting her paddle to the right side for a power stroke, the wave gets past her. Oh well, nature will always make more waves.*

④ *Michelle takes a seat as Noam goes it alone.*

① *Noam does well—you know, for a kayaking baseball/football/basketball/Sports Center fanatic. He catches the wave paddling parallel, then steps back with his left foot into the goofyfoot stance. Wait a minute, wasn't Noam a regular foot? Apparently not. Sometimes the stance test on land doesn't hold up in the water. So Noam is a goofyfoot, cool. Now there won't be any family arguments over whether to take a surf/SUP vacation to Mundaka—a famous left point in Spain—or Jeffrey's Bay—a famous right point in South Africa. Moving the foot back and putting weight on the inside rail turns the board and puts it on an angle. "His paddle position is good, and his eyes are up and looking down the line," Skylar says. "But his balance is not ideal: He is a little too far forward, and he is going a little straight, but maybe he will recover."*

② *Oh! Oh! Oh! By George, I think he's got it! "He's using his paddle to steer and propel himself down the line," Skylar agrees. "He has a bit of a stinkbug stance, but that will be corrected. I was impressed when he did that. He sat out there and watched and watched and watched and paid attention. That is the benefit to spending time on the beach watching."*

③ *Kowabunga. Using subtle weight shifts on the rail and the tail, Noam squeaks a turn out of his beginner barge and makes a nice angle down the line, heading right, toward the Malibu Pier.*

④ *Once those 12'1" Lairds get up and running, they can be remarkably fast, like an offensive lineman running the 40-yard dash in 4.4. But this wave doesn't really allow any trim or planing, as the wave "sections" off, leaving Noam behind.*

⑤ *Noam gets out of this as best he can. "He doesn't yet have the skill to sink the tail and steer the board out the back of the wave," Skylar points out. "Instead, he goes back to his knees where he is comfortable and stable and pulls the board out of the wave."*

⑥ *But Noam turns sideways. "The problem is that he didn't straighten out and go directly at the beach," Skylar says. "It takes skill to ride a wave in the whitewater at an angle versus going perpendicular. Noam was probably aware he was headed for the rocks, so he got out as best he could. He 'caught a rail' as the board went parallel to the whitewater." A little bit of wave catches a lot of surfboard, and then it's time for a capsize drill. But little mishaps like this are all part of the process. Better to get wet than hit rocks.*

① *Noam is nonplussed. He's a goer, he has grit, which is important when learning how to ride waves, whether prone or standing. It takes time, and you are going to fall, wipe out, get wet, get cold, get frustrated. But if you're one of those who can get knocked down and get back up again, you will persevere to enjoy that most supreme pleasure.*

② *Noam takes off with decent form, but he is on the wrong side of this wave. An experienced stand up paddle surfer might be able to stroke madly and get into the meat of the wave in front—"Or probably wouldn't have taken off at all," Skylar says. But Noam's skills aren't there yet, and he gets caught behind the section.*

③ *This is called "digging a rail," in which the wave is tipping Noam to his left, and his balance is off. "Similar to what he did on the previous wave when he was in the whitewater," Skylar says. Noam makes a splash and will soon fall. The water is shallow here, and there are some sharp rocks, all part of the perils of learning to stand up paddle surf. "One thing that's important when it's shallow like that is to fall flat," Skylar says. "In other words, spread your surface area out. Don't jump out with your legs out. Fall on your back as opposed to falling on your face. And always, always, always protect your head, especially when you come up."*

① *Noam is knee stroking back out, and that is a good idea. "Sometimes you don't have the time to get back to your feet, or there are too many waves coming, and you can't control your board," Skylar says. "So stroking out on your knees is a safe idea." Skylar gives Noam a front row seat to what he has to look forward to: stand up paddle surfing with style and grace and making it look easy and good. Skylar catches the wave in a parallel stance.*

② *For a moment Noam thinks Skylar is going to go "straight off Adolf," and run him over. "Noam is kind of doing this wrong," Skylar says. "If a surfer is on the wave, Noam should not race him to shoulder when he is paddling out. Better to cut inside [to Skylar's left] and maybe take a little punishment and not get in anyone's way."*

③ *Going about it properly, Noam should change course and pass to Skylar's left, taking a little punishment from the breaking wave.*

④ *Skylar and Noam are still on a collision course here, but Skylar has skills, so he cross-steps back to the tail and turns the nose of his board down the line.*

(5) *Collision averted as Skylar scoots down the line, and Noam steers to the inside of Skylar.*

(6) *Skylar now has a nice wall in front of him. Malibu is a pleasing wave, even when it's little.*

(7) *Even experienced SUP-erstars like Skylar can glitch. Skylar's balance is off, he is a little too far forward, and he is bogging and pearling at the same time.*

(8) *By using his paddle and his skills, Skylar will recover from this and speed on down the line.*

① *Left to his own devices, and with no one in front of or behind him, Noam sets up a nice little wall.*

② *He is too far forward, and maybe his balance is a little off, but he is making a nice angle.*

③ *With both hands on the paddle, Noam uses it to gain speed and correct his angle.*

④ *The more experienced guy on the shoulder sees this beginner dude charging his way and gives him some space.*

Cruising in Hobbitland: Jeremy Stephenson on Starboard's 10'5" × 30" Drive striding on the South Island of New Zealand.
Photo: Jeremy Pierce/courtesy Starboard

CHAPTER 5

TAKING STAND UP PADDLE-BOARDS ON LAKES, RIVERS, AND ALL KINDS OF WILD ADVENTURES

The steelhead trout is a sturdy fish that is born in freshwater rivers, gains strength as it swims downstream, goes out to sea for a couple of years, gets supersized on diet and exercise and survival, then swims back upstream—as long as 40 inches and weighing as much as 42 pounds. The steelhead is considered the world's finest fighting freshwater fish, as they are turned to steel by their migration from river to sea and back upriver.

In theory, stand up paddlers could follow this same path: taking first strokes somewhere inland, protected and safe, then slowly moving into bigger water and out to sea.

In theory, you could paddle out of the lake and down a creek, to where that creek connects to a river. And you could paddle down that river through the countryside and through cities and deal with whitewater and boats and other hazards natural and artificial and paddle for as long as it takes for that river to connect to the ocean.

By the time you have paddled all that way downriver, your skills and balance and strokes and turning will be refined, and you'll be ready to head into the ocean. Maybe the river leaves the land through a harbor channel, but eventually, you will be at sea, and there will be a whole new set of challenges.

In the ocean, there are waves. There could be waves breaking at the mouth of the river, and depending on the board you are riding, and your skills, you could try to ride those waves. Or you could paddle up the coast or down the coast, close to shore or out to sea, depending on wind and tide and swell and your comfort level in an environment that is generally more threatening than lakes and rivers.

Paddle up or down the coast, and there will be different kinds of waves, based on the geography they are breaking over: river mouths, beach breaks, reef breaks, point breaks. There are places where waves break up into rivers, and there are places where waves break on reefs far out to sea—as far as 100 miles out at a place called the Cortes Bank off San Diego, for instance. But you probably don't want to paddle way out there.

Most waves break within 100 yards of shore, so a stand up paddler with ocean skills can cruise a comfortable distance offshore, watching waves breaking from the back and venturing closer when a break looks tempting.

Ideally, there will be no wind, because wind is a foe for stand up paddlers. If you are paddling into the wind, you could find yourself making more backward progress than forward. If the wind is coming from the side, you will find your stable, comfortable paddling platform trembling and bucking and drifting and sliding, and if you can go into shore and wait out the wind, you probably should. Paddling in headwinds or sidewinds is no fun; it's a lot of work and potentially dangerous— if the wind is blowing from the land to the sea, you could be taken out with it and find yourself waving frantically at passing oil tankers for assistance.

The charming and glamorous (and remarkably efficient) Margareta Engstrom taking the fall foliage tour paddling a Starboard 9'8" × 30" Element on Simmelangsdalens Lake in the south of Sweden. Peter Anjou

However, if you are heading down the coast, and the wind is at your tail, well that's a different story. Hooking into a wind that is going your way is called a "downwinder," and that can be a lot of fun. The ocean is still rough, and it's work staying stable and upright as you ride the winds and the swells created by the winds. But do a downwinder right, and it's as good as a Nantucket sleigh ride.

The wind will push you as fast as or faster than you can paddle, and you will find yourself doing a combination of sailboarding and surfing—catching the wind, catching waves, and flying down the coast with the combination of speeds.

Where will you end up when the winds die? Who knows. Like a steelhead trout, your ocean skills are improved, you are stronger, you have survived many perils. But now you are tired and want to take it easy, so you find a river mouth or a harbor entrance or a bay or an arm or a fjord, and you turn inland, out of the wind and the swells and the tides and the current.

Inland waterways have their own perils: boaters, shipping, currents, rapids, winds, randy river otters, accurate fishermen. Just as a steelhead trout has to adjust its own skills to moving upriver through freshwater, so does a stand up paddler have to deal with fewer waves and less wind, perhaps, but other challenges. But steelhead do it, so it could be done on a stand up paddleboard.

There are many adventures possible out there, from the Pacific Northwest to Chesapeake Bay to the Mediterranean to the Black Sea.

People around the world are using their stand up paddleboards on lakes, rivers, bays, estuaries, and anywhere else that is liquid. They are experimenting and pushing the boundaries of what people might think is possible on a stand up paddleboard, inspiring others to do the same. Here are some of their stories.

Getting deeply barreled at Puerto Escondido, Mexico, is also a killer place for a stand up paddleboard. Here Sean Poynter gets a stand up barrel on a Starboard 9'1"× 29" Pro.
Photo courtesy of Starboard

Charles MacArthur
The Origins and Commandments of Stand Up Paddling Down Whitewater Rivers

During the writing of this book, I got into a debate about the history of SUP with Dave Parmenter of C4 Waterman over various facts and firsts. Before withdrawing all his notes and quotes, Parmenter made clear the contribution of the Makaha surfers on the west side of Oahu, and also the pioneering design and riding of Todd Bradley, Brian Keaulana, Mel Puu, and the founders of C4 Waterman. In his notes on various firsts in the evolution of stand up paddling, Parmenter listed C4 team rider Charlie MacArthur as a "whitewater kayak expert and (Aspen) ski instructor doyen," and "the first SUPer to take on whitewater rapids." Parmenter also noted that C4 developed "the first whitewater/river-specific stand up board, the ATB, or All-Terrain Board."

Q: Tell us about yourself.

A: As far as I know, I was the first stand up paddleboarder to paddle whitewater rivers. Not intentionally, of course. I just like doing different cool combinations of different sports. For instance, my friends and I decided to go snow kayaking back in 1996. The plastic river kayaks of the day had just begun to be designed with a flat bottom and relatively defined edges—like a surfboard. This gave us greater control than a typical round, sausage-shaped boat and hence, way more fun.

Wanting to share and teach the fun of the new hybrid sport of SUP on the river, I started the Aspen Stand Up Paddle School along with the Aspen Kayak Academy in 2007. [Charlie was also a longtime instructor of alpine skiing, telemark, and snowboarding and an instructor-trainer for the American Canoe Association in whitewater kayaking.]

Q: Are you from Hawaii originally?

A: I grew up in the summers on the south shore of the island of Oahu. My father had just got the part of "Danno" Williams in the original Hawaii Five-0 *series when I was 7 years old.*

Q: No way! You're the son of James MacArthur?

A: I am.

Q: Funny. The guy playing Danno on TV now is Scott Caan, who was a Malibu surfer before he went all Hollywood. Actually, he was born Hollywood, because he is the son of James Caan. But Scott's a good surfer and a cool guy. Not sure if he likes stand up paddlers, though. Sorry. Carry on.

A: I was fortunate that I was schooled in the ocean by surfing legends Keone Downing, Fred Hemmings, and others. Training with these guys was never limited to surfing of one type. They instilled the Hawaiian waterman ethos. We would bodysurf, paipo board, longboard, ride the new shortboards (it was the late '60s and early '70s), paddle and surf outrigger canoes, swim, snorkel, sail catamarans, and trail run. This was the beginning of my fascination for all things water.

After moving to Colorado for school and missing the surf, I discovered the rivers. I soon got into rafting and kayaking. I joined a group of accomplished extreme kayakers, including Paul Tefft, John Placek, Scotty Young, and Bill Mellenthin. We put up first descents in the Roaring Fork, Crystal, Frying Pan, and other drainages. The new shorter, plastic, creek kayaks allowed these once-impossible steep and narrow

Charlie MacArthur getting some thrills on Pine Creek rapid, a Class V section of the Arkansas River. Gwyneth Tefft

streams to be paddled. Eventually we took our kayaks to the oceans and rivers of Hawaii.

In 1996 we did the first descent of the Seven Sacred Pools below Hana, on the island of Maui, in our 9.5' kayaks. Later in 2000 we surfed some huge days at Hanalei Bay on the island of Kauai (13- to 20-foot faces) in our SIN Squirt Boats outfitted with fins. We did the first whitewater descent of the Hanalei River from the source at the base of Mount Wai'ale'ale (the wettest place on Earth) to the sea in Hanalei Bay—a fantastic, 10-mile paddle through Class IV and Class V rapids. The next season Paul, John, Scotty, and Sam Drevo did the first descent of the hefty Koai'e stream and the Waimea River, also known as the "Grand Canyon of the Pacific."

Q: I've flown over that in a helicopter. When did you move to the Rockies?

A: I moved to the Rockies in 1978 to go to college. All I knew is that I wanted to ski and teach skiing. I started teaching skiing in Aspen while I was in college. There I discovered telemark skiing and early snowboards like the Winterstick. We would ride these in the powder on Loveland Pass. At that time, tele was more versatile, as you could ski on any snow surface, while the snowboards were still limited in their design to powder only.

Patti Banks and Charlie and Riley MacArthur chillin' on the Colorado River. Riley is in a 5' 1¾" Jackson Shooting Star. Charlie is on the 10' iSUP, and Patti is on the 10'6" C-Mac ATB. Jenny MacArthur

Telemark skiing was intriguing, as it was about doing more with less gear. Lacking the heel piece of alpine skis, tele was immediately a greater challenge and beautiful when executed properly. Stand up paddling lives soundly in that place of doing more with less, and its demanding and playful nature is addicting.

Q: When and where was your introduction to stand up paddleboarding?

A: I first tried stand up paddling in 1973 as a teenager in Hawaii. My friend and I would watch this 50ish Hawaiian gentleman casually and effortlessly paddle the waves in front of Diamond Head in Waikiki. We badly wanted to surf like this guy. We floundered around for a day, trying to catch waves, standing on longboards with short canoe paddles. We didn't do so well.

I tried SUP again in the fall of 2003 on my honeymoon in Fiji on a tandem board and using a proper length stand up paddle. Shoulder-high waves all afternoon had never been so much fun—I was hooked.

Q: There is a word for that now. We call it the SUPiphany: when people realize how much fun it is.

A: As a surfer and kayaker, this perfect combination of SUP was electric. Back on the mainland I bought a 12' longboard and started paddling the rivers around Aspen and Glenwood Springs, Colorado, in 2005.

In 2007 a friend of mine urged me to put some SUP river video on YouTube. We posted video of SUP in Snowmass Canyon on the Roaring Fork River, surfing and running Class II and III rapids. I was paddling a friend's donated Mistral sailboard. Very tippy: 12'6" × 24" wide with a domed deck and a mast stay threatening to batter delicate anatomy from a fall onto the board.

Q: At some point you hooked up with the Makaha boys?

A: About two weeks later, I received an e-mail from Todd Bradley of newly formed C4 Waterman in Oahu. I happened to be traveling to Hawaii with my family later the same week. The day I landed, Todd and I got together immediately and tested different length boards. We ended up at master shaper Dave Parmenter's house, with Brian Keaulana sharing ideas about what would make a great river board.

In January 2008 I tested the first prototype C-Mac ATB [All Terrain Board]. At 10'6" × 29" and 4⁵⁄₁₆" thick with a volume of 187 liters and weighing 26 pounds, it handled the river very well.

Dave designed the board with a flip rocker in the nose and tail, very flat bottom, and thick beveled sidewalls. These kayak-like features helped the board handle really well in fast current and whitewater rivers. In 2008 we started paddling big, pushy Class III and medium-flow Class IV rapids. I ran my first 5-foot waterfall and actually landed it after at least six attempts.

I was interested in what it would be like to attach footstraps to the board for stability and Eskimo rolling. Yes, weird as it sounds, you can roll the board like a kayak with a little practice. Last year I used no footstraps and focused quite a bit more on footwork by walking the board and changing stances more often.

The ATB was a big hit and helped jump-start river paddling. By now I had gotten a lot of my friends into stand up paddling on the river. My friend Paul Tefft had an idea to put on the first National Stand Up Paddle Championships in Glenwood Springs. We had three events: downriver, slalom, and surf.

Q: How were those events run, judged, and so on?

A: Competitors signed up for individual events or all three for the overall title of White Water SUP National Champion. The morning downriver race runs 5 miles west from Glenwood Springs to South Canyon and is a timed event. Board length is now kept

to a 12'6" maximum limit with a single-blade paddle. Competitors battle each other in a mass start at Two Rivers Park and ply their way through Class II and III rapids to the finish at the South Canyon boat ramp. The large 5-foot standing waves in South Canyon rapid are the pinnacle of the event.

Noon is the start of the SUP paddle cross. Picked in favor of the traditional slalom run in '09, SUP paddle cross proved to be really exciting with elimination heats and a finals heat. Four racers sprint down a boat ramp and into the water and bounce off each

Charlie MacArthur paddling rapid number 5 on the Arkansas River in Colorado on the new 10'8" x 34" C4 XXL iSUP, summer 2010. Gwyneth Tefft

other vying for the hole shot into the first turn of the 150-meter long course. After another eddy turn, it is a mad, 40-meter sprint to the finish.

The last event is the surfing event at the G-wave. This is all about freestyle: Front and back surfs, cutbacks, spins, headstands, and stylish cross-stepping are all part of the afternoon. Surfers compete on *boards from 7' to 12' in length with a variety of short-board and longboard maneuvers. They use the paddle to initiate and enhance tricks on an endless standing wave hoping to win over the judges and the crowds. They compete in three one-minute rides for the title of best SUP surfer.*

We had competitors from Hawaii, Connecticut, Montana, California, Colorado, and Australia. We had no idea how many people would show up. We were very happy to have a field of twenty-five our first year. Thank-you, C4 and CKS, for the help.

We did it again in 2010, and other events have since popped up around the country in Reno, Nevada, Salida, and Vail, Colorado, for the Vail Teva games.

I was also doing quite a few SUP first descents. I soloed Shoshone (Colorado River) and Toothache (Roaring Fork), both Class III rapids in 2006, West-water Canyon (Class III), and Slaughterhouse (Class IV) in 2008 with kayak support. It is always safer to run rivers with other people.

After the championships in 2009 with a mixed Colorado and Hawaiian crew, we did the first SUP descent of the Class III Gunnison Gorge. I paddled Pine Creek (Class V) and the Numbers (Class IV) section of the Arkansas in 2010 on the new C4 XXL iSUP. Wider than the C-Mac ATB Boardworks or iSUP models by 5 inches, the new C4 XXL made paddling Class IV much easier. This board is even opening Class V rapids, as well as being a fantastic board for really big people.

I wanted to do an instructional and adventure DVD on river SUP, so I teamed up with Paul Tefft and C4 Waterman to produce and release RiverSUP *in March 2010. This is the first video to showcase SUP on the rivers with easy-to-follow instruction up through Class II whitewater. We wanted to focus on standard techniques as well as skills that are specific to the river. There is also a large segment on reading the river and river safety. The DVD has a big desert*

river trip as well as tons of action accompanied by great blues guitarist Andy Putnam and some fantastic Indian-inspired music by drum master John de Kadt.

Q: From working on this book, watching the Teva SUP video by Dan Gavere, and talking to inland stand up paddlers like yourself, I am getting the impression that rivers are dangerous. Could you give your ten commandments for stand up paddling on rivers and elsewhere?

A: *Sure.*

Charlie MacArthur's Ten Commandments of SUP

1. Thou shalt rejoice in the paddle stroke felt through thy whole upright body.
2. Thou shalt practice the etiquette of river, ocean, and lake paddling.
3. Thou shalt not disparage riders of other craft.
4. Thou shalt learn to surf before paddling a SUP into a lineup.
5. Thou shalt take a swift water rescue course before paddling whitewater rivers.
6. Thou shalt not strike the rails of thine board with thine paddle blade.
7. Thou shalt attach a board leash to thy quick release belt on thy life jacket and never thine ankle while running a river.
8. Thou shalt not catch every wave just because thou can.
9. Thou shalt attach thy boards properly and securely to thy vehicle.
10. Thou shalt explore many stance, stroke, and board variations in different waters for the growth of thy soul.

Q: Thank thee. That was as good as the burning bush.

A: *Thou art welcome.*

Norm Hann
Expedition Exploring by SUP in British Columbia

I've driven from California to Alaska and back twice, by way of Puget Sound, the San Juan Islands, Vancouver Island, Tofino, Port Hardy, the Inland Passage to Prince Rupert, the Cassiar Highway, Hyder/Stewart, Juneau, Homer, Turnagain Arm, and a lot of places in Alaska, the Yukon, northern British Columbia, Alberta, Montana, Idaho, Washington, Oregon, and even Nevada.

The Turnagain Arm Tidal Bore, Tofino, and a lot of these places are high on my SUP-it list because there is a lot to see up there, and a stand up paddleboard would be a great way to see it, as there are endless nooks and crannies (and isolated steelhead creeks) that can only be accessed in a small craft.

In February 2011, as the deadline for this book was approaching like a tsunami, Norm Hann answered an e-mail and shared his experiences and advice as a solo SUP explorer and group guide in northern British Columbia.

I have been SUPping in Canada for the last three seasons, and I own Mountain Surf Adventures, a stand up paddleboarding and expedition company here in Squamish, B.C. [40 miles north of Vancouver]. [Visit www.normhann.com for more information.] As a qualified wilderness and ocean guide, I offer multiday SUP expeditions to the Great Bear Rainforest of British Columbia. [The Great Bear Rainforest is a vast expanse of temperate rain forest that covers 25,000 square miles from Vancouver to southeast Alaska. British Columbia contains 25 percent of the remaining intact temperate rain forest in the world.]

In May 2010 I did a 400-kilometer conservation expedition called Standup4Greatbear, where I paddled my SUP along the proposed oil tanker route on the north coast from Kitimat to Bella Bella. My goal was to bring awareness to the potential threat of oil tankers in the Great Bear Rainforest and to highlight traditional food harvesting areas of the First Nations and the rich marine ecosystems.

British Columbia is a world-class destination with vast expanses of unexplored terrain. The coastline is a powerful place and begs the stand up paddleboarder to push new levels of adventure. From majestic fiords to remote windswept beaches and pristine river valleys rich with life, the north coast and Haida Gwaii [formerly known as Queen Charlotte Islands; the Haida First Nation recently gave the name back to the Crown in a ceremonial bentwood box] are a paddler's dream: remote and untouched. When the salmon make their way back to the Great Bear Rainforest in September, the rain forest ecosystem goes into high gear. This is a land of grizzly and rare spirit bears, humpback and killer whales, bald eagles, coastal wolves, and sea lions. At this time of the year, thousands of salmon will pass silently under your board on their way to spawn, die, and give back to the forest.

I have also surfed the North Beach on Haida Gwaii, "Islands of the People." With permission this spring [2011] I am planning to stand up paddle from the Haida Village, Old Masset, to the totem poles at the UNESCO World Heritage site—the Ninstints—as part of Standup4Greatbear 2011 [about 400 kilometers by paddleboard].

These islands are on the edge of the continent: powerful and spiritual. Oil tankers, if allowed, will pass right by Haida Gwaii, and my goal will be to visit traditional and culturally important sites and talk to the people of Haida Gwaii to find out what they are risking in the event of an oil spill. More so, this exploration will highlight a magnificent area and people.

My first exploratory expedition to the Great Bear was in 2009 with Explore Magazine, *and last*

summer I ran the first commercial SUP trip up there. Guests made their way to Prince Rupert, where they took a four-hour ferry ride to the Gitga'at village of Hartley Bay. Our seven-day expedition began and ended in this small native community. Six clients spent a week exploring the Great Bear Rainforest, searching for the spirit bear, paddling with whales, visiting culturally important areas, and watching wild salmon spawning at their feet in local rivers and creeks. We stayed in native longhouses and watchman cabins and paddled close to 100 kilometers. More importantly, though, the clients developed an appreciation for such a magical place and an area at risk.

Norm Hann leading Jen Segger and Explore *writer Masa Takei through and along the misty mountains of British Columbia.* Taylor Kennedy

This summer [2011] Mountain Surf Adventures has two commercial SUP trips booked for the end of August and September. It is my privilege to show guests this area and to spend time experiencing the traditional culture of Hartley Bay. The SUP is the ideal vehicle to explore the Great Bear Rainforest. I am also looking to offer mother ship SUP trips up there. Mother ships allow you the comfort of a large vessel and become the platform to travel larger distances and explore by SUP.

(left) Jen Segger and guide Norm Hann pull through a narrow strait somewhere in British Columbia. Taylor Kennedy

(above) Norm Hann takes point as his Explore Magazine *team follows in his wake on the first exploratory SUP trip of the Great Bear Rainforest, North Coast, BC.* Taylor Kennedy

Gear

Before going on any SUP expedition, be sure you test out all of your gear. Your expedition is not a good time to realize your paddle is too long, your life jacket is uncomfortable, or your board sinks with added expedition weight.

Board

Andy Lambrecht of Pemberton, B.C., built me a 12' red cedar stand up paddleboard that I used for the Explore *magazine trip. Red cedar is the tree of life to the First Nations on the coast, as it was used for everything. Andy reclaimed the wood himself and built a board that was a tribute to the temperate rain forest.*

I did my Standup4Greatbear expedition on a 14' Surftech Bark Expedition board [14' × 29" × 5.25" × 235 liters × 32.5 pounds—named Best Stand Up Paddleboard in the 2009/2010 Gear of the Year issue of Men's Journal*]. This was an amazing board for the trip. I loved it, and it performed beautifully in all conditions. For my clients on the Great Bear SUP, I give them the option to bring up their own boards, or I will provide boards around 12' in length that are stable in an ocean environment yet paddle well. There are a number of displacement hull boards on the market that I think would work really well in the 12' to 14' range. These boards also have built-in attachment points and bungy cords that can hold expedition gear.*

It is really important to test gear on your board before you go on a trip. Find the right balance points and paddle with the gear in more challenging conditions to see how you, your board, and the gear perform.

Norm Hann with his custom-made, 12' red cedar stand up paddleboard, shaped by Andy Lambrecht. Taylor Kennedy

We cover a lot of area on our trips, and it's important to be efficient. The ocean conditions can change quickly, so you want a board that can handle variable conditions. Paddle and test your board in all conditions so you know how to handle it, what to expect, and to trust it.

Paddles

For my expeditions, I use a Kialoa Nalu [108" surface area, blade width 9.25", blade length 16.5", 26 ounces]. I like the bigger blade face, and once my body becomes conditioned to the blade size, I can move a lot more water and weight more efficiently. In downwind conditions, there is more surface area for the wind to blow against. I really love the Kialoa blades; they just feel really good in your hands. I like the narrower shaft on the Kialoas, as they decrease the chance of gripping fatigue in your hands—important over long distances.

I recommend that clients bring their own carbon fiber paddle on the expedition, as I think this is one piece of personal gear that paddlers should own and be comfortable with even before they buy a board. The paddle should not be a secondary item to purchase with a board. There are a lot of blades out there, and I recommend you find one that works for you. Test it out and spend the money—it's worth it. Paddles can make a really big difference in your technique, power, and efficiency.

I also use wooden Whiskey Jack paddles. Danny Brown from Whiskey Jack sent me some to use, and they are works of art, are beautiful to paddle, and look amazing in the Great Bear Rainforest.

Clothing

As a qualified guide, safety is my number one concern. The SUP can get you in a lot of trouble really quickly on the ocean. The waters in Canada are cold and unpredictable. When I run my commercial trips up north, I

have clients outfitted in a layering system. The layering system on our expeditions consists of a wicking base layer, a midlayer of insulation, and a Gore-Tex shell for the upper and lower body. On rainy days most clients will paddle in rubber boots, but some prefer booties or, like myself, bare feet in warmer conditions. We receive 10 to 15 feet of rain annually, so we always have to be prepared to get wet any time of the year. We also have to have the appropriate clothing when the temperatures are warm: 25 degrees Celsius (77 degrees Fahrenheit) days are not uncommon, but generally it stays cool and moderate during summer.

Clients are required to wear a life jacket.

I have boat support on these commercial expeditions, so if the conditions deteriorate, I can call for a pickup. Some clients will bring wetsuits, though, and can wear them if they want. Clients who come up are experienced, and the boards are stable, so the chances of falling in—combined with boat support—allow us to not wear wetsuits. Although wetsuits provide a safety net, the chances of falling in are low, and that outweighs the cumbersome chaffing and overheating issues with wetsuits. Another really good option is to wear a drysuit.

Wetsuit

On my first exploratory trip up there on stand up paddleboards, I did wear a 5/3 wetsuit, although I could have gone lighter: 4/3, even 3/2. Hopefully, someone will design a SUP-specific suit that protects you in case of a dump but does not overheat.

There are numerous times when I personally paddle with a wetsuit. In Canada I paddle and train all year long. I look for strong downwind conditions to train in, and I will be wearing a wetsuit at all times. I wear wetsuits, of course, for surfing in Tofino and wear them anytime of the year on big crossings when on exploratory expeditions. The wetsuit provides a really big safety net when you are paddling on the Canadian coast. I am also hoping to purchase a drysuit this year, which I think will be really effective for expedition paddling on the coast.

If the conditions are calm, it's rubber boots, layering, and Gore-Tex. Paddling on the ocean requires solid decision-making skills both personally and with clients.

Leashes

On the ocean, clients always wear a coil leash. I always wear one as well, even when I'm with a buddy, since your buddy can get blown away from you pretty quickly. You can lose a paddle, but you don't want to lose your board. The leash is your lifeline on the ocean.

PFD

I wear an Astral Green Jacket PFD that was given to me as gift from Walter Bucher, owner of Raven Rescue, who set up the safety logistics for my stand up4greatbear expedition (www.astralbuoyancy.com). The Green Jacket is ideal for guiding and expeditions. It has a lot of pockets and a rescue belt. I am able to carry a VHF radio, spot tracker, compass, knife, and energy bars in the jacket.

Attachments

My old boards are kitted with EZ Plug attachments, bungee cord, and Outdoor Research bags. Outdoor

Norm Hann maintains a stealthy, low profile as he watches a rising transient orca that had just made a kill. This is directly on the proposed tanker route in Squally Channel. If a whale surfaces near you, keep your distance and do not approach any closer than allowed by marine law. Brian Huntington

Research has some lateral dry bags that provide easy access, and I love their Dry Comp Ridge Pack: It carries well on deck, and then you can just grab and throw it in your pack on hikes into the forest, a great day pack for SUPing. With a few tweaks specific for paddleboarding, this would be the go-to day bag for stand up paddleboarding. All Outdoor Research bags are fully waterproof and seam-sealed. Prior to my expeditions, I would test the weight of the bags on the deck in calm water. Once I found out where the bags balanced best, I would set the EZ Plugs up and bungee the bag. We use big Sealine dry bags if we do not have boat support for multiday expeditions.

Also, when paddling with gear on your board, you better make sure it is tied down well. I call it West Coast ready. Waves lapping over the board can slow your pace down considerably, and you do not want to lose gear out on the water when the conditions become heightened and the waves clear off your board.

Accidents and Close Calls

I have learned a lot of things while stand up paddling on the ocean. I try not to have accidents or close calls. If I am doing personal expeditions, I can increase the risk level, but when I am with my clients, I try to keep them very happy and safe. As a guide, I have been

Norm Hann with Jen Segger and Explore *writer Masa Takei during the 2009 exploratory expedition to the Great Bear Rainforest. They are checking out red sea urchins during a stunning day of north coast weather.* Taylor Kennedy

mentored to be safe and to make sound decisions. You may know the formula to make a good decision, but you need to combine technical knowledge with experience. There is no substitute for experience on the water. We all strive to be watermen who can make good decisions personally and for groups we are guiding. The ocean can teach a lot of lessons, and if you're ignorant and not watching the signs she gives you, she will make you pay. Never become complacent on the ocean.

Wind

On a stand up paddleboard, your weather window is a lot smaller than in a sea kayak. The wind affects you so much, especially if it's in your face. We are like a big sail. If wind and water get really bad, then you can always go to your knees to create a more stable and efficient platform.

Stay a good distance away from sea lions and other marine life so as not to disturb them. Taylor Kennedy

Wind can mean the difference between minutes and hours, between grueling upwinders and exhilarating downwinders. The ocean is dynamic, and you have to consider a lot of factors when paddling, one of them being the wind.

Talk to experienced people in the area to figure out local wind effects, and look at the topography on your charts to see what terrain features will create winds. Fjords and sounds usually create daily inflow and outflow winds during the summer as the land warms and cools. Land will also create onshore and offshore winds during summer months. You must also consider what the winds will do to the sea state as they continue to blow. You should know the predominant winds in both *high pressure (good weather) and low pressure (bad weather) systems and what types of systems you're most likely to experience throughout the year.*

Really, it's about being a waterman, but converting all that knowledge and combining that with the soft skills of guiding. The leadership pie includes:

1. *Self*
2. *Group*
3. *Environment*

A good decision model uses the four pillars for decision making:

1. *Weather: wind, temperature, precipitation*
2. *Sea state: calm, waves, tides, currents*
3. *Terrain: bathymetry, land topography, boomers, shoals*
4. *Human factors: age, experience, fitness level, health of both yourself and those you are with or guiding*

Another thing: Leave a trip plan with a reliable person, and when planning an expedition, consider the seven P's: Prior Pretrip Planning Prevents Piss Poor Performance.

I went out this winter in the strongest winter out-flows I have ever seen in Howe Sound. The winds were pushing 80 miles an hour, and the waters were ice-bucket cold. I was at the edge of my limits and I had to make sure of a few things before I enjoyed the surf:

1. *I had someone drop me off and wait for me at the end of the run with a general time of completion.*
2. *I had to make sure all of my gear was in proper working order, especially my leash, and I wore a full wetsuit with life jacket.*
3. *Mentally and physically I felt ready.*
4. *I had my cell phone with me in a Sealine drycase.*
5. *I double and triple checked everything.*

It was pretty intense, but you don't want to be saying coulda, woulda, shoulda when you're out there. Obviously, most people would not paddle in such conditions, but there is a lot to learn in the extremes. There are so many people out there who are not yet conscious when they are on the water. Stand up paddling has opened up the water world to so many people, and they need some proper training and experience to enjoy the sport safely.

Eric Stiller
SUP in the Waters around New York City

Stand up paddleboarding has transitioned a lot of kayakers from *homo sittus* to *homo erectus*, and the new sensation has made kayak companies stand and take notice.

Such is the case with Eric Stiller, the owner of Manhattan Kayak Company (MKC), located on Pier 66 at Chelsea Pier in west Manhattan, overlooking the Hudson River. Stiller has kayaking in his DNA. His father, Dieter Stiller, came to the United States by way of Rosenheim, Germany, and introduced modern kayaks via Klepper Kayaks, a store that sold the Klepper folding kayak and other small craft for thirty-six years. "Klepper was first on Greenwich Avenue [in New York City]," Stiller said, "then Union Square, and finally Park Ridge, New Jersey, from 1959 to 1995."

In 1992, at age 32, Eric Stiller teamed up with Australian Tony Brown in an attempt to kayak entirely around Australia—a trip of anywhere from 12,000 to 20,000 miles, depending on how they went. By the title of Stiller's book about the (mis) adventure—*Keep Australia to Your Left*—they went counterclockwise around Australia, but it didn't go well. Beginning in Sydney in February 1992, Stiller and Brown survived a thousand perils by land and sea and made it as far as Darwin before

they canceled the trip in July 1992—2,000 miles in a diagonal line from Sydney as the kookaburra flies, and God knows how many miles by kayak: "Then I pedaled a bicycle from Darwin to Melbourne," Stiller said, "finishing the whole trip in November 1992."

Stiller's relationship with his girlfriend didn't survive that adventure, but Stiller did, and he came back to the United States to start Manhattan Kayak Company. He got the title *Keep Australia to Your Left* from David Lee Roth: "David was my first paying client ever," Stiller said. "He helped me pioneer many New York City kayak routes because he wanted to do big things around the town. He gave me the title of my book while discussing the Australia trip at Chumley's in the Village over tequilas."

David Lee Roth is the first of many stories Stiller is distilling into a book about his adventures running a kayak company on the cusp of New York City and the Hudson.

That company led to his present pioneering of stand up paddling on the Hudson and in New York Harbor.

Stiller first became aware of stand up paddling when he saw Laird Hamilton doing it in a magazine. "It was in *Outside*, I believe," Stiller said. "I said to myself, 'Now, that is a way for me to enjoy a surfboard!'"

As a kayaker growing up in Manhattan, I always looked at surfers with a lot of curiosity. I would kayak-surf waves at Gilgo Beach in Long Island and catch them all day long while the surfers often waited and

Reformed kayaker Eric Stiller, paddling his 10'6" × 29" wide C4 from Manhattan Kayak Company at Pier 66, overtaking some kayakers and headed for Hoboken, New Jersey. Erik Olsen

... waited. The waves they caught and the way they surfed those waves were images of grace—but those waves came few and far between.

I suppose I was not that patient. The kayak allowed me to be more active even while I was waiting.

However, SUP changed the formula: You did not **have** to catch a wave to be doing something. To me, SUP was about having a good time, perfecting one stroke, working on balance, different paddling positions on the board. I immediately liked the look and concept of it. And if Laird seemed to really like it . . . then it was a legit way to enter the board-surfing world. It was not "surfing with training wheels."

The opportunity to manifest my SUP fascination

Eric Stiller hasn't entirely turned his back on kayaking, but he has become a convert to the pleasures of stand up paddling and is hoping a good percentage of the huddled millions of New York City will come down to Pier 66—for the waters.
Erik Olsen

came three years ago when a man named Simon Tetlow came to us from working with Kayaks Kauai Outbound, an outfitter my father helped set up over twenty-five years ago.

Simon wanted to start a SUP program. I gave him carte blanche, and he went to Outdoor Retailer 2009, met some folks from C4 Waterman, and arranged for two 11'6" and one 10'6" and three paddles to be sent to us. C4 Waterman delivered within the month. When the boards came, they were quite beautiful, and I **knew** they were the right way to go.

I had developed a moderate case of sciatica in my right hip/butt and could not sit in the kayak for more than ninety minutes without a dull ache developing. This presented quite a conundrum for me, as this was how I made my living, and I was very concerned. Sitting in the kayak was never going to allow the sciatica to go away and in fact would likely make the condition go to chronic. Not a pleasant prospect.

Stiller took his first strokes on a C4 Waterman that was 11'6" × 30"—a fairly classic beginner's board: "The water conditions around MKC at the Pier 66 Boathouse at Twenty-sixth Street and the Hudson River are usually bumpy, as ferry wakes collide against breakwalls and create continuous oscillation," Stiller said.

So, there is no "bunny slope," no flat, calm section. Nevertheless, I had good faith in my basic balance, and the 11'6" × 30" board seemed generous, particularly compared with the 17" wide Surf Ski I had been paddling.

I knew that a proper progression would be to evolve into the standing position—what I like to call the "walking on water" look. I started by kneeling on the board (although these days I start people by prone paddling the board just like a surfboard).

I learned to paddle and control the board and enjoyed the vertical angle and leverage it provided. When I had that down pat, I went to do the basic stand up in the center of the board and extended the paddle to full length. I automatically started with reach and torso rotation, as this is our gospel at MKC: using the hips and torso to paddle from the core and not use arms and shoulders. The board immediately surged ahead faster than I expected. After a number of strokes, the board developed that wonderful schussing sound with the occasional patpatpat sound as the board reverberated over waves.

My experience with E. J. Jackson (www.jackson kayak.com) and his "Strokes and Concepts" method of learning freestyle kayaking immediately applied to keeping the board straight while paddling on one side should I choose to. I could also apply a number of these K-1, C-1 style strokes to various turns.

I experimented with the surf stance technique to "squirt turn" the board and then practiced slalom around some large, standing pylons in our embayment. Needless to say, I took my dumps and popped right back on . . . so easy, so uncomplicated, so playful.

Going in the Hudson River seems like not such a good idea—for passenger jets but also for human beings. Jamie Brisick is a Malibu surfer who spends most of his time in New York City. When asked what he thought about taking a stand up paddleboard around the Hudson, Brisick spoke in terms of a caveat:

The water is definitely a concern. Sure, there's tons of trash that gathers in certain pockets, but it's more the overall hue and aroma. I would think Eric could give you more help with this than anyone. He's the one getting in there. Does he ever fall into it? Does he get ear infections? It's a good thing to explore. There are probably lots of people who live near sketchy bodies of water and wonder about these things. Westlake, Lake Sherwood, Malibou Lake, to name but a few close to home.

Eric Stiller said this about the perceived water quality in the Hudson and the truth:

Once upon a time from early in the twentieth century to about 1975, the Hudson was very bad, famously bad, as was Lake Erie. Then, beginning in the 1970s, the federal Clean Water and Water Quality Acts, along with Pete Seeger's Clearwater group and Robert F. Kennedy Jr.'s Riverkeeper/ Waterkeeper groups, made the Hudson River one of the great success stories in modern urban waterway history.

New York City also added at least five major water-cleaning centers that did not exist prior to 1985, when it relied only on the very powerful and pretty effective tides to clean the water. Almost all industry and industrial farming has been gone from the Hudson Valley for decades now. The full food chain is reestablished, and many large striped bass are caught in New York Harbor. This year many seals, dolphins, and whales have been flirting with the lower harbor.

We have been actively kayaking, rolling kayaks, doing rescue days, been out in many windy, wavy conditions, and we have heard of no sicknesses like ear infections or stomach issues or other things like that.

The bacterial count is actually quite low the vast majority of the time except after heavy rainfalls, and then it is elevated for about a twenty-four-hour period. The tides are very strong and dismiss the vast majority of these kinds of problems within two or three cycles.

I will dare say, and you can look it up, the Malibu coast has some very serious discharge issues and can register off-the-chart kinds of bacterial numbers. I cannot swear, but on average it may be worse than anything New York City can throw at the Hudson.

The exceptions in New York City are Newtown Creek, the Bronx River, and the Gowanus Canal [in Brooklyn]. Those are some very toxic, stagnant backwater areas.

Yes, I have seen trash congregate in the nooks and crannies of the piers at certain slower tide cycles now and then, but it is truly the exception.

Odor? No, not on the Hudson side where we are. I would say there may be more chances for that on the East River / Harlem River side after very heavy rains.

Yes, we fall in the river all the time on the boards, especially when practicing squirt turns and slalom stuff. But the Hudson River / NYC Harbor is way cleaner than the Thames, the Seine, and Venice, that's for sure. And maybe even Malibu.

While some people saw stand up paddling around the Hudson as being potentially hazardous to one's health, Stiller discovered the health benefits of this new form of exercise.

Three years ago the kayakers barely paid heed to my novel method of paddling around, but by last summer, the detached approach changed to interest.

Simon and I were a titch ahead of the curve when he was with us a half season. A big article in New York magazine in 2010 seemed to change the impression about the sport. This was good because there was always a concern that the perception of the water quality around New York might prevent people from wanting to do it. This mainly imaginary threshold seems to have been crossed, and MKC (aka SUP NYC) intends to teach many people this wonderful pursuit.

SUP helped me dispel my sciatica. It is long gone, and I can kayak all day long should I choose, but these days you will see me on the paddleboard as often as in the kayak. They are both great sports, and the core of the paddling technique shares the same roots. This year I intend to add the wave-surfing elements and put the whole concept together.

I have been a fitness instructor for over fifteen years. I run an underground [word of mouth] boot camp called Primal. SUP connects balance, dynamic motion, and efficiency. SUP can be a wellness tool, to get out in open spaces on the water and casually cruise about, or it can be a hard-core fitness pursuit when the paddler is truly engaged with his or her full body on each stroke.

The forward stroke in SUP is never perfected, and that is the beauty of it. It brings the paddler into the present moment to "connect all the dots" from the soles of the feet to the ends of the fingertips. You can hear and feel the connection when it is going well and not so well.

As with recreational kayaking, many beginners will adapt a very casual, arm-centric stroke. If this is allowed to continue for many thousands of strokes, *then this will be how they paddle, and converting to a more dynamic torso-rotating style may be hard.*

In New York we have a tidal river and potentially strong winds. We often have to paddle against these forces and make progress. A solid core-centric "body" stroke is essential to this. I do believe it is good if beginners can see and learn this sooner rather than later, should they want to be more than casual about the pursuit.

You may want to watch a few of Dave Kalama's YouTube videos if you have not already. . . . The "Tahitian" technique is quite compelling and seems to be the stroke of choice among racers.

In order for SUP to contour to some of the preconceived notions of fitness regarding heart rate, endurance, strength, speed, and power, the seeds of good full-body technique need to be planted early.

SUP is still new to New York, and Stiller says it is not yet close to outranking kayaking. Stand up paddling in the Hudson River between Manhattan and New Jersey has hazards and pleasures:

We do not have a flat, calm learning area, so the quest for standing balance will be more challenging. We will make sure our people know how to paddle with their whole body as it is more required for using the paddleboard to go someplace cool than on a lake or sheltered cove.

I have seen that the "I can do it" effect kicks in with great satisfaction after about one hour. This usually involves ten to fifteen minutes of wobbling about and then taking a break, fifteen minutes of wobbling with decent strokes and turning around ability and taking a break; then in the last thirty minutes I watch the new SUPers moving pretty well. . . .

There is something about learning in a somewhat more vigorous environment that gives people that wide-eyed, "I accomplished something!" look.

What stand up paddling on the Hudson doesn't lack is places to go and things to see, and it's more

than a little invigorating to be out on the water and in the elements, so close to a great city. "As soon as people leave the embayment and head south on the Hudson, they get a panorama view of the southern Hudson and Upper Harbor," Stiller said.

They will see the new Hudson River Park Trust park system lining the west side of Manhattan. They will see Hoboken and the sizable skyline of Jersey City. The farther they go, they will see Greenwich Village and the "Gold Coast" of fancy, new, all-glass private apartment buildings, then Tribeca, then Ellis Island and the Statue of Liberty. The latter will be more visible with higher degrees of skill advancement.

The cross-town traffic on the Hudson includes Waterway ferries, giant cruise ships, and sailboats, but hopefully no more belly-flopping passenger jets.

Going north, we see the Jacob Javits Convention Center, the Empire State Building, and ideally we get to the Intrepid *aircraft carrier, which should make for excellent photo opportunities. Better paddlers will get up to the Trump Tower complex and the Seventy-ninth Street boat basin for a little brunch and a paddle back.*

Even better paddlers will get up to Sushi Town in Edgewater, New Jersey. . . . As we go north, the city skyline starts to mix with the open views of the Palisades on the Jersey side and the lower Hudson Valley.

There is a lot to see going north or south from Manhattan Kayak Company on Pier 66, and Stiller is now seeing stand up paddling go through the same arc as kayaking: media, celebrity, popularity. Once people get past the idea that contact with the waters of the Hudson will not melt their clothes or their skin or cause birth defects, people flock to the opportunity to get outdoor exercise on the fringe of the city.

I believe this is just the beginning. I do not have enough of a client sampling to tell you about too many aspiring SUPers. We have a big South African rugby guy who did it in the Hamptons. He is the athletic director of a fancy micro gym called La Palestra. We have a couple who use the Austrian inflatables. We had [actor] Ed Norton drop in who said he SUPs all the time. I know the bulk of my clients are going to come from the social media sites this year for the SUP Basics class. It will be up to us to see if they have a sufficiently rewarding experience to come back again. . . .

We intend to work some synergy with Paddle Diva to get our folk to enjoy the Hamptons experience and have some of the Hamptons people give New York City a try. Our website is being fully redesigned and will have stills and videos on SUP, as well as descriptions of the various trips and lessons we offer.

Stiller has kayaking in his DNA, but he is sold on stand up paddling and believes it will become the Next Big Thing around the Big Apple, although as of now, kayaking is still more popular.

SUP does not outrank kayaking in popularity by a long shot . . . yet. I think it will take some time and some faster boards to do the trick. The currents, winds, and paddling distances required to see cool things are better suited for touring and sea kayaks right now. We will need to educate and train people to paddle stronger and faster on good equipment to open up the same types of trips we do routinely on kayaks. It took over twelve years to get people consistently on surf skis; now quite a few people are on those.

Back in the 1990s, Stiller became famous for attempting to kayak around Australia and writing a book about a valiant but doomed attempt. Now that he is sold on stand up paddling, Stiller was asked whether he would attempt to circumnavigate Australia: "No, I won't try to go around Oz on a SUP, but I am thinking about the Greek Isles or the coast of Israel. Maybe Alexandria, Egypt, to Israel. Call it the Walking on Water Tour."

The Geft Family Goes Hawaiian
Stand Up Paddling around Both Sides of Oahu—and Right up the Middle

If Michelle and Noam Geft could pack up the kids, crank up the RV, and drive to the Hawaiian Islands, they would do it. A long, 6,000-mile round-trip it would be, but worth it. The Gefts love Hawaii. To healthy water people and nature lovers, the Hawaiian Islands are better than Disneyland and one of the few places they like more than Malibu—even better weather, more sun, warmer water, and better waves.

But the RV thing isn't possible, so every year the Gefts step onto a big old jet airliner and spend the Thanksgiving holiday in some new part of Hawaii. For Thanksgiving 2009, they stayed on the south shore near Diamond Head. For Thanksgiving 2010, they rented a house with several other families on the north shore of Oahu, near Haleiwa.

But this time, they flew over with about a month of stand up paddling experience under their belts, and their heads dancing with visions of places they had visited before but were eager to visit again, standing tall on stand up paddleboards, gliding along swiftly and smoothly across the sea.

If the Gefts could drive their RV from Malibu to Oahu, they could have brought their own gear: boards and paddles and leashes, but no need for wetsuits (yay!) although they would have brought PFDs for the kids.

Transporting stand up paddle equipment, especially oversized stuff for beginners, is an expensive pain in the back, but the Gefts did some research online and found several places on Oahu that rented equipment for reasonable prices, sparing them the expense of carting their own gear and giving them the chance to try a variety of boards, and perhaps find the ideal size and feel for them to buy.

For Thanksgiving weekend of 2010, the family settled into a house on the water looking out at the outer reef surf spot called Avalanche, which breaks just to the west of the popular Haleiwa Ali'i Beach. Before you could say "Duke Kahanamoku" they were up and at 'em and having stand up adventures on the north shore of Oahu, the south shore of Oahu, and even right up the middle on the Haleiwa River.

Haleiwa River

The Haleiwa River empties into the ocean on the north shore of Oahu, forming Haleiwa Harbor, which separates Ali'i Beach from Pua 'Aena Point (where the TV show *Lost* was filmed). Anyone driving into or surfing Haleiwa has crossed that bridge, looked upriver, and wondered what's up there. Noam and Michelle and the kids took their paddleboards to find out.

The Gefts got to poke around for about a mile upriver and see things up close and personal that most people just glimpse as they are zooming across the Haleiwa River Bridge. Lili Foster

The Haleiwa River has carved a valley that goes for miles into the interior of Oahu. Somewhere upriver there is a waterfall that was used in the filming of Lost. Lili Foster

Waikiki

Waikiki is the spiritual and physical home of surfing, but also of stand up paddleboarding. It was here, in the first half of the 1900s, that the Hawaiian beach boys began standing up on giant surfboards and paddling them with oars and paddles. Some say the beach boys developed the technique to help instruct tourists. Others say they did it to keep their cigarettes and cameras dry.

(above) The Gefts parked in the Ala Wai harbor lot and launched in front of the Hilton Hawaiian Village. There is a small, protected Hilton Lagoon where some newcomers were practicing their stand up paddling skills, but the Gefts were well beyond that phase and headed to sea. Lili Foster

(below) Evan took to Michelle's 10'6" Pearson Arrow and headed for Diamond Head. If Malibu were a little warmer and bluer, he would be doing this every day back home. Lili Foster

Michelle catching a small right and keeping both hands on the paddle as she rode, just like Skylar instructed her. Lili Foster

Waimea Bay

In Hawaii there's a place called Waimea Bay, where the best surfers in the world come to play, when giant waves are rolling out of the north Pacific toward Oahu. But when the surf is small—and it can be, even in winter—Waimea Bay is one of the best beaches on Oahu and in the world, and a great place to go swimming, snorkeling, stand up paddleboarding, or all of the above.

(above) Michelle and Noam left the keiki *(children) on a beautiful beach and paddled out into Waimea Bay to surround themselves with sky and water and jungle views.*
Lucia Griggi

(above) Water clarity at Waimea can be 30 feet or more, even in winter. Two proper forward strokes, as seen from below.
Lucia Griggi

(left) Michelle saying hello to the critters below. Lucia Griggi

Pua 'Aena Point

Michelle and Noam paddled off the beach at Pua 'Aena Point. This is across the harbor channel from Ali'i Beach and a place where the TV show *Lost* was filmed. When the surf is giant on the north shore, Pua 'Aena is one of the few places where beginner to intermediate surfers can go and catch waves that aren't life-threatening. They'll be back to Hawaii. Oh, you betcha.

When the surf is small, the waves at Pua 'Aena are perfect for stand up paddling because they break, back off, and reform. Lili Foster

Skylar Peak, Morgan Runyon, and Christian Shubin

The Lost Coast from Shelter Cove to Westport

Skylar Peak, Morgan Runyon, and Christian Shubin: aquanuts, restaurateurs, entrepreneurs, raconteurs; known to the authorities from Malibu to the Hawaiian Islands and all the way to Surabaya. All longtime surfers from the Malibu area, Peak, Runyon, and Shubin like to get in the water as much as possible, and they all have become SUP devotees. In the summer of 2010, they traveled to an isolated corner of northern California to get a taste of something wild—because there are parts of California that are surprisingly well off the beaten path. They got lost, they saw orca, they wiped out, but they survived, and Christian Shubin—co-owner of Poseidon SUP in Santa Monica; www.poseidonstandup.com—used his raconteur skills to tell the story of their adventure along the Sinkyone Wilderness. (For their summer 2011 trip, they are headed for the west coast of Vancouver Island.)

Our goal was paddling from Shelter Cove to Westport along what is known as the "Lost Coast" of Humboldt County, California. This is a rugged yet amazingly beautiful stretch of the northern California coast that is declared wilderness and untouched except for the occasional hiker, fisherman, or kayaker.

I [Christian Shubin] have had the fantasy of doing a multiday stand up paddle trek for a few years before it actually materialized. In the summer of 2010, I told my neighbor Skylar Peak that I was planning on visiting some friends in Humboldt County and that while I was there I wanted to paddle a section of the Lost Coast. All we needed were some big SUP boards, dry bags, food, and a few supplies. Once Skylar committed

to the trip, longtime friend Morgan Runyon soon found out what we were up to and eagerly joined in on our plan. I drove our three boards up from Malibu solo, stopping in Cayucos to swap out one of our SUP boards for a 12' board that was perfect for our trip. The plan was for me to pick up Skylar and Morgan from the Arcata Airport and from there drive about 100 miles south to Shelter Cove to start our three-day, 28-mile paddle adventure.

Skylar and Morgan's original LAX to Arcata flight was on the verge of being diverted to Redding due to heavy fog. I was pondering the idea of leaving them in Redding after finding out that the original one-hour drive to Arcata to pick them up would be turned into a three-hour drive to Redding. Luckily, the fog cleared, and from Skylar's report the pilot landed hard onto the Arcata Airport runway.

We got dropped off at the boat launch in Shelter Cove at noon the next morning by my good friend Dave. On the boat slips before we departed, Skylar questioned a few local fishermen on what we should be using for bait. The fishermen gave us the rest of their frozen anchovies. An old weathered character on a moped tried to sell Morgan some weed, and a young teenager on a BMX bike tried to sell us a bamboo peace pipe.

NorCal, dude.

We finally set off south on our paddle, leaving behind the local vendors and fishermen. We knew we were headed south, but we did not know what we would find. We had ample gear and food in dry bags strapped to the decks of our boards. It was summer, but we were wearing hooded 4/3 wetsuits pulled on halfway, preparing us for unknown conditions.

What we found, amazingly, was mostly glassy conditions. Typical June gloom conditions prevailed in the mornings, but none of us complained, knowing that the sun can often bring wind as well. Only a light breeze pushed at our backs, and we felt lucky

SUP Team One, up a creek with their paddles.
Photo by Christian Shubin

that the weather was cooperating. What we were taking in through our senses were breathtaking rugged cliffs lined with pine and redwoods. These bluffs edged the wide-open coastline that stretched before us. The ocean moved under us, and we could feel the energy of a small swell that would stay with us over the next few days. We kept paddling, knowing that we had to make up some lost time because of our late start. We came upon giant sea stacks and sea arches that enticed us to paddle through them. Timing is critical going through these sea arches, as the rising waves can easily mash you into the top of the arch.

After 12 miles of paddling, we found a small protected bay for us to set up our first night's camp. One of the most fun parts of our trip was figuring out which route to take to get in through the surf and rock outcroppings. Negotiating rocks and riding waves into the bay's shore and finally stepping off our boards, we found ourselves in a perfect place to camp for the night. A small tidal lagoon stretched across a broad pebble-strewn bay. We had running water in the stream to filter and giant driftwood trees to use as tables, chairs, and windbreaks.

We made a fire and ate a full meal of burritos complete with beans, cheese, couscous, avocado, and Trader Joe's hot sauce. Morgan threw on the fire a few out-of-season mussels that we collected. They opened up quite nicely, and they were tasty. If Morgan would have had it his way, we would have all survived by eating mussels, and our only condiment for the trip would have been a bottle of olive oil. (Morgan inherited a legendary Malibu restaurant called the Old Place, which used to serve two things: steak and clams.) That trip could still happen.

I had the great idea to set up my tent in the tidal area of the rocky pebble lagoon. I only shrugged and laughed at Skylar and Morgan's suggestions to set up farther up the beach. Well . . . at what was probably two in the morning, I awoke to the feeling of sleeping on a waterbed. I felt around the floor of my tent, and yes, it did seem as though I was on a waterbed. I pulled up my sleeping bag to hold it up out of the water and panicked to get my tent zipper opened. I spent at least an hour that night drying out my tent near the fire. We had some good laughs the next morning as my friends found me and my tent on new, higher ground.

The next morning we made some breakfast and paddle surfed the cove out front, which was pretty fun even on our big boards. The waves were breaking right off a reef in the middle of the bay, and then it would reform on the inside to a left all the way to the beach. It was pretty amazing to be miles away from anyone else and surfing fun waves all to ourselves.

Setting out for our paddle south on the second day, we left our camp and looked forward to our next destination. We paddled for miles, and then a few more miles. We could see endless coast stretching in front and in back of us as far as the eye could see. Every distant point turned into another distant point, and we just kept paddling. Lunch and snack times were spent in the water, floating, taking in the vastness of the ocean all around us.

Christian Shubin framed by the Sinkyone Wilderness.
Morgan Runyon

We soon realized that there are few places to go ashore that would provide protection from the tides as well as providing fresh water. We had a handheld GPS device that we reluctantly used and for the most part did not use very well, because we overshot our second night's camp by at least 3 miles. We decided not to backtrack, so we kept paddling, hoping we would find another suitable campsite. After a few more miles, we paddled around a protected bay that offered a broad beach landing in the trough of a creek. The waves in this bay were much bigger, and we hugged the left side of the bay coming in.

Pulling our boards up the sandy beach, we crested a sand ridge, which led us to a broad creek flowing out of a canyon. We curiously and instinctively pushed our boards into the fresh water and explored further. We paddled up the creek, sometimes moving large dead branches out of the way. The creek led us to beautiful shallow pools of clear water under half-shaded ferns and trees. We filtered our water, Morgan picked and fed us some tender fiddleheads as a snack, and we made our way back to the mouth of the creek and our campsite for the night.

Before setting up camp, we caught a few waves in our newfound bay. There were a few bombs coming

233

through, and Skylar was loving the left peak. I caught a nice right on my 11' single-fin Jimmy Lewis, trying to bury the fat, round-edged tail on the bottom turn. I proceeded to break my leash trying to get out through the rest of the waves of the set. A few fun waves satisfied our souls after a full day of paddling. We will spend at least a full day at this spot next time.

Building a fire for the night, we collected wood along the creek and paddled it on our boards to get it closer to our campsite. We chose a sandy bluff above the shoreline as our camp. We built nice chairs with driftwood and set out cooking our meal for the night. One of the highlights of our meal was super-burn-your-mouth-hot ramen noodles that Morgan brought along. Not sure where he picked those up: the 99 Cent Store? We poured off the broth and tried to eat what we could of the noodles alone, and they were still very spicy. Tuna in a bag worked pretty well on our trip as well, and we enjoyed some tuna pasta with olive oil.

Our next and final day of paddling was relatively short, but slightly rougher conditions made it feel a lot longer. I know my body was feeling a little fatigued as well from two solid days of paddling.

Around noon, or maybe it was closer to three, we reached our final destination in Westport. We ended our trip under a highway bridge at the mouth of a creek. For an audience there was a large family who were fishing for the day. They watched as we caught our final waves into the beach. Morgan gave us a spectacular wipeout off his board on his final wave, and I rescued the board from hitting the rocks by sacrificing my body, as the board took me out at the legs and I fell forward over it. We had to give the fishing family some entertainment, and yeah, they did laugh a lot.

I had strategically left my car at Westport, and we loaded it up and drove north to drop my compadres off at the Arcata Airport. As we drove, we talked immediately about our next trip. The possibilities were
endless as we thought of coastlines, lakes, and rivers that we could explore.

Take that oversized board that you learned on and load it up with some gear. I guarantee there are a million possibilities and adventures waiting for you, too.

Ken Hoeve
Making the Transition from Kayaking to Stand Up Paddling

I have never been to Colorado for some reason. Apologies to that state, and its people. Not even a layover on a flight. I have been to Nevada, Wyoming, Utah, Idaho, and Montana, but never to Colorado.

I have also never shot a river on a stand up paddleboard, but I am fiending to do that—and also do some fly fishing from a stand up paddleboard. As soon as this book is done, it's back up to the Smith River in northern California and then after that, maybe six months of wandering, back through Montana and British Columbia and the Yukon up to Alaska, to SUP and SUP fish a lot of rivers I've seen in the past.

So, knowing very little about Colorado or kayaking or running rivers on a stand up paddleboard, I had to feel my way through an interview with Ken Hoeve, a newscaster from Colorado who is one of the leading innovators in riding stand up paddleboards on rivers.

Q: Charles MacArthur sent me the start of his personal history, and it was very good. He claims to be the first to ride whitewater on a stand up paddleboard. Is this true?

A: *He may be the first person to try whitewater on a board, but he's not the first to ride whitewater while standing. That title belongs to Jeff Snyder, who has been standing in an inflatable ducky and paddling Class V for at least fifteen years.*

Q: Is it possible to give a brief history of how whitewater SUP evolved? Who were the major participants, and what were the evolutionary events? When was the first competition? First media mentions, and so on?

A: *The first major players in stand up river running were certainly Charlie MacArthur, Dan Gavere, Taylor Robertson, Jay Kincaid, Luke Hopkins, and Corran Addison. Not surprisingly they are all world-class kayakers.*

Q: Can you say what year the experimenting with river SUP began, approximately, and where it was and what equipment they were using at first?

A: *Its roots could really be traced back to Snyder and his striding in an inflatable kayak, as far as river running is concerned. As for the more current form and recent progression of actual boards in rapids, I would guess it started around 2005. The equipment was really just normal ocean surfing SUP boards, and then came the inflatable SUPs. Their durability makes them great, but the lack of structural integrity makes it more like riding a sponge in wave trains.*

Q: What are the advantages of SUP over kayaks and vice versa?

A: *The main advantage is its ease of use and minimal equipment. All you need is a board and paddle (and PFD), and you're out there paddling flat water. I also like the visual side of it. In a kayak you can't see too deep underwater, but on a board I can actually see deeper. It's awesome to fish off of for this reason. You can see the fish and cast to them.*

Q: Do you still kayak, or are you SUP only?

A: *I still kayak all the time. SUP has helped it tremendously. I have dropped a ton of weight and have become super fit because of it. SUP is far more of a*

workout and has helped me train for whitewater races. *This year I won or placed in the top five of every kayak race I entered.*

Q: How long have you lived in Aspen?

A: *I live in the Vail area: Gypsum, Colorado, to be exact. I have been here for twenty years, since 1991.*

Q: Ooops, apologies. I have somehow never been to Colorado. What was your whitewater and/or ocean experience before you started SUPping?

A: *I grew up surfing in north Florida, starting in 1984. When I moved to Colorado, I had no way to get my water fix, so I took up kayaking on the local rivers. Within five years I was a safety kayaker for a local rafting company, and two years after that I was a sponsored professional kayaker paddling for Dagger kayaks. I have been on their team for thirteen years now.*

Q: When did you first become aware of SUP?

A: *I had seen it on a trip back to Florida in 2007 and then tried one at Outdoor Retailer in Salt Lake City the following year. As soon as I got on it, I thought, "This would be such a sick toy for the river." I got an inflatable C4 ULI at the show and immediately took it down a Class III stretch of river by my house. I got worked but realized this was a direction in river running I wanted to go.*

It was fun, but there was a ton of room to advance the sport's design and progress. And there still is. Manufacturers still have not even come close to what can and will be done in future boards.

Q: Where did you go for advice on how to get started?

A: *I pretty much taught myself. With a history in surfing and paddling, I had a good idea of what I needed. The board and paddle are part of it, but the* real necessity is safety gear and river safety education. You can get truly jacked up running rivers, so having years of safety instruction is the major benefit.

Q: What was your first experience: where, what board, did you have an instructor, how long did it take you to be competent?

A: *My first river experience was on the Colorado River near my house. I had no instruction but did have my buddy Matt Solomon along with me. We just felt our way into it. Kayakers pick it up quickly, as they already know how to brace and stroke. It's just a matter of working on your balance and learning to drive the board where you want it to go.*

Q: Were you thinking about whitewater all along?

A: *Yeah, the whole time. Being a landlocked surfer is difficult, and all I kept thinking was how this brings the surfing feel and lifestyle to those without a coast nearby. With stand up, I can pretty much surf the earth: rivers, lakes, ponds, inlets, ocean, bays, or channels. It takes riding a board to anywhere there's water.*

Q: Describe your evolution into riding whitewater: boards, which rivers, safety equipment, techniques.

A: *The only major change I have done is my safety gear and padding. You learn fast that falls hurt. Rocks make rapids, and falling on them is devastating. I even wear a cup, shin pads, and hip pads when running the rowdy stuff. Also, my board (made by Surftech) helps a lot. It's thicker and wider, so it's more stable and has extra flotation in aerated water.*

Q: While researching this book, I've heard some hair-raising stories about stand up

Ken Hoeve negotiating whitewater rapids during the Colorado off-season. Photo courtesy of Ken Hoeve

paddlers getting blown out to sea by offshore winds and getting bumped by white sharks. What kind of stories of near death are there in the world of running rivers on stand up paddleboards? Any major incidents you can name? Drownings? Crocodiles? Unexpected waterfalls?

A: There have definitely been some incidents on the river, but fortunately for us, we have not been the victims. But the danger is always there. I have heard of leash entrapments, low head dam drownings, foot entrapments, and joint dislocations from rock collisions. The river never lets up, so once things head south, they tend to get worse.

Q: **Watching the Teva instructional video, they advise people running river rapids to never put their feet on rocks, because your legs can be pinned by the current, and you drown. What other advice would you give to first-timers who want to run rivers and ride whitewater on a stand up paddleboard?**

A: Always wear at least a helmet and PFD, make sure you have adequate gear that keeps you warm (drysuit), and never paddle alone.

Q: **I want to go back to Greg Noll's house on the Smith River and run it on a stand up paddleboard. I regularly use a 12'1" Laird with a carbon fiber paddle. What advice would you give an experienced ocean person in running a river like the Smith? What board, paddle, leash, and safety equipment should I use? Are there special fins for river SUP? I have broken out three fins on the rocks at Malibu, and I would imagine rivers are even worse on fins. Do you recommend a single fin or tri-fin setup?**

A: Wide and stable is good when looking for boards. Also, thickness counts for a lot, as whitewater

is aerated, and a board needs extra girth to keep it at the surface. Fins are a must for me because I love to stop and surf all the little waves along the way. However, fins can act like a stick being tossed in your bike's spokes if they catch a rock. You get tossed, the fin breaks (maybe even the fin box), and you are swimming. Rubber/soft fins are ideal. They work when you surf, forgive when you bash rocks, and won't cut your hand off if you're getting tumbled in a hole alongside your board.*

Q: **Do you recommend wearing leashes for whitewater? I could see them becoming as much a hazard as a safety device.**

A: Wearing a leash is the big safety question and concern in river SUP. Whitewater paddlers have known for years that ropes or lines attached to you are a bad idea. If they grab onto a branch, rock, or debris when you are floating in the river, they act like an anchor that will literally pull you underwater. For that reason if I ever wear a leash on a river, I always wear a safety PFD with a quick release harness. If things go bad and I get hung up, I can pop the release and be free of the leash.

Q: **Can you describe your equipment quiver as of right now (February 2011)?**

A: For summer cruising on flat water and slow-moving water, I mostly wear shorts, a hat, sandals (sometimes), and my iPod. If it's unlikely I'm going to fall in, I like to wear as little as possible because you work up a sweat quickly. I always have a shell along in case it turns windy or cold and of course have a PFD handy. When I'm river running cold rapids, it's another program. If you fall into the water here, it can kill you just from the temps. River runoff in the spring is freezing here in the Rockies. It was snow just hours before and has now made its way a few miles downstream and has remained at near-freezing temperatures. We often paddle when there is ice on the banks. So for those reasons I don't mess around when it comes to dry, warm gear. From the skin up I wear a fleece one-piece suit, a fleece top over that, Kokatat drysuit with dry footies with fleece socks underneath, gloves, full-face neoprene glacier mask, and a helmet.

Q: In the world of wave-riding on stand up paddleboards, guys are regularly surfing Pipeline, Teahupoo, Piahe/Jaws, Mavericks, and other extreme-wave situations. What is the equivalent of that in whitewater SUP?

A: All rivers are sketchy. I surf and understand the hazards of big wave surfing and reefs, but I truly feel river running is just as dangerous, if not more so. When you run a Class IV rapid, you are hauling ass over and around/through large, sharp rocks. They are everywhere, all the time. Sometimes the water is deep, sometimes it grabs your fins and wants to send you over the handlebars like riding a bike and having someone throw a stick in your spokes. And when you crash on a wave, you may get held down a good spell, but eventually the sets ease and forgive a bit. The river never lets up. Ever. You crash and burn—prepare to be shoved relentlessly downstream into logs, rocks, debris, and rapids.

Q: Is there a record for shooting a waterfall on a stand up paddleboard?

A: As of now, no. I'm sure someone will huck and stick a 20-footer soon. But finding the right waterfall to do it on and then running it a bunch of times and beating yourself senseless is tough. Someone will—but sticking a beast drop will be difficult. It's much easier to drop waterfalls in kayaks. I have run a 40-foot drop in California and cannot even imagine how it could be done stand up paddling. If someone does it, I will go take the pictures.

Josh Kuntz
Surf Montana: In Pursuit of Mrs. Bubbles and Rising Trout

Montana is to a fly fisher what the Mentawai Islands are to a surfer: the promised land, etched with promising waterways from streams to rivers to glacial lakes. Around every corner in Montana there is a new stretch of water, most likely loaded with trout of every stripe. I try to go fishing once a summer somewhere in Montana, but I don't always make it. Now that I am a SUP addict, I am fiending to go back to Montana and try whitewater running and fly fishing on the Big Hole, the Madison, the Lamar, the Clark Fork, and all those creeks, rivers, and glacial lakes I have seen in the past. Thanks to Josh Kuntz for sending words and photos of the Montana SUP experience, and I'll be up there soon.

My Introduction to SUP

My business partner and lifelong bro, Peter "PK" Kirwan, has always had a landlocked kid's love affair with surfing. PK grew up in Bozeman, Montana, and went to college in Tacoma, Washington, from 1995 to 1999. There he met Art Griffith from northern California. Art was an avid surfer, and they did a few surf trips in Washington, Oregon, and California. After college, Art spent a year in Montana snowboarding, hunting, mountain biking, and so on. A few years after Art returned to Cali (2005 or so), PK went for a visit, and Art took him stand up paddleboarding. PK was hooked instantly, and as former kayakers, PK and Art believed the next logical step was to paddle the river and surf waves. The next few years PK introduced me to SUP, and we ran dozens of trips down the Yellowstone River near Livingston, Montana, in pursuit of surfing a wave called Mrs. Bubbles.

Word spread that we were doing something crazy and new, and we soon had a long line of friends asking

to join the river trips. PK was the only one with a SUP (11' ULI), so we all took turns rotating from the SUP to canoes, kayaks, and rafts. I really enjoyed SUP, but I wasn't sure I wanted to spend the money on a setup since I was already saturated with outdoor pursuits and gear.

My first SUP experiences were on an 11' ULI (inflatable). The first board I eventually purchased was a 12' SUP ATX. For our earliest experiences, we used water ski wetsuits and water ski PFDs or a few kayaking PFDs. I even tried wearing a scuba wetsuit from 1986 (5 mm, I believe). It was completely purple, and people started calling me Barney (as in the dinosaur), and I overheated in about three minutes of paddling, so I scrapped it.

However, I have worked as a special events consultant for the past ten years, and one of my clients is a luxury guest ranch in Montana. In the summer of 2008, they asked my opinion of new ways to amp up their activity offerings. SUP came right to mind, so I designed a program for them. While doing the research on that program, I took a closer look at SUP and realized that the sport was absolutely booming, and there

Want a challenge for your balance and coordination? Try fly fishing from a stand up paddleboard. Livingston native Tyler Erickson uses a stealth 9' Liquid Shredder and a Stendy paddle by C4 Waterman to sneak up on unsuspecting brown trout on the Yellowstone River, east of Livingston. Balancing yourself on a 9' Liquid Shredder while casting is a good trick. Hook up and you might get an even better trick. Some of the brown trout lurking along the bottom of the Yellowstone are big enough to take a local on a Livingston sleigh ride.
Photo courtesy of pinkcowboy.net

was an opportunity to start a business ASAP. That is how my SUP business, Pink Cowboy Fitness and Recreation, was born. (The strange name is in reference to our support of Breast Cancer Awareness programs.)

Two Types of Stand Up Paddlers in Montana

It is first important to understand that Montana is usually a few years behind when it comes to adopting trends, so SUP is still in its very early stages here. However, it has already become apparent that there are two separate segments of stand up paddlers in Montana.

Ben Ruffato (left), Kara Kuntz (center), and Moira McKinnon (right) paddling the Bitterroot River near Missoula, Montana. Ben is on an 11' ULI inflatable, Kara is on an 11' Liquid Shredder with a C4 Stendy paddle, and Moira is on a 9' Liquid Shredder. Photo courtesy of pinkcowboy.net

The earliest adopters were some of the hard-core adventure athletes, mostly kayakers, snowboarders, and skiers. These young, athletic types quickly realized that river (whitewater) SUP provided the biggest challenge and most similar thrill to their other "extreme" sports pursuits. Kevin Brown (KB) and Luke Rieker, owners of Strongwater Kayak in Missoula, are undoubtedly the guys most responsible for spearheading the whitewater and river surfing SUP in Montana. These guys are the best whitewater paddlers and river surfers in the state, and they have done a great job taking their vast whitewater kayaking experience and integrating it with SUP to get people psyched about whitewater SUP. Their shop is now a kayak/surf shop, the only one of its kind in Montana. If you want to learn more about whitewater-specific SUP in Montana, give Strongwater a call.

In my business, the river SUP interest is growing like crazy. It is a natural summer activity for all of the young athletes that live in Montana and spend the winter skiing and snowboarding. I describe downriver SUP as "the love child of a crazy three-way between kayaking, surfing, and skiing." What I mean is that downriver SUP incorporates many of the skills of these sports, such as reading water currents, having agility, altering balance, and using your legs as shock absorbers. I find it amazing how similar paddling a large wave train is to skiing a line of moguls.

The second segment of stand up paddlers in Montana is what I call the "lifestyle" crowd. These are the folks we typically see on lakes and occasionally on a mellow river. These folks are drawn to SUP for three reasons.

1. Fitness: They are into health and fitness and recognize the great benefits of SUP.
2. Serenity/nature: Montana is freaking beautiful, and seeing it from a stand up paddleboard in the middle of some of our lakes is simply breathtaking.

3. Family toy: A lot of the "lifestyle" paddlers have a cabin on a lake, and they see a paddle-board as one more lake toy for the family to enjoy. They get a stand up paddleboard for the whole family to just play around on.

My business primarily focuses on the "lifestyle" crowd. I try to give people a great introduction to the sport and allow them the opportunity to see how it can be a unique addition to their outdoor lifestyle. I think SUP has the chance to be a truly huge sport, pursued by people of all ages and athletic abilities. The adventure athletes will always push the sport to its edge with whitewater and surfing, but I think it is the average person who stands a huge chance of falling in love with SUP. It is easy to learn (on flat water), it gives you a fantastic connection to nature, it promotes strength and cardiovascular health, and the equipment requires minimal maintenance and can often be shared by multiple people (great for families).

Kara Kuntz paddling the Madison River in Montana. Kara is on a 9' Liquid Shredder with a Liquid Shredder adjustable-length fiberglass paddle. Photo courtesy of pinkcowboy.net

SUP Challenges in Montana

I would estimate that 90 percent of the Montana population has still not heard of stand up paddling. People see my boards on my truck and start heckling, "Kind of far from the ocean, ain't ya?" When I am out on a lake, I have boats come racing over because they are so perplexed by what I am doing.

Because very few Montana residents have a surfing background, they are easily confused by SUP. Most people I talk to assume that it must be extremely difficult to learn or that it can only be done in the ocean. The lack of surfing knowledge also means that most inland residents have no clue what type of board to purchase or even rent. They have no background in

(left) Josh Kuntz paddling the Flathead River just outside Glacier National Park in Montana. Josh is on an 11' Liquid Shredder with a personally customized fiberglass paddle. Photo courtesy of pinkcowboy.net

(below) PK paddling on Fairy Lake (Montana) on an 11' ULI with a homemade wood/fiberglass paddle. Photo courtesy of pinkcowboy.net

board shapes, sizes, materials, and so on. Unfortunately, this leads to some people purchasing boards that are a very bad fit for the application they had in mind (for example, someone purchasing a narrow, fiberglass board for whitewater river SUP).

Because of Montana's remote inland location, shipping SUP boards is expensive, and damage is more likely to occur than in shipping to most other areas. This is more of a frustration for the SUP retailers.

Due to the cold water and air temperatures around Montana, most people wait until July before really pursuing water sports (at least on the lakes). July and August are busy, but right after Labor Day, the lakes are quiet again. Obviously, a two-month season is hard for a SUP business to work with. So we are trying to educate our potential customers that you can quickly become competent enough on a SUP to make the likelihood of falling in very low when paddling on a calm lake or pond. This flatwater paddling obviously extends the season greatly, since you stay nice and warm on top of the board.

David "Catfish" Adams
Surfin' the Mighty Mississippi

As I was searching for stories about people far from the ocean having adventures on a stand up paddleboard, David Adams came highly regarded by Clay Feeter, the editor of *Standup Journal*:

Vietnam vet David lives near the Wisconsin/Illinois border town of Galena, Illinois. He called me out of the blue about a year and a half ago. He said he had kayaked for a while, had never seen a live stand up paddleboard, but had seen it on TV, and he was hooked.

He had called to subscribe to the Journal, and we got to talking. His first and only surfing experience was in Vietnam on R&R. He tells me, "I was a radio operator on recon patrols and was the squad leader during the big Tet Offensive of 1967–1968. When I surfed in Vietnam, it was near Pleiku in the central highlands. It wasn't really R&R but a one-day party at a local lake there. Flat water and no wind. There was a surfboard, and nobody wanted to use it, so I would paddle as fast as I could, then jump up and surf about 10 yards, lose speed, fall off, and do it again—almost all day. I have never surfed a real wave yet.

"These wind waves on the Mississippi River are real close together, and my board is on three or four waves at the same time, so there is no 'drop' to negotiate. In Vietnam I learned when you got the thing moving, it becomes more stable. I got pretty good at it but never did it again. Now I can surf again!"

And so he has. I told him about Gary Stone at Paddleboard Specialists in Madison, Wisconsin. So he drove the three hours up to Madison and bought a board.

Here is David's story about SUP on the Mississippi in his own words:

The Mississippi is 2 miles wide where I live near Chestnut Mountain, a ski resort in Galena, Illinois. I live about 100 yards from the river, so I go out about four times a week from the Illinois side: That's where the backwaters are and lots of forested islands. There are nesting bald eagles, deer with their fawns, and for the first time this summer I heard and saw coyotes on one of the islands. I have had beavers sneak up behind, splash their tails, and get me wet. But they never attack, and I just get a good chuckle.

Getting Started Stand Up Paddling on the Mississippi

I've been kayaking these waters for thirty-two years. I was a dorm director for college hearing-impaired students, so I had my summers off for eight years. I spent those summers camping on the islands and riverbanks and eating catfish and other fish, frogs, turtles, and snakes.

Then late fall of 2009 I saw a bikini babe on a stand up paddleboard in the background of CSI Miami. *My boss at the Aurora YMCA Child Care Googled it, and that led to me contacting Clay Feeter and subscribing to his* Standup Journal. *He gave me the number for Gary Stone, who owns Paddleboard Specialists in Madison, Wisconsin—about 100 miles from where I live.*

(left) David Adams (aka Catfish) stroking his 12'6" Joe Bark racing board in the upper reaches of the mighty Mississippi, near Blanding Landing / Chestnut Mountain Resort.
Photo courtesy of David Adams

(below) Taking a break in the shade on his 12' × 30" Hobie ATR somewhere in the trees on the upper reaches of the Mighty Mississippi. David Adams

Gary pointed me toward my first board, a Hobie Surf SUP that was 12' × 30" wide, 4" thick, and 30 pounds. It was winter, so I bought three instructional SUP DVDs and watched those or parts of them almost every day through the winter of 2009 and 2010, and continue to do that. They helped me learn and were fun to watch.

My learning experience began in April 2010. I just needed to get time on the board, and I soon made a huge jump in skill and stability after getting in the surf position and feeling the board while shifting my weight from side to side and doing the paddle techniques for turning and steering. That made me much more confident and caused me to search out rough water and weird wind conditions. I've been blown off my board two times by wind gusts while practicing pivot turns.

After one hundred hours on the Hobie Surf SUP, Gary Stone upgraded me to a Joe Bark racing stand up paddleboard that is 12' × 6" × 30" wide. At first the Bark was a bit tippy but barely noticeable, so no problems getting used to it. With the Bark I bought a non-adjustable Quickblade paddle. I like the Quickblade best because it's so light.

The biggest advantage for me with SUP is the view—standing on the board versus sitting in a

Father otter checks out this odd creature standing on the water. David Adams

kayak. I can see way better and can read the wind and rough water. I snuck up on a coyote pup on an island because I'm a lot stealthier on a paddleboard.

I carry my camera in a waterproof fanny pack. One day I was sitting on the board under a low-hanging branch in the shade when an otter family came to play about 20 yards away. I got some photos of the dad otter. The bald eagles are used to seeing me in my kayak, but they seem more interested when I'm on my board.

Safety Concerns on the Mississippi

In some areas of the backwaters, I have to paddle from the kneeling position because the danger of hitting a stump with the fin is too great. I have "finned" stumps and fallen off, and it's like walking the plank—only really fast. I always wear a DaKine coil leash and a Cabela's mesh PFD in case I "fin" a stump and fall on it. I haven't done that yet, but a PFD would offer me some protection if I fell into a stump. And if I hit my head and got knocked out or injured to the point where I couldn't swim, it would keep me afloat.

My advice for stand up paddling on the Mississippi is to get a river map that shows the stump fields and avoid those. When I'm not in a small-boat channel that I know is deep, I keep shoving my paddle down to test the depth. In certain areas I just get on my knees because I'm expecting to hit stumps, weeds, or maybe even the bottom. I've hit weeds with my fin and been able to stay standing. That took some strong abs and balance. I keep remembering Gary Stone's advice: "Tighten your core! Tighten your core! That helps a ton!"

In Vietnam I came so close to dying several times, but I don't have that invincible attitude anymore. The reason I've been able to avoid danger when stand up paddleboarding on the Mississippi is that I have immense respect for the river. I tend to avoid the main channel in a kayak or on a paddleboard. I do have to cross the main channel sometimes, and I always make sure there's no boat traffic—then I go as fast as I can.

I would like to surf boat waves, but I don't want any part of being behind a barge up close, so I try to catch the side waves. So far I haven't been close enough to catch a decent wave. I was a little surprised to discover that houseboats and big pontoon boats actually make bigger waves that last longer than those made by the barges. But I haven't been close enough to catch one of those yet, either.

Two times I've been hit with boat waves ["wake waves"] from the side while simultaneously paddling against wind waves, and I fell. Two other times the same thing happened, but I managed not to fall. I kind of panicked and just shoved my paddle real deep and jiggled it back and forth real hard, and it was like holding on to a post. I hung on and surprise, surprise, no dunking. Turned out I did a canoe and kayak technique called "bracing." I didn't know that at the time, but it sure worked good.

Once I crossed the channel near a buoy—a huge steel float anchored by a cable to the bottom—and the normally 4 mile per hour river current was moving pretty good at this spot. I used the current to go fast, but it started pulling me toward the buoy. I could tell it would smash me into the buoy, and I was worried it would suck me under it. I paddled like crazy and got away from it. Now I give those buoys a wide margin.

I have been out in some pretty big winds on the Mississippi. When I first started stand up paddling, there were a few times I didn't go out because the wind and waves were too much. One time the wind was out of the west, and it was so strong I couldn't even get 10 yards away from the riverbank. As I got better, though, I started wanting to go out in all the wind I could handle. I just needed that time on the board to get used to crazy conditions. Being able to see so much better on a stand up paddleboard has

David Adams's Hobie ART SUP at the Blanding Landing Campground boat landing. "I roll my board to the river from my front yard, then put the wheel stuff in the carry bag and bungee it to the front of the board," he says. "I attach the WindPaddle sail to the front, too. I always bring my cell phone in a dry bag. I wear a hat and sunglasses for sun protection and bring frozen water bottles to drink (when they melt, I have cold water) and always sunscreen. I wear shorts (or wetsuit shorts if it's cold) and whatever kind of shirt or sweater that suits the weather, or no shirt if it's really hot. I paddle barefoot unless it's very cold. Then I wear wetsuit booties. David Adams

been a real education for reading winds. It's amazing how the islands and the trees (or lack of trees) affect the winds. When the wind is more than I can paddle into, I take the kayak. That's only happened twice this summer, though.

I also have a WindPaddle sail that works on my SUP. If I can sail with the wind, it's fast enough to get in the surf position and do paddle turns and steer. I have fifty minutes of actual surfing in the "surf position" this season on 2½-foot wind waves. Cowabunga!

I want to ride waves again, but I'm 1,600 miles from the Pacific and 800 miles from the Atlantic. I *know there is a beach in Chicago on Lake Michigan that's been dedicated to surfing. I plan to go there for sure once the weather warms. You can't imagine how bad I want to surf on a real wave! Next year around Christmas time I plan to go to Sydney, Australia, rent a car, camp at Bonneyvale campground, take a surf lesson, and spend six weeks SUP surfing.*

Dane Jackson
From Tennessee to Ottawa to Uganda

As this book was coming together in January 2011, Duke Brouwer at Surftech suggested: "Another great whitewater guy you should contact is 17-year-old Dane Jackson. His family owns Jackson Kayaks. Dane and his sister Emily are two of the top freestyle whitewater kayakers in the world. Dane's a stud and is absolutely hooked on SUP." Sounded good, so we contacted Dane, and in between his travels in the United States and all the way to Africa, Dane detailed his transition from world-class kayaker to SUP addict.

I am a professional kayaker, and I have traveled all over the world kayaking the greatest rivers. I am 17 now but started kayaking when I was 2 years old. I started with a little fiberglass kayak and did it as much as I could growing up. My dad was already a professional kayaker when I was born, so I was always around the rivers. It didn't take me long to get into a kayak. But even when I wasn't kayaking I was still swimming in the rivers or playing with miniature

kayaks in the little creeks. All I wanted to be was a kayaker. I still go kayaking almost every day.

But a couple of years ago I got into stand up paddling and loved it, so now I do SUP, and I kayak. I try to do both all around the world.

Where I live in Tennessee is right next to the Collins and Caney Fork Rivers. They are both dammed up at their confluence. We live right by the dam, but just downstream of the dam is a hydroplant that releases water almost all fall, winter, and spring, but not very much in the summer. We kayak down below the hydro plant almost every day.

I was born in Washington, D.C., but when I was 4 years old we sold our house, moved into an RV, and traveled all over the country kayaking and going to competitions. So the rivers I grew up around are all around the country. Where I currently live used to be one of the most popular places to kayak in the South. Now it is not super popular but still one of the most beautiful, and there are still quite a few kayakers that come down.

I pretty much became a professional kayaker when I was 11 or 12 years old, and I have done more things as a professional than I can remember. I was the youngest person to run some of the biggest creeks and whitewater all over the world: the Zambezi and White Nile Rivers in Africa.

I went on my first expedition in Newfoundland when I was 14 years old. Expeditions for kayakers usually means going to do rivers and creeks that no one has ever done before in a kayak, in unexplored rivers in different countries.

To the untrained eye, this looks like Dane Jackson on his Laird Surftech about to get sucked into a vortex or crevasse or whatever river runners call trouble like this. In reality, this is Dane on the Ottawa River, and he is about to punch through what kayakers call a hole. "A hole is what they call something like an ocean wave after it has already broken," Dane said. "It looks terrifying, but it is not that bad." Photo courtesy Dane Jackson

I am a two-time silver medalist in the world championships of freestyle kayaking. I was the 2010 gold medalist in the World Cup of freestyle kayaking in my age group. I am a four-time national freestyle kayaking champion in the junior men's class, which is 18 and under. I am a three-time C1 national champion, which is using a freestyle kayak on my knees with a canoe paddle. Those are a few of the main things, but I also have been all over the world kayaking and going to events.

I try to do as many things as I can that involve being on the rivers. So last summer I started SUP, and I thought it was a blast. I think it was 2006 when I was at the Outdoor Retailer Show in Salt Lake City. I was there representing Jackson Kayak—my family's company in Tennessee—to help sell kayaks and help out with our booth.

I was at the Surftech booth and saw a stand up paddleboard. They explained what it was, and it sounded really sweet. I didn't see stand up much until 2009, when a lot of kayakers started to do it.

When I was in Salida, Colorado, this past June [2010], some people were demoing boards, and I tried one out. I wasn't worried or scared to get on it because I have spent my whole life around and in rivers, so I felt fine if I fell in the water. I do not know what company made the board, but it was an inflatable, and I took it out on a little wave. I couldn't stay on it very well, but I still had a great time.

The first place I ever got to try my own SUP was in Canada on the Ottawa River, which is one of the most beautiful in the world, and in the summertime it is one of the warmest. It is already one of the most famous rivers for kayaking. But I think it is one of the greatest SUP rivers out there.

There weren't many surfing options for me at the beginning because I still wasn't very good. But I found this little hump wave, and I would spend hours just getting better and staying on and learning how to

In the world of surfing and stand up paddle surfing, this is called "pearling," which is short for "pearl diving," when the nose of the board goes under water. "In the world of river running, this is called pearling as well," Dane said. "But if your board or kayak goes vertical after pearling, it is call an ender."
Photo courtesy Dane Jackson

control my board a little better. I was on the Ottawa for a month. I rode a SUP almost every day because it was just so amazing. I arrived at the Ottawa barely able to stay on the board, and I left able to run the biggest rapids on the river without falling off.

I started learning to carve and stay on better. When I got home to Rock Island, I went straight to the Collins and Caney Fork Rivers. We live a mile from one of the coolest places to kayak, but I didn't even realize how amazing it was for SUP. I got good at running the rivers on the Ottawa. But here at home I got a lot better at surfing: I could carve and stay on a lot longer.

For beginners I would just say don't even care if you fall in the water. If you don't care that you go for a swim, then you will try more things and progress faster.

Last year at the Outdoor Retailer Show I bought my first stand up paddleboard. I didn't actually know what board I was getting. Surftech decided to send me what they thought was best for me: a Laird 11'6" Softop. I had no knowledge of what boards are

better, so I felt that the Laird was a great board for me. And it was.

My first paddle is the one I still use, which is the Surftech Ventana paddle. I do C1 in kayaking, which is freestyle kayaking sitting on my knees using a canoe paddle and doing tricks, so I was already used to the one-bladed paddles. Stand up paddling with a single blade was not weird for me.

Whether I am kayaking or stand up paddling, I always wear a PFD and helmet, but I only use the leash if it is safe. On a shallow river with lots of rocks, it can be unsafe to wear a leash because it might get hung up. On a deeper river without rocks, it can be okay.

I also wear a drysuit. It has latex gaskets on the neck, wrists, and ankles so water doesn't get inside of it. I wear some form of fleece underneath it. I stay bone dry and warm all day even in cold water.

When I first got into SUP, I wanted to get better so I could take the board on some bigger waves like those we surf in our kayaks. But the biggest challenge for me was just figuring out how to stay on the board. In the ocean you either fall off or you carve off. But after that you are practically in flat water. In the rivers you have waves and breaking waves and rocks after you fall off the wave.

I stand up paddle as much as I can now. When it is sunny, I go SUP and then kayak later. It is just so sweet, I do it as much as I can. My goal is just to keep getting better and better at surfing and take my board to different rivers all over the world.

Caroline Gleich
Getting Salty in the Middle of the Desert

Originally from Minnesota, Caroline Gleich relocated to the mountains of Utah and has been an avid outdoor adventurer ever since. In the winter she can be found skiing the powdery slopes around her Salt Lake City home. She's pretty good, too—Caroline's been published on the cover of *Ski* magazine three times and in countless other media outlets. In the summer she likes to stand up paddle Utah's lakes, rivers, and reservoirs and even makes a few trips to the beach to paddle and surf in the ocean. She competes in local races and is an enthusiastic ambassador of the sport. Through the miracle of Internet communications, Caroline responded to the following queries.

Tibble Fork Reservoir, American Fork Canyon, Utah. Paddling a Surftech Universal 10'6" Softop and Nautical paddle. Picture shot on a GoPro. Photo courtesy of Caroline Gleich

Q: When did you first become aware of stand up paddling?

A: *I became aware of stand up about five years ago, in its infancy. I may have seen SUP for the first time at the Outdoor Retailer summer trade show in Salt Lake City, although I can't remember for sure.*

Q: Did you jump into it right away, or were you wary? Surfers are wary, but maybe river and lake people aren't so much.

A: *As soon as I saw it, I wanted to do it. I saw its utility on the lakes and on the ocean when the waves are flat.*

Q: Why were you at Outdoor Retailer?

A: *I was meeting with some of my ski sponsors.*

Q: What were your athletic proclivities before getting into stand up?

A: *Before getting into stand up paddling, my primary summer activities were climbing, mountain biking, trail running, hiking, and going to the ocean to surf whenever possible.*

Q: When did you first try a stand up? When and where and what board?

A: *The first time was spring 2008 on East Canyon Reservoir, which is in the mountains near my home in Salt Lake City, Utah. My best friend, Iris Noack, worked as a sub rep for DaKine and Reef, and her boss, Ben Buehner, had two Surftech Laird boards. We took them out during a wakeboard competition. We had so much fun messing around on them. First, we paddled around on one board tandem, which was a riot. We had to time our paddling so we wouldn't fall off. The boat drivers for the wakeboard competition would drive circles around us to get us to fall off, but we were both such proficient skiers and athletes that we were able to stay standing. At the end of the day, we*

paddled all the way across the reservoir. I was hooked.

The next time I went stand up paddling was for an outdoor documentary show that I hosted for a local television station. The producer wanted to do a piece on the sport, and I found myself attending Nikki Gregg's stand up paddle boot camp for the show. After Nikki's class, I felt ready to race.

Q: How long did it take you to become proficient, and what advice do you have for other beginners?

A: *I became proficient in the first few hours I did it, but after Nikki Gregg's class, I knew about proper technique. My advice to beginners is to start by sitting or kneeling on the board to get your balance. Once you stand up, keep a wide stance, and keep your eyes up—don't look down, or you will fall. As you begin to refine your stroke technique, remember to use the big muscles in your body rather than the little ones. Keep your arms straight as possible, and torque with your obliques and core muscles to power yourself forward.*

Q: What was the first stand up you owned?
A: *A Surftech 10'6" Universal Softop.*

Q: When you first started paddling, what goals did you have in mind?

A: *I just wanted to have fun on the water and cool off from the hot Utah summers. After my first season, I was ready to start running some rivers and try to compete in the local race series.*

Q: At some point, most people have an epiphany when they really get hooked. For Laird Hamilton, it was when he found he could make the transition from small surf in summer Malibu to giant surf in winter Maui, and his legs were ready for the stresses of towing giant Piahe. Anything similar with you?

A: *The first time I stand up paddled down the river, I was addicted to the adrenaline rush and the excitement of having moving water under my feet. I love the perspective and the way you can experience the river. After a season of river SUP, I was in great shape for my ski season. My core was toned, my legs were tough, and my balance had been put to the test. Unlike most workouts, SUP is something you want to do everyday. I cannot get enough of it.*

Q: **Describe your evolution in equipment, ability, and experience. What was your first really big challenge?**

A: *The first few times I paddled, I either rented or borrowed boards from people. It was so difficult to have paddles that were way too big and boards that I wasn't used to. Having too long of a paddle can really tweak your shoulders. One of my first challenges was when I got my own paddle, deciding where to cut it. I ended up cutting it a little bit too long, but I'd rather have it a little too long than too short since I was racing. Another challenge was figuring out how to load up the board by myself, but I figured this one out pretty quick—I just put it right on my roof rack and tied it down.*

Q: **Do you stand up paddleboard mostly in summer and hang up that equipment when the snow starts falling?**

A: *My SUP strategy is to be on the water until I can be on snow. This fall, I paddled through mid-November, at which point I hung my boards on my ceiling in my living room. However, we had a nice day last week (mid-February), so I busted out my AirSUP and took it to the river.*

Q: **How often do you paddle now, and where do you mostly go? What are your goals and challenges in the future?**

A: *When the fall ended, I was stand up paddling three to five times per week, mostly at mountain lakes and reservoirs, but also on the rivers whenever I could get a posse together. I also love taking my SUP boards to the ocean and paddling for distance during a small swell. My goals for the future include running more rivers and possibly becoming a whitewater SUP guide so I can share my passion for the rivers with others. I want to keep competing, too, both in the local race series for distance and in the Teva Mountain Games for whitewater.*

I'd also love to do the Battle of the Paddle just for the experience. My biggest goal is just to have fun with it and keep a smile on my face.

Q: **What places or events are on your SUP-it list?**

A: *This spring, I want to go to Reno, Nevada, for their river festival and to Vail, Colorado, to compete in the Teva Mountain Games. I want to go to Southern California when the waves are small or flat to learn how to surf. I'd also love to go to Minnesota to do a SUP trip through the Boundary Waters. Pretty much I'll SUP anywhere.*

Q: **What boards, paddles, PFD, and other equipment are you using now?**

A: *My current quiver includes the inflatable Air-SUP for the rivers and for portability, the 12'6" Lahui Kai board for racing and flatwater paddling, and the 10'6" Universal Softtop for general cruising, some rivers, and surfing the ocean. I have an adjustable aluminum paddle for rivers and for friends, a Ventana paddle for a lightweight paddle, and a Nautical paddle that is fully carbon for racing.*

I have three wetsuits—a 3/2 mm short-sleeve shortie, a 3/2 mm full suit, and a 4/3 mm long full suit. I also have booties and gloves. I use a Peak UK Airlite vest as my PFD. When I do rivers, I attach my surf leash to a quick release belt for safety.

Caroline's Ten Commandments for SUP on Rivers

1. *Practice on flat water. You want to be very comfortable on your board and feel balanced and strong. Practice J strokes and support/brace strokes for stability. Once you get on the river, you want to be sure you have excellent board control.*

2. *Be comfortable in the water. When learning how to SUP whitewater, you will inevitably fall and have to swim through the river. Staying calm is essential.*

3. *Know before you go. Make sure you've scouted your river line and know where to put in, take out, and how to navigate obstacles in between.*

4. *Go with people more experienced than you, and never go alone.*

5. *Always wear your life jacket, no exceptions to this one. Same with the helmet.*

6. *When you fall, keep your feet in front of you, and don't try to put your feet to the bottom. You could get caught on a rock or tree. Keep them up and stay calm until you can get back on your board.*

7. *In difficult rapids, keep your eyes up. I like to focus on a tree or feature on the horizon. If you look down, you will certainly fall.*

8. *Know what eddies are and how to use them. This is where the SUP skills come in—it can be difficult to get out of the current into an eddy, but it is an essential skill.*

9. *Start small and work your way up. Practice on easy rivers before tackling the harder, bigger rivers.*

10. *Keep your group together. After each section of rapids, wait up for one another at the next eddy to ensure safety.*

Robert "Wingnut" Weaver
Sea Bass Sleigh Ride: Stand Up Paddle Fishing

Star of *The Endless Summer II* and appearing in surf magazines and other media from California to Japan to Iceland, Robert "Wingnut" Weaver has been one of the faces of modern longboarding. Originally from Newport Beach, California, Wingnut splits his time between the east side of Santa Cruz and the world, and he has found that SUP is a good way to increase his water time—and also put fresh, flopping food on the table.

The rig I use is made by BoardFisher and is called the BoardFisher—attached to an 11' Wingnut Model SUP, of course, and a Werner paddle. BoardFisher has a great, upgraded milk crate with quick release tie-downs that stick to the rails of the SUP. The crate has a rod holder, paddle holder, pockets for tackle, window for your fishing license, and so on. Makes it easy.

I head into the kelp beds off Pleasure Point and find holes in the kelp bed—10 to 30 feet across—then start casting lures across the holes, five across the top, then start letting it sink before bringing it back.

If the sea bass are in the holes, you know it pretty fast. And yes, it's a sleigh ride. They pull you right away. I stand the whole time. That's the fun and challenge. It's only when the fish has quit and is right next to the board that I get to my knees and pull it up.

The limit is 28 inches, and that is the width of my board, so it's pretty easy to know if it's a legal fish. If it is legal, the leader goes through the gills, but I still keep it onboard so the sea lions don't take it away. And then I put it into the BoardFisher crate with the leader tied to the crate because those sea bass are sneaky. After not moving for twenty minutes, they will spaz and try to get out. Pretty fun.

Catching a wave into shore with two 12- to 15-pound fish in the crate is exciting, too.

The legal minimum for sea bass in California water is 28 inches, and that just happens to be the width of Wingnut's 11' Wingnut Model. If the fish goes rail to rail, you won't go to jail. Photo courtesy of Robert "Wingnut" Weaver

With so many paddleboarders and surfers on the water these days, knowing proper etiquette and how to avoid running into other people is essential, even in Waikiki's Battle of the Paddle. Pat Huber

CHAPTER 6

SURF ETIQUETTE

HOW TO

KEEP THE PEACE AND NOT GET PUMMELED BY THE LOCALS

Around 2007 the Association of Surfing Lawyers placed a SURFER'S CODE sign at the top of the stairs at First Point Malibu, overlooking a chaotic surf spot where the well-established rules of surfing etiquette are routinely, flagrantly stampeded when the surf is up and the break is crowded.

The sign and those well-intentioned rules were ignored by just about everyone but the City of Malibu, which demanded that the sign be taken down because this group of lawyers didn't get a legal permit to install it.

Taking down an etiquette sign in Malibu is on par with removing all the traffic lights and signs along the Pacific Coast Highway, or playing football or hockey without rules or referees: Chaos reigns, and chaos can be harmful to children and other living things.

IN THE SURFING WORLD, out in the ocean, there are rules and laws both written and unwritten, spoken and often shouted with great vengeance and furious anger, over how surfers in the surf zone should behave themselves. Now that stand up paddlers are routinely surfing into waves, these same rules of etiquette apply to them.

The rules are pretty simple and practical, really, but at places like First Point Malibu, and any popular surf break in this crowded world, the rules are broken every couple of minutes.

Surf etiquette rules appear on signs at other breaks, and they are also learned verbally and even physically, as experienced surfers will regularly correct with harsh words and sometimes fisticuffs those inexperienced surfers who transgress the written and unwritten laws.

The rules of the ocean really aren't that difficult. Essentially, stay out of the way of other surfers. If you are paddling out through the break and another surfer is on the wave, it is the paddler's responsibility to get out of the way of the surfer on the wave, even if that means steering into the breaking part of the wave and taking it on the head.

Ideally, surfing is a one-man, one-wave situation, but in this crowded world, that ideal is harder and harder to find, as more and more surfers are taking up the sport, and Internet surf forecasts and web cams seem to teletransport crowds directly into the lineup.

Ideally, the surfer taking off closest to the curl of a breaking wave has the right of way on

One surfer, one wave, good etiquette: Lance Hookano catches a nice wave. The paddler in the foreground is backing off and staying out of the way. Photo courtesy Surftech

that wave. Surfers paddling "down the line" are expected to pull back and not take off on the wave but let the surfer who is up and riding continue on, unimpeded and uninterrupted.

But at places like First Point Malibu, it is not uncommon to see as many as seven surfers up and riding the same wave at the same time, a situation that often leads to collisions, injuries, uttered oaths, fights, and even lawsuits and jail time.

The introduction of stand up paddleboards into already crowded surfing lineups has caused more than a few problems, not just around Malibu but all up and down the California coast, to Hawaii and around the world.

Stand up paddling in the surf is a lot of fun, and once people start doing it, they find that just cruising the coast on a board and sightseeing doesn't really compare. Riding waves on a stand

up paddleboard is challenging even to experienced surfers, and for some stand up paddlers, it is their introduction to the surf.

The problem is that many beginning stand up paddlers have not been traditionally indoctrinated into the etiquette and rules of surfing. A beginner on a stand up paddleboard is many times more mobile than a beginning surfer paddling prone on a surfboard. Whereas most beginning surfers will sit timidly off to the side and maybe occasionally get in the way of more experienced surfers, a stand up paddler can approach the surf break from any direction, go blundering into the middle of it all, and cause a lot of trouble on a 12' long, 30" wide, 30-pound board they can't control. Once a board gets out of control, with the rider either standing on it or swimming after it, it can take out surfers on waves, surfers paddling out, even kids playing on the beach.

Or Beverly Hills plastic surgeons. On the morning after Halloween 2009, Dr. Ken Siporin was surfing near his house at Latigo Beach, just north of Malibu. He related the story for this book while sitting at Malibu Kitchen, waiting for the tide to drop:

It was an unreal day and an unexpected head-high south swell hit my home break, a mellow point break where many beginner stand up paddlers were starting to show up regularly.

There were only five people out: two SUPers and two other lay-down locals. I picked off a really fun, shoulder-high wave. I was just beginning to get to the best inside section of the wave, and I was impervious to a couple of muted warning yells.

I looked to my left, and this Barney on a 12' Laird board was yelling at me to get out of the way, while I was just beginning the inside little bowl. His board slammed into my left fibula, smacking me pretty damn hard.

I floated in the water for five minutes, in too much pain and too pissed to respond to his comments. It was such a good day, I didn't want to get out, so after I composed myself, I tried to catch another wave, but I couldn't put any weight on my leg, and I fell after a short ride. I looked down to see blood coming from my wetsuit, so I swam in.

I had X-rays at Malibu Urgent Care, which I paid for, and I was on crutches for a few days but out of the water for six weeks.

I was lucky. The fibula is a twig of a bone in your lower leg. It is the same bone Jack Youngblood broke during a Super Bowl game, but he continued to play.

I ain't no Jack Youngblood.

The territorial battles between surfers and stand up paddlers at San Onofre and Doheny in Orange County became so troublesome that county officials were forced to cordon off sections of each place into areas where stand up paddlers could and could not go.

In the *Orange County Register* for June 1, 2010, Brittany Levine detailed the problem under the headline "Beach Restrictions Ruffle Stand Up Paddlers":

It all started in 2008 when the U.S. Coast Guard and the California Department of Boating and Waterways declared stand up paddleboards to be vessels, putting them in the same category as kayaks and wave skis. That definition, adopted last year by state beaches in Orange County, has led to restrictions on where stand up paddlers can be at some beaches and, consequently, to conflicts between traditional surfers and paddleboard surfers.

San Onofre south of San Clemente is one of the most popular beaches in Southern California. In the summer there is a line of surfers in RVs and other vehicles that wait an hour or more to drive down to the sand's edge and ride the easy, gentle waves that break over rocks and sandy beach.

San Onofre is a perfect wave for beginning stand up paddlers to learn their strokes and ride waves, but the influx of *surfers erectus* caused the State of California to issue order 925-96-024, which segregated stand up paddlers from prone surfers:

In accordance with the provisions of Section 4326, California Code of Regulations, the water area extending from the high water mark waterward 1000 feet, along the entire length of beach known as San Onofre Surf Beach, from the northwest boundary of the Military Enlisted Men's Beach extending southeast to the "Dog Patch" surfbreak, is declared a prohibited area to

Some welcoming graffiti for stand up paddlers at San Onofre State Beach, on the San Diego/Orange County line. In 2010 the state passed a law regulating stand up paddlers to the south end of the beach, at a place called Dogpatch. Ben Marcus

all vessels (ref Definition harbors & Navigation Code Sec, 651 and 651.1), except law enforcement, lifeguard, research and commercial fishing vessels, while in the performance of their official duties. The prohibition will continue indefinitely.

While most of the new rules and regulations segregating surfers and stand up paddlers have been in California, Hawaii is also popular with stand up paddlers. Lately there have been conflicts with offshore swimmers at Ala Moana on the south shore of Oahu that also inspired some regulation.

The conflict began in May of 2009, when a surge of stand up paddlers inspired as many as thirty complaints a day from swimmers who felt crowded out. There was at least one report of a swimmer injured from a collision with a paddleboard. The state invested $1,400 to anchor seven buoys outside the swimming zone, which stand up paddlers can enter at any point. The channel is not mandatory, and there were no signs put up by the state on the city-owned beach. Longtime users of Ala Moana Beach Park called the new channel and the lack of signs confusing.

SUP RIVER ETIQUETTE

Stand up paddleboarding is a relatively new thing on the rivers of Montana, according to Josh Kuntz of Pink Cowboy Fitness and Recreation. Montana is a big, empty state with more than enough moving and flat water to satisfy everyone, but he has seen some issues arise involving river etiquette for stand up paddleboarders:

The two issues I see most often are conflicts with fishermen and play-boaters (kayak wave surfers). Montana is home to a ton of fly fishers. So on the rivers, SUPers need to take precautions to not get in the way of lines being cast and also try not to paddle or splash when passing a drift boat or bank fisherman so as to not spook any fish.

The other issue is simple. Wait your turn and try not to crowd any kayakers surfing a wave. Some kayakers feel SUPers are annoying because we wreck frequently on river surf waves.

One other nice courtesy is to not use the boat ramp for loading. Since stand up paddleboards can easily be carried, I try to launch and load off to the side, leaving boat ramps clear for drift boats and rafts to launch.

History of the SUP Etiquette Controversy

Around Malibu, the same surf spot called Privates where Laird Hamilton first began experimenting with tandem boards and custom-made stand up paddleboards also became one of the early flash-points for conflicts between surfers and stand up paddlers—usually over breaches of etiquette.

It was at this little known surf spot where a local surfer hung the "oaron" tag on the masses of stand up paddlers that began to appear around 2004, when stand up paddling came out of the shadows and companies like Surftech, C4 Waterman, Paddle Surf Hawaii, and many others began making production boards for the world.

According to one local resident from Privates:

Most accidents happen when SUPers get cleaned up by a set [of waves], and instead of holding onto their board as surfers do, they hold onto their precious oar [paddle] and let their board fly through the whitewash like a battleship in a tsunami. Oftentimes their leashes break because the leashes can't stand the force of the wave with the mass of the board (and some idiots don't even wear leashes because they are "watermen").

That local resident from Privates is a particularly vocal opponent of stand up paddlers, but he is talking about a place where the local surfers have always felt a sense of entitlement. This place is a bastion of old-school surfing "localism," which is a tradition that has been diluted by Internet surf forecasts and web cams, but also the increasing severity of criminal punishment for fighting and intimidation.

Privates is a place where outsiders on normal surfboards are not given a whole lot of space or respect, so to have stand up paddlers coming in from all over in groups of five, ten, or twenty—well, that just would never fly at this stretch of beach.

There have been incidents that justify some of the ill will expressed by the locals, and others who regularly surf at this area west of Malibu, which is a string of a half-dozen surf spots.

One of the worst incidents happened between a Malibu surfer with the most-excellent surfer name of Patrick Stoker, who had a run-in (run-over?) with an unidentified, inexperienced, injurious, and not entirely truthful stand up paddler. While this story and others in this chapter take place near Malibu, they serve as cautionary tales for any surf break anywhere in the world where traditional surfers and stand up paddlers share the water. As the first edition of this book was being written, a well-known surfer/lifeguard from the north shore of Oahu named Kolohe Blomfield was struck and injured by a stand up paddler at Chun's Reef. And there were reports from Hookipa on Maui and the Big Island of stand up paddlers just not getting along with surfers and other water people. Hopefully, beginners reading this chapter will avoid adding to the turmoil.

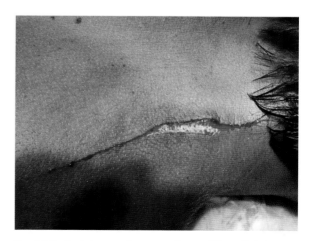

Patrick Stoker's injury after a stand up paddler collided with him. Photo courtesy of Patrick Stoker

This is how Patrick Stoker described his incident at Privates:

I had a very unfortunate run-in with an inexperienced stand up paddler in 2010. I was out in the lineup for about five minutes. A few other locals were out along with a couple SUP boarders that I did not recognize. I caught one wave and was paddling back out when I saw a SUPer paddling into a wave. I had a bad feeling about it because he did not look very comfortable while on the wave. I started to paddle over to the left to try and go around the wave, but he just kept coming right at me. He was not looking at the wave in front of him or looking out for other surfers.

I was scraping at the wave, trying to get out of the way, away from this 40-something guy with a 12-foot, 65-pound log and a lame paddle. I dove down with my board, deeper than I ever had before, and breached out the backside. As I came up, BANG, this huge board slammed me right on the back of the head, slicing my thick-chained Saint Christopher necklace off my neck, and also slicing my neck.

I am telling you about the Saint Christopher necklace because I believe that it took a lot of the blow, and without it—my neck would have been dreadfully worse!!! But anyway, the guy apologized to me in the water. I asked him if it was bleeding or if the back of my neck looked alright.

He said, "No, it's not bleeding. I am really sorry, man."

I replied, "What the [bleep] are you doing? It's people like you that ruin surfing!" I was absolutely livid. He very quietly and quickly paddled away, back toward the Beach Cafe restaurant.

My buddy Russell paddled over and said, "You almost got your head sliced off!"

I angrily replied, "I did, man. He just slammed me. Does it look alright?"

Russell said, "You gotta go in, man, that doesn't look good. You're going to need stitches!"

My [anger] skyrocketed. He lied to me, telling me that everything was okay, and now he's gone.

I paddled in, and a few people came to check it out. I ran down the beach to try to find him, but everyone insisted I go to Urgent Care, and they would find him.

I went to Urgent Care and got thirteen stitches. The guy who hit me showed up and offered to pay for everything—and kept saying how sorry he was.

It was about $800 total for stitches and bandages. I was not allowed to do anything too active, or go in the water for two weeks. It was a horrible experience and one that possibly could have been prevented if a sign was up, or SUPing was banned!

You know, the motto on that Saint Christopher's medal says, "Saint Christopher, Protect Us." Well, it did, and that medal ended up lodged in the wax on my board.

A local doctor is knocked out of commission for several weeks, and a local surfer kid nearly gets his head taken off. These are the kinds of incidents that caused some surfers in the Malibu area to take up pitchforks and lanterns and start an anti–stand up paddler campaign.

Blame Laird?

During the summer of 2010, stickers began appearing around Malibu, proclaiming BLAME LAIRD.

This wasn't entirely fair, kind of like blaming the Wright brothers for all the air accidents that followed their messing about at Kitty Hawk. Because for all the local surfers who wanted to blame Laird for the fleets of stand up paddlers bungling into the lineup, there was a growing population of surfers who were taking up stand up paddling and actually praising Laird for coming up with yet another way to find joy on the water.

Some anti-pranksters would alter the stickers to read BE LAIRD. Toward the end of the summer, Laird Hamilton himself usurped the "Blame Laird"

campaign and began selling shirts and hats with the BLAME LAIRD logo. Since then, the BLAME LAIRD signs and stickers have mostly disappeared, but there still is plenty of ill will between surfers and stand up paddlers around Malibu and in other places around the world.

Anti-SUP sentiment stickered on the tile bathroom at First Point Malibu. Ben Marcus

The Controversy Comes to a Head

The friction between surfers and stand up paddlers began to come to a head in 2009. The local surf club—which was about 50 percent surfers and 50 percent stand up paddlers—got together and made up their own little signs, which they placed at strategic entry points to Privates.

According to Skylar Peak:

After the summer of 2009, SUPing was in full effect, and people from all over were trying it out. Safety in the water became an issue. A few groms got taken out by SUPs, and people got pissed off. I was

part of a group of about one hundred key surfers and SUPers in early 2010 in Malibu who got together because of some ongoing issues in the water and in our community. I felt we were losing some of our community and needed to regain it. Friends were getting into arguments with friends over surfing and SUPing.

It was actually kind of amusing seeing some of the newbie rich folk trying to justify themselves with guys that were born and raised here. In any event, the point was clear: The ocean will always police itself when the waves get big, but the problem is they don't get big around Malibu all too often.

Safety was the number-one reason for the sign. Just trying to get those that don't have a clue to get a clue on what they are doing. After five group meetings

The 10 commandments of surfing Malibu, as illustrated by Ariel Medel. Image courtesy Ben Marcus

at various houses on the Point, and ten or so versions of the sign, the sign is what we came up with. There are two of them installed on the point and one at Paradise Cove. They were installed in June 2010.

The aforementioned local resident who coined the phrase "oaron" expressed the emotion behind the sign:

There is a surf club made up of surfers and stand up paddlers. The few SUPers who understand and respect lineup protocol are tired of getting a bad name because of the influx of never-surfed-before oarons. It's like peace-loving Muslims getting called terrorists because the Jihadists grab the headlines. We need the SUPers in our group to educate the influx of scarecrows on floating sidewalks. Have you ever seen one of them coming at you on a wave? It's truly frightening. They are good enough to row into a wave (so is my dog) but not good enough to control their battleship on a wave. They should NOT be in a crowded lineup.

Sam George lives in a mobile home park close to Privates and regularly paddles up there for health and to catch some waves. He is aware of the squabbles between local surfers and "outsider" stand up paddlers and believes the blame is not fairly laid: "Watch Malibu or Outers on an average day, and you can see guys and gals running over each other constantly," Sam said. "Bailing their boards in the soup, paddling in the way, shoving drop-ins, boards and expletives flying. Stand up paddlers aren't a bigger problem figuratively but literally. So when it comes to good etiquette, what's good for the stand up surfer is good for all surfers."

It was Sam who translated the anti–stand up paddler emotions of people like the local resident into a kinder, gentler sign that lays down the rules to anyone approaching Privates.

When asked to list his Ten Commandments of Stand Up Paddling Etiquette, Sam responded with this:

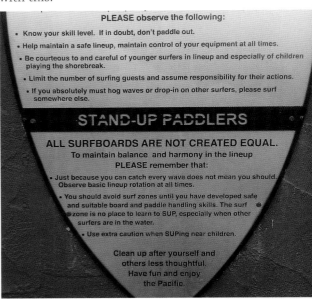

The etiquette sign placed at Privates, with a special message for stand up paddlers. Ben Marcus

1. Don't learn to paddle in the surfline. Until you can paddle and balance comfortably enough to perform a tail spin-around "jibe" turn, stick to flat water.

2. Control your board and your paddle at all times. Meaning: Don't bail off your board while surfing or paddling out.

3. If you absolutely have to bail off your board paddling out, look around and behind you before doing so. If there are other surfers in the way, grab your rails and take the pounding.

4. Avoid crowded, traditionally established lineups.

5. Never paddle out past a crowd and take the first wave that comes along. Respect conventional lineup rotation at all times.

6. Never take two set waves in a row. The ability to catch more waves comes with responsibility to share more waves.

7. After riding a wave, never paddle straight back out through the lineup. Take a wider course and take your time.

8. Read rule #2 again. More specifically, it's imperative to learn how to kick out at the end of the ride. And if you can't kick out, then straighten out. No bailing off the board.

9. Never stand looming over conventional surfers. Give everyone a bit of space. And sit down to chat.

10. Realize that all surfboards are not created equal, and act accordingly.

Most of these rules are just basic surfer etiquette, amplified a bit because of the range of motion that stand up paddlers have, and also the potential damage their boards can inflict.

There are more than ten rules of etiquette, and the local resident added this: "If a kid wants a wave and a [stand up paddler] is on it, then the [SUPer] must kick out. Don't be a kid killer."

And also this: "Wear a leash. Not wearing one is mean and evil. You are not Laird. And even he should wear one."

I agree with all of this. I began stand up paddling in the summer of 2009, when there was a fair bit of hostility around Malibu toward stand up paddlers in the surfing areas.

I learned to paddle in flat water between First Point and my apartment on Pacific Coast Highway, about a mile east of the Malibu Pier. I was eager to get into the surfline at First Point, but it was summer, and it was crowded, and I didn't want to injure anyone or myself. At the time there was talk about stand up paddleboards being banned at Malibu. Los Angeles County had passed a forward-looking rule banning kayaks and bodyboards from First Point, so to me it did not seem out of the question they could tweak the existing rules and do the same to stand up paddleboards.

Since then, I've taken to stand up paddling at First Point every day, and for the most part I've felt welcomed because I strive to be a paragon of stand up paddling etiquette and manners.

I used to feel frustrated at just the thought of surfing Malibu—because the rate of waves there is almost always inconsistent, the crowds are notorious, and I grew up surfing Santa Cruz in the 1970s and had it drilled into my brain and body that taking off in front of another surfer was bad form.

But even with all of that, I feel I've found a comfortable place in the lineup at First Point. I no longer feel any frustration when paddling out there on a stand up paddleboard, because after two years of surfing First Point almost daily, I've learned that I will always get waves, and almost always come out satisfied, even behaving 100 percent with the heart of an aloha gentleman. And I think that you,

Skylar Peak gives four of his youthful wards a free ride at a place where tensions between surfers and stand up paddleboarders are high. Skylar and his friends took off on the wave first and were closest to the curl, so they have the right of way. But this stand up paddleboarder apparently was not schooled in the etiquette of surfing, and he just goes, forcing Skylar to sink the tail of his board and take his students out of harm's way. Courtesy of Skylar Peak

as a new stand up paddler, can find your own comfortable place in your own local lineup if you show consideration toward surfers and other paddlers.

Here are my own Ten Commandments of SUP Etiquette:

1. When first entering a surf zone, you are going to get bad vibes, and you will come to understand a little bit what it might feel like to be racially profiled. Combat that by behaving yourself. When you see a set coming, let people around you know what is coming. On a stand up paddleboard you have thirty seconds of early warning compared with people who are sitting. You can see sets coming, how many waves are in a set, and how the waves are moving. Stand up paddleboards are the perfect thing for the information age. Share that information with people around you. Help them get into better waves. Talk one person into a bomb, and they will love you.

2. Never, ever drop in on another surfer when you are on a stand up paddleboard. Would you steal candy from a baby? Steal an elderly woman's purse? Of course you wouldn't, so never take advantage of the *advantages* of the stand up paddleboard by dropping in on another surfer. Inexcusable. Death penalty.

3. Help beginners, tourists, and others who appear to need it. When you are paddling back out after a wave, keep your eyes peeled for inside waves and the kinds of little waves that experienced surfers don't want, but beginners do. Direct beginners where to sit and how to catch waves. This was one of the original purposes of stand up paddleboards as used by the Waikiki beach boys. It works. Share a wave. Make a friend. Get a date, maybe.

4. Be patient. Wait out the sets. Rewards await you. Even when it's ridiculously packed on a

This sort of wave-sharing etiquette could lead to fisticuffs on the west side of Oahu. But these two wave riders appear to know each other and are okay with it. Shutterstock

big day, if you are patient and there is a set of maybe seven waves coming, the prone paddlers will scramble for the first waves of the sets. You can see what's coming, and they can't, and often the first waves of a set will clear out everyone, and you will be out there facing down one of those beautiful 4- to 5-footers, with no one near you. Then you can just go, without guilt or recriminations. It's so damned fun.

5. Be aware of people inside of you. When stand up paddling at Malibu on a crowded day, I am usually 20 to 50 feet outside the pack, so when a set comes, I can see everything happening in front of me, sometimes thirty guys all turning and paddling at once. And then it's like Terminator targeting: Drop in. Flailer. Sarlo. Andy. Go/Don't Go. Because stand up paddleboards are big and bulky and don't turn on a dime, if someone does something stupid in front of me, we are both in trouble. So I have to be responsible for what I am doing, and what they are doing. Look all the way down the line, anticipate problems, and if there are big problems coming, don't go.

6. Don't be a wave hog. You are on a stand up paddleboard. You have at least thirty seconds of early warning and can get anywhere twice as fast as anyone else. Use the stand up board to go after weird-angled waves and inside waves and other waves that surfers can't see or don't want. Mix it up. Move around. Be mobile. Catch some bomb sets, but also catch some insiders.

7. Let people know you're not a wave hog. If someone is inside of you, paddling and looking back with disgust because there is a stand up paddler about to hog the wave, surprise them by being nice. Yell, "Go!" and pull out of the wave. They'll paddle back out and thank you, and you won't get any stinkeye from them, ever again. Or at least until the next wave.

8. When in doubt, paddle in. Sometimes you will paddle for a wave and miss it, or catch a wave and be "caught inside" a set. Resist the temptation to try to paddle back out through the incoming waves. Stand up paddleboards can be awkward, and anything can happen in a crowd, so it's best to avoid trouble by staying out of it. Turn your board toward shore, ride the whitewater in until the set is over, and then paddle back out. You're going to get plenty waves.

9. If you are inside, and a loose board comes bouncing in, show your command of paddling. Pick the board up, place it at your feet, and paddle it back out to the surfer swimming in. He will like you. Maybe he has a good-looking sibling.

10. If you are surfing a beach break or somewhere with a lot of different breaks and peaks, go to the place where surfers aren't. Stand up paddleboards make just about any wave a challenging wave, so go challenge yourself away from others. You'll still have fun and will avoid the guilt and recriminations.

Does this all sound complicated? Well, it is a little complicated. Throw twenty or thirty wave-starved surfers into any surf break, and life gets complicated. It gets more complicated when a stand up paddler enters the picture, so if you are going to mix it up with the surfers, understand there is some bad voodoo out there—but also understand what you can do to increase the peace.

Mike Sandusky using his SUP as a fitness platform on Lake Ontario.
grantkennedy/surfontario.com

CHAPTER 7

LOSE WEIGHT HOW?

GO SUP NOW!

THE HEALTH and FITNESS BENEFITS OF STAND UP PADDLING

Stand up paddling equipment takes up a bit of space, so do yourself a favor: Go out to the cabana or toolshed or garage or some covered, secure space, and make some space for your tools of the new sensation: That Thigh Master ($29.99) you bought on TV is taking up some square feet, so gather up that, along with the Ab Circle Pro ($199.99), the Abdominizer, Shake Weight ($36.95), Stair Master, and all that other exercise equipment that is sitting around wasting space, and sell it on Craigslist or give it away now, and make way for the exercise machine that actually accomplishes everything Suzanne Somers, Christie Brinkley, Chuck Norris, and Wesley Snipes promise.

And while you're at it, cancel your Weight Watchers subscription and tell your chiropractor you've gone SUPing.

If you get into stand up paddling and do it properly and do it diligently, you will find that the results you get from this one "machine," done for an hour or two outside in the fresh air and

Four-time Battle of the Paddle winner Candice Appleby getting a workout on Lake Tahoe. Photo courtesy of Surftech

sunshine, on the water, away from stinky gyms or your living room floor, will live up to and surpass all the TV pitchmen and women put together.

Listen instead to the likes of Marisa Miller, Laird Hamilton, Chris Chelios, Rick Rubin, and other celebrities and civilians who use stand up as part of their daily regimen to run faster, jump higher, and look maaaahvelous. These people aren't being paid to hype stand up paddling, they are talking about being jazzed at finding an activity that gets results in the most fun way possible—out on the water, in the sun, riding waves, cruising rivers, checking the perimeters of lakes.

Marisa Miller

A surfer girl born to hippie/surfer parents in Santa Cruz, Marisa Miller is someone who is more than a little surprised to find herself living *la dolce vita*

Alexandra Westmore took most of the instructional photos in this book, but she is also good in front of the camera. This is Alex (aka "Aflex") putting her yoga skills to the test on a 12'1" × 30" stand up paddleboard, standing calm in a shaky ocean off the Malibu Pier. Ben Marcus

as a very much in demand swimsuit and fashion model in Southern California.

She is seen around Malibu from time to time, popping into the "Starstrucks" at Cross Creek for a cuppa or surfing out at Third Point. Tiny and ultra-fit, and even by Southern California actress/model standards, she is remarkably healthy and pretty. The winner of the Nordic combined: eyes, teeth, hair, and sleek physique.

Marisa grew up surfing in Santa Cruz, and her father, Mark Bertetta, was a contemporary of Randy French, the founder of Surftech. Her uncle

Four fit folk: Guy Pere, Slater Trout, Candice Appleby, and Mikey Cote photographed at the Turtle Bay Hilton, Oahu, during the 2009 Molokai-2-Oahu paddleboard race. Photo courtesy of Surftech

Kevin Useldinger is a longtime Santa Cruz surfer, and Kevin's daughter Jenny is a super-fit water-woman who is one of the few girls to charge the big surf at Mavericks.

Marisa has nature and nurture on her side, but the camera can be as vicious as getting caught inside at Mavericks, so she lives a clean life and works hard, every day, to stay fit, energetic, and camera-ready.

In April 2010 Marisa posted a notice on her website blog about her project with Surftech on a stand up paddle board line: "The boards I'm design-ing are great for women because a lot of the SUP boards are super heavy and really difficult to carry, so Randy [French] and I worked on making it

super light and built for a woman's body."

True to her blog, Surftech did come out with a Marisa Miller model, and in February 2011 Marisa was on the cover of *Shape* magazine looking great. Inside, she continued to espouse the health ben-efits of SUP:

Anyone who has made her living wearing swim-suits and lingerie has to be familiar with the gym, if only to enhance her superhuman DNA. But Marisa Miller is not your typical gym girl. She prefers a more "fluid" environment, so you'll often find her skimming the waves on a stand-up paddleboard. "It doesn't just tone the big areas like your butt, abs and back: it also targets those tiny, supporting muscles that pull every-thing together."

Heels over head for SUP fitness on Lake Tahoe. Photo courtesy of Surftech

Some bodies are more pulled together than others, and Marisa does have genetics on her side. But staying healthy, energetic, camera-ready, and fabulous still takes work, and she has discovered what more and more are discovering: Stand up paddling is a fun and efficient way to pull yourself together.

Karen Seade

Karen Seade is another SoCal transplant and surfer girl who sometimes swears at stand up paddlers who hog waves at First Point, but swears by stand up as a tool for rehab. Originally from Humble, Texas, Karen earned a bachelor's degree in kinesiology at the University of Texas at Austin.

She continued her education at the University of Puget Sound in Washington, where she received a master's degree in physical therapy. She moved to Los Angeles in 2001 and began surfing around 2006, "after agreeing to face one of my biggest fears: drowning," Karen said in an e-mail response to my questions when I was researching this book. "I was instantly hooked and started to plan my life around catching waves."

Karen has worked at SportsMed at the SportsClub LA for the past four and a half years evaluating and treating patients with various orthopedic injuries and postsurgical conditions. Before that she worked in Beverly Hills as a certified Pilates and Gyrotonic-based physical therapist.

In 2009 Karen obtained a board certification by the American Physical Therapy Association as an orthopedic clinical specialist, ranking her among the top 1 percent of all therapists in the nation.

For fun, Karen goes back and forth between her stand up and an Ian Zamora single-fin noserider. For work, she is very aware of the almost-magic therapeutic and healing effects of stand up paddling.

Asked for her experience with stand up paddling, Karen responded nicely:

Karen Seade catches a wave on her stand up paddleboard.
Photo courtesy Karen Seade

Working as a board-certified orthopedic clinical specialist for the past twelve years of my life, I have explored several exercise forms to most effectively treat patients with all sorts of pain. Pilates, Gyrotonic, and traditional weight training have all been exercises I have incorporated in clinics to treat patients with tendinitis, arthritis, spinal disc bulges and stenosis, balance impairments, chronic fatigue, and pain.

As a water girl, I have personally experienced the amazing benefits of stand up paddling and envision a new dimension in rehabilitation without clinical walls.

Stand up paddling challenges the joints of the entire body, making it especially effective in rehabilitating musculoskeletal problems and preventing injuries. The main movements of rotating side to side while paddling, as well as pulling to propel, strengthens the abdominals and back—otherwise known as the "core"—improving postural stability and alignment. It strengthens the muscles around the shoulder blade and the rotator cuff, optimizing mechanics for throwing, lifting, and reaching overhead. Anyone who has tried stand up paddling can also attest to experiencing "the burn" in their hips and arches of the feet, proving its effectiveness in conditioning the muscles controlling walking, running, jumping, and balance.

Therapeutically, stand up paddling provides an extraordinary means of exercising for people who have suffered from arthritis. It is low impact and is an excellent means of strengthening for extreme cases of limited range of motion and flexibility. The low impact and aerobic benefits also provide for a safe and effective environment for overweight individuals to exercise without developing injuries. For those suffering from chronic fatigue and pain, flatwater paddling improves muscular endurance, circulation and endorphins—all necessary to help break through endless patterns of pain and suffering.

Not to mention a good dose of sunshine will most likely change these chronic sufferers' focus on pain and fatigue to pure joy!

Laird Hamilton

At 6'3" and 215 pounds, Laird Hamilton is about half a foot taller and 50 pounds heavier than your typical pro surfer, who usually run around 5'9" and 165 (Kelly Slater's dimensions exactly). He is a linebacker-sized guy in a world of gymnasts, and that has both helped him and hurt him.

Laird outgrew traditional competition physically and emotionally and had to look for other pursuits, and those pursuits have led to him innovating and setting world records and doing all kinds of crazy @#%@ in a number of disciplines: sailboarding, kitesurfing, tow surfing, hydrofoiling, and now, stand up paddling.

The genesis of Laird's stand up paddling was simply that he wanted to ride tandem with his daughter. But what sold him on stand up was that he could spend a summer paddling around Malibu on a 12' × 24" tandem board, and all that work got his legs ready for the big-wave season on Maui, at Peahi/Jaws, and other places on other South Pacific islands.

Stand up gave Laird something he didn't have before, and gave it to him in a pleasurable way. He is known for running the sandhills at Thornhill Broome with his daughter on his back, a grueling, sweaty, football-style training regime. Stand up paddling was less sweaty, less grueling, and a lot more fun.

In the January phone interview for this book, Laird explained:

Stand up is physically as hard as anything I've ever done because it's so thorough. It's the nonstop aspect of stand up. It's not like sitting and waiting, you're standing and it forces you to be balancing the whole time. Your muscles are firing, your arches, your feet. Every little thing. Your equilibrium. Forcing you to stay stabilized.

So there's two sides to each coin, but somehow it's easier but somehow it's a lot harder.

Laird spent a lot of time doing stand up on a tandem board that was made for prone surfing, and at 12' long and 24" wide would be considered a needle in the modern world of stand up paddling. But the 30" standard was still a few years off, Laird didn't know any better, but that struggle gave him an important side benefit that served him well when he made the transition from summer in Malibu to winter on Maui:

Well, I started noticing after doing it in the summer, coming back to Maui and then go tow, at big, giant Peahi, just how strong my legs were. And how my transition from the summer into giant surf and onto my giant guns was just like no transition. The transition was seamless. It was one of the aspects of why I liked it so much. The way it made me feel and the whole act of doing it, but also just the seamless transition into giant surf.

The Malibu Mob

Laird Hamilton has been living in Malibu every summer going back to 1997, and in that eighteen years he has become one of the leaders of the "Malibu Mob," a group of surfers, celebrities, and civilians who understand the importance of staying fit for good work and good living and who have discovered the benefits of stand up paddling.

The Malibu Mob is "on for young and old," as the Australians would say, as it is includes the likes of septuagenarian fitness fanatic Don Wildman, 40-something hockey player Chris Chelios,

ALL YOU NEED IS SUP: LAIRD'S REWARD

Lose weight how? Go SUP now! From Malibu to Maui and around the world, people are discovering the sometimes miraculous healing and fitness qualities of stand up paddleboarding.

And you know who gets a big kick out of this? Laird.

He has taken a lot of lip from people—sometimes to his face, a lot behind his back—for being one of the pioneers of stand up paddling. But for all the "Blame Laird" stickers and invective on the Internet, Laird says his best reward comes from the effect of stand up paddling.

In the interview for this book:

The bottom line is I couldn't get enough grief, compared to the joy. Just seeing a lot of guys . . . their rotator cuffs were screwed or their neck's jacked and they can't paddle anymore. They surfed for forty years, and they don't surf anymore because they can't even paddle.

And now they are like little kids again with these big giant smiles. And I'm like, You know what? That's what this is for. You can have all these other things happening, and people can say all the stuff they want, but that alone: the joy that it brought some old-timers who had dedicated their life to surfing but couldn't do it anymore because maybe they did it too much. They're back out again doing it.

You know what? That right there, that's all I need.

Crucify me. I don't even care. It's for them. That's who it's for. It's for all these people that deserve to enjoy the ocean.

musicians Flea and Anthony Kiedis from the Red Hot Chili Peppers, tennis star John McEnroe, and actors John C. McGinley, John Cusack, and Tony Danza. These are the familiar faces among a crew of a couple dozen Southern Californians who take to the waters around Malibu to experience the most supreme pleasure of stand up paddling, and use their time on the water to stay fit and ready to bounce around on stage, check defenders half their age, and look good on camera.

Rick Rubin's Transformation

In 2010, record producer Rick Rubin made headlines not only for producing Kid Rock's latest album but also for his remarkable physical transformation, losing 130 pounds. According to a profile in *GQ* magazine: "Rubin dropped the weight with a fish-and-protein-shake diet and by working out six days a week with big-wave legend Laird Hamilton."

Poking around online, it's easy to find photos of Rubin stand up paddling with Flea and other members of the Malibu Mob, and according to Laird, stand up paddling played an important part in Rubin's transformation from bearded, Buddha figure to bearded, lean, Kwai Chang Caine.

Chris Chelios

According to Wikipedia, when Chris Chelios was called up from the Chicago Wolves to play for the Atlanta Thrashers during the 2009–2010 NHL season, he became the oldest active player in the NHL, the second oldest of all time, and played the most games of any active player in the NHL. Born in 1962, Chelios's hockey career began in 1978 with the Moose Jaw Canucks and then covered 1,651 games played over thirty-two seasons. He joined the NHL in the 1983–1984 season and played with the Montreal Canadiens, Chicago

Blackhawks, and Detroit Red Wings then ended with the Atlanta Thrashers at 47 years old, playing against guys less than half his age in one of the most physically demanding sports on Earth.

Swooping around on frozen water with a big stick in his hand is second nature to Chelios, and during the summer he is a frequent figure on the unfrozen waters of Malibu, paddling his board to keep his legs ready for the ice.

In a December 2006 ESPN interview, David Amber declared, "Chelios has no intention of calling it quits yet," and Chelios divulged one of the secrets to his remarkable longevity:

Q: At age 44, what is your offseason training like?

A: *At my age, I can't run the way I used to, so I started mountain biking, surfing and other water sports. I train with guys in California.*

Q: Surfing?

A: *Yeah, but I don't get into the crazy stuff. I don't surf the 30-foot waves. I do get a good workout with Laird Hamilton, a buddy of mine who is the big surfing guru. We work out every day, we do a thing called stand up paddling. It's like sprinting on surf boards and you catch waves as you paddle into waves with an oar. It's the love of my life in the offseason. You're out in the ocean, and it's a great exercise, and it's becoming a fad out there. It's a blast.*

A few years later, in March 2008, Chelios was still using stand up paddling as a part of his workout, according to the story *So Not Done* by E. J. Hradek in *ESPN Magazine*:

One killer workout per summer day isn't enough. After cruising home along the Pacific Coast Highway in his 1972 Chevy K5 Blazer convertible, Chelios grabs his mountain bike and meets a group led by Don

Wildman, the 74-year-old founder of Bally Total Fitness, and surfing legend Laird Hamilton. They push one another for more than 90 minutes in 90-degree heat up and down the dusty hills that rise from the beach toward the Santa Monica Mountains. After lunch, Chelios and one or more of his four kids—sons Dean (18) and Jake (16), daughters Caley (14) and Tara (12)—paddle-surf in the ocean, the day's final workout. "On that board, in the elements, you have to work everything," Dad says.

Apparently stand up paddling and the effect it has on Chelios longevity caught the eye of other hockey players, as there are more than a few off-season hockey players gliding around on liquid water with big sticks, keeping their legs ready for the ice.

According to the story "NHL'er Kyle Quincey Stands Up to Recover" posted on www.okSUP.com:

The native of Kitchener, Ont., was first introduced to the sport in 2007 by Chris Chelios while a member of the Detroit Red Wings. Three years later and he's a partner in Boardworks Canada, a company that distributes paddle boards across the country. Kyle trades in his stick for a paddle and his C4 SUP in the summer.

"The first thing that attracted me is the fun factor—the health benefits are just a bonus," said the 25-year-old, who used paddle boarding as a way to rehab from a herniated disc in 2009. "Everything happens for a reason—the business side literally fell in my lap. Looking forward this can be very good for when I retire, but right now it's fun and it's a passion I have."

Avalanche teammates Scott Hannan, John-Michael Liles and Ryan O'Reilly are all proud owners of paddle boards and Quincey says he knows upwards of 30 National Hockey League players who use the

sport for both recreation and as an off-season training device.

"There's just nothing quite like going for a nice paddle on the lake in the morning, finding a nice quiet area to do some sit-ups and squats on it," said Quincey, whose partners include childhood friend John Kuyper and clothing designers Chip and Pepper Foster. "The balance factor is amazing. I'd go out for a mile or two, paddle and I could really feel it in my core, shoulders and back after just an hour."

Suzie Cooney

Suzie Cooney is the owner of Suzie Trains Maui in Paia, only a few miles from Peahi and Hookipa and Spreckelsville, which makes it ground zero for the Maui side of the stand up paddling revolution. At one time a professional motocross racer from Sacramento and the Bay Area, Suzie competed for two years, starting on an RM80 Suzuki, then moving to the 125 cc class. "I was young and unbreakable," Suzie said in an e-mail.

Active in windsurfing, surfing, motocross, mountain biking, skiing, snowboarding, golf, and tennis, Suzie moved to Maui in 1999, "to take two

Suzie Cooney stoking her Naish 9'0" Mana into a winter bomb at Kanaha, on the north shore of Maui. Courtesy of Suzie Cooney

Suzie Cooney working out on the beach and getting ready to hit the water. Courtesy of Naish

years off of a very stressful career/life on the mainland. I came to windsurf my brains out and better my surf skills."

She began fitness training in 2001, "when it was time to get refocused and with my background and love of people, it was a great match. And I could do it outdoors on the beach if I chose."

Around 2006 Suzie first saw stand up paddling on Maui at Hookipa, "a famous surf spot which never allows SUP unless you're Laird, Dave Kalama, Loch Eggers, or a few others. People have been paddling here though for at least six years."

Suzie first tried SUP on a Starboard 10'5". When asked to comment on her experience, Suzie e-mailed:

To me the benefits for my body and the ease in which you can literally step into the face of wave is mind-blowing to me. Yes indeed, I love it all. The downwind racing is my favorite where we get pushed down big open swells here on Maui's North Shore with deep troughs, huge swells, and rides that are literally half the length of a football field.

The most recent huge day—December 2, 2010—we had wind gusts to 50 mph and 8- to 10-foot faces. Sticking a ride down a breaking wave on a 14' rocket, now that revs my engine!

Naish took Suzie onto their team in June 2010: "As a fitness specialist and professional team SUP rider for Naish, I've seen it transform bodies in a very short time—including mine."

Suzie has also personally experienced the rehab powers of stand up paddling. In April 2009 she came in from a four-hour SUP session and was looking forward to a photo shoot in a week, but by the end of that day she was in the hospital with two broken legs:

I wish I could say I was on my 250 cc and missed a jump, but it was lame. I simply missed the bottom two stairs at my home and broke my legs. Instead of doing that photo shoot, I ended up in a wheelchair with two busted legs: left distal fibula, left tib/fib, and right ankle. I was more mad than anything but grateful I didn't bust my face or anything else. Devastated was one word, but not knowing when I'd walk again was another.

Suzie showed some grit, continuing training students while working from a wheelchair, and she did that determined to get back on her feet as soon as possible, and knowing that her stand up paddleboard would get her there fast:

My background is sports orthopedics, and I knew that this platform of training would soon rebuild all the fine stabilizing muscles around my bad ankles and legs. It was also great mental aqua therapy besides my own physical therapy.

My rehab was long and painful. Compression stockings at night, very sexy! Because my profession is so physical it still talks to me. My strength is at about 90 percent, and SUP was a HUGE part of my rehab. As soon as I was able to fully bear weight, in July 2009, I got on that board at least four or five times a week. That's when I knew I needed to tell the world,

and that's what I did: 430 women from around the world responded, and so did 30 sponsors. My event at the Four Seasons Hotel on Maui was the first, large SUP event in the world. The event heard round the world: "STAND UP" for Women's Health and Fitness.

Back on her own two feet, Suzie was an even stronger believer in the strengthening and therapeutic powers of stand up paddleboards:

I introduce SUP to everyone in my practice, and the day they come to me, I put a paddle in their hand. Boards are stacked in the studio to inspire and promise how this will be the best form of cross-training they will ever experience. I train all ages, all types of folks, pros and non-pros, and they will all agree that all you need—well, almost—is SUP. I agree. My studio is INDO Boards, INDO Gigantes, Vew Do Boards, free weights, medicine balls, body bars, pull up bar, plyometric boxes, resistance bands, great music, and a SUP board without fins. Also, my gym is the ocean.

My training style is functional first. I educate that SUP creates your "base" as the machine would in the gym, your levers (arms to paddle) are the extensions to stress the machine or, better yet, your core. As you may know, the core is everything excluding the extremities. I train people to SUP better on and off the water. When my clients are not with me, they are surfing, SUPing, and doing other sports. They all agree that SUP, even over surfing, has strengthened their body in the shortest amount of time. It enhances their surfing and their entire life.

Gina Bradley

Gina Bradley is the founder of Paddle Diva, a SUP school for women-only based in the Hamptons out on the east end of Long Island, New York. A former fitness instructor, windsurfing teacher, and PADI-certified scuba instructor, Bradley tried SUP for the first time in 2006 and pretty quickly discovered the physical and spiritual benefits of stand up paddling. In the summer of 2009, she started informally giving lessons to her friends—so she didn't have to paddle alone all the time—offering beginning SUP instruction and paddling tours of the bays and surrounding waterways, ocean awareness courses, "beach boy surfing" on a SUP, and children's lessons.

She was in the right place doing the right thing at the right time, and her classes are popular with Hamptons' locals and the many visitors who flood into town in the summer.

Bradley's time on the water and experience with women and beginners also led to the development of the DIVA board: a women's stand up paddleboard, custom built by Nature Shapes, that allows women to pick their own colors and size—ranging from 10' to 12'. The DIVA board is very easy to maneuver in the water and most importantly is lightweight, so women can carry the boards easily.

Bradley now shares her passion for stand up paddling with an ever-growing collection of Hamptons' locals, celebrities, and visitors who want to look good, feel good, and have fun getting there. Having a keen eye for business and marketing while also having athletic prowess makes Bradley a leader in the industry. Rather than trying to become a competitive athlete in the sport, she has decided to build her name and reputation on serving women in the sport, which is a very new market segment for many traditional manufacturers and retailers.

When contacted for this book, Gina shared her experiences of learning how to stand up paddle and what led her to start Paddle Diva:

The inspiration for me to start the business came while I was paddling with two of my girlfriends, headed into the mouth of Three Mile Harbor, one of the East End of Long Island's most beautiful and protected

Gina Bradley and three students out for a group SUP in Three Mile Harbor, East Hampton, New York. From left to right: Gina Bradley, Jennifer Ford, Sydney Jones, and Meg Salem.
Photo courtesy Gina Bradley

bays. I announced I was going to start a business teaching this amazing sport to women, and the three of us brainstormed for the rest of our workout. That evening at dinner, my husband came up with the name. The inspiration came from something very silly: I used to call a great parking spot "diva parking" and claimed that I was a parking diva, as I always managed to park as close to wherever I was going as possible. Paddle Diva was born in an evening as I raced home, registered the URL, and made my first run of business cards and car magnets through one of the many printing websites. Overnight I went from a mother of two and athletic housewife to a business owner.

Paddle Diva started out with a small quiver of boards and paddles in the summer of 2009. If I needed more, I would borrow them from girlfriends who were so supportive of my idea and wanted to see me succeed. That was a great way to start my business: very organic with slow growth.

The following summer in June 2010, I added about four more boards to our quiver. Two included my own custom DIVA board, a 10'6" handmade fiberglass

board that was light and designed with women's needs in mind: lightweight, stable, no chine rails, flatter bottom, but still had some curve for maneuverability. Another great feature about DIVA boards was that women could pick their own colors and even graphic.

We also added two 10'6" Core Four boards that I was able to obtain at a reasonable cost. So by the beginning of that summer I had about 8 boards. I became a Kialoa Paddle dealer in late spring, so I was able to sell paddles to my clients and have great paddles available for my clients. By the end of the summer, Paddle Diva had taken off to such an extent that I ended up with over fifteen boards in my quiver and

Three on the tree in Puerto Rico in January 2010. From left to right: Jennifer Ford of Bent on Learning, Jessica Bellofatto of KamaDeva Yoga, and Gina Bradley of Paddle Diva, all devotees of the sport of SUP who incorporate it into workouts to stay in great shape. Photo courtesy of Gina Bradley

twenty paddles. I was a JP board dealer and was able to populate my quiver with more lightweight gear that women seemed to respond well to using on the water.

Paddling on the East End of Long Island is amazing. There are so many bays and waterways that my business went from slow to 100 percent go! in about two weeks. The interest women had for learning how to paddle and the willingness to pay for the lessons and group tours only slowed down with the arrival of the cold winds of winter. Paddle Diva was able to still capture plenty of business through the fall when we introduced our Adventure Paddle Tours that were longer and slightly challenging distance paddles. And our winter retreats to locations in Rincon, Puerto Rico are also very popular.

Paddling for women is different than for men. Two of the first things I learned were that women need much smaller boards and the perfect paddle length. In the beginning women (me included) used what was in the garage—husbands' or boyfriends' gear. So the boards were too heavy and unwieldy and the paddles too long, and sometimes the blades were too wide. Having a lightweight paddle also makes a huge difference for paddling. As soon as I got my skills honed and got tired of lugging our 11' Jimmy Lewis, I started to gravitate towards my husband's SUP surf boards, as they were shorter—between 10' and 10'6". They were so easy to load on the truck and even easier to maneuver in the water.

I believe that when trained properly women can be on much shorter, lighter boards, and because of those two factors, they will get out on the water more frequently! One of my biggest reasons for not SUPing in the early years was the fact that I could not load onto my truck any of the boards in our quiver: We had a Jimmy Lewis 12' distance board, an 11' all arounder, and one of the 10'8" tri-fin surf models. At first I was terrified to get on the 10'8" because I was told it was for "surfing" and that seemed so daunting. But that particular board became my board of choice for everything from group distance cruising to sup'ing small waves.

One thing we are finding is that SUP boards are getting smaller and lighter for both men and women. There is definitely a need to have a board for cruising and one for surfing (should you choose to do both). One of my absolute up and coming favorite boards (as I am

still trying to master it while spending the holidays at our place in Rincon, PR) is the small 9'3" wave boards made by JP. Finding balance and coordination are important with the smaller boards on the ocean and in waves, as is having a perfectly tuned paddle blade size as well as shaft size. I am finding that for riding waves, I need a narrower blade as I need less energy to pull quick short strokes through the waves and a shorter shaft than I typically use for cruising. Using a smaller board is also my board of choice for lessons and shorter group tours as I work my core even harder keeping balanced and tracking the board straight.

A critical component to having a successful paddle session is the size or the length of the paddle. Generally speaking for flatwater cruising paddles should be about 10 inches over your head. For SUP surfing you want about 2 inches off your normal length. When I size up my clients I usually have them hold the paddle and reach their hand up and if with a straight arm they can wrap their hands around the blade, it is the right size. As women get more and more experienced, they tend to be pickier about paddle length and can tell if they have a paddle that is the wrong size.

SUP is still in its infancy on the East Coast. There are so many who have yet to experience what I have been so lucky to indulge in every day. Even in the winter, I still suit up in my Kokatat drysuit and head out. For me SUPing has become my livelihood, but it has also become a way of life. We are surrounded by water on the East End of Long Island, and I live about five minutes away from the bay and only ten from the ocean. I paddle every day as long as there is water and not ice! Winters are a challenge so in lieu of hitting an iceberg, we pack up and spend as much of the winter time in Puerto Rico as possible. When I step out on the board and start heading out to sea and slosh over the waves, everything and anything that stressed me out dissipates. It's just me and the board and the water, all in unison, all working together to move forward.

Kate Nelson (left) and Michelle Caranto (right) practice some cautious SUP yoga in the canals of Venice, California. Careful, because the water quality through there is a little sketchy.

Photo courtesy Pau Hana/Jake Albrecht

CHAPTER 8

BEND IT LIKE DASHAMA

SUP YOGA
FOR THE WORLD

The practice and art of yoga has been traced as far back as 3000 BC to India and has expanded in recent years to all regions of the globe from the White House to Hollywood, waterfalls to football stadiums. With over thirty million people in America practicing regularly, the health-enhancing benefits of yoga have been studied, researched, and confirmed now by the Harvard College of Science and many other trusted authorities worldwide.

On the other hand, stand up paddling is no older than AD 1900—some say originating in Australia, some say Hawaii. Yoga and stand up paddling are both physical, mental, and spiritual disciplines that each have a variety of schools: Yoga has Anusara, Ashtanga, Bikram, Hatha, Hot Yoga, Iyengar, Pranashama, and Vinyasa, while stand up paddling has wave-riding, racing, downwinders, rivers, touring, and now . . . SUP yoga. Around

2009 the ancient practice of yoga combined with the fresh practice of stand up paddling to form a subgroup of both pursuits: SUP yoga, which is also known as yoga boarding or paddleboard yoga.

Whatever you call it, since around 2009 more and more yogis are discovering how practicing yoga outdoors, on the water on a shaky, vibrating paddleboard, enhances the practice and experience of yoga. SUP yoga takes yogis out of the enclosed, sometimes stinky four walls of indoor yoga studios and places them in the sun and fresh air of the great outdoors. The vibration of a stand up paddleboard on even the most placid waters adds a muscle and balance workout that also offers a more supreme pleasure—adding value to the practice of yoga, even for the most experienced yogis.

There is no reliable metric on the number of stand up paddlers in the world, but take a look out your window at the nearest lake, bay, or beach, and you most likely will see stand up paddlers—solo, or in flocks. They might be fervently paddling—toning their bodies from foot arches to core muscles to frontal lobes—but more and more stand up paddlers are laying down the paddle for a few moments to sit, kneel, stretch, and pose on their boards—practicing yoga asana for healthier bodies and healthier minds.

Dashama Speaks

SUP yoga has become so popular, there is now a magazine dedicated to the practice: *Samata, A Woman's Paddleboard Magazine for the Body–Mind–Soul*. The first issue of *Samata* is a healthy 120 pages of technique, travel, profiles, and articles written by women for women who have taken to the water on stand up paddleboards.

The magazine is chockablock with full-page and spread ads from the major SUP companies that are

Gimme a Y! Gimme an O! Gimme a G! Gimme an A! What's that spell?! Annelise Brosch twists into asana to spell her passion. Photos: Jodi Caplan

Day or night, night or day . . .
Photo: Dashama/Christian de la Iglesias

taking SUP yoga seriously enough to design boards specifically for women, and even more specifically for practicing yoga on the water.

The magazine and the ads feature some spectacular photography of healthy women doing yoga in exotic places, but perhaps the most eye-catching photo shows a yogini named Dashama (DA-sha-ma) on her signature inflatable Starboard Astro SUP yoga board doing a hollow-back extended wheel pose, her back beautifully arched and her left leg and toes straight up in a tribute to the Sanctuary of Truth temple in Pattaya, Thailand.

Flip through *Samata* magazine or plug "SUP yoga" into the Internet and you will find hundreds if not thousands of SUP yoga instructors and schools around the world, from Thailand to Tennessee. It's not possible to interview all of them about their techniques and philosophies, so it was up to Dashama to represent and explain her history as a SUP yoga instructor: when she began, where it has taken her, what she has learned, and where she is going with SUP yoga.

Dashama is in motion constantly—whether it's traveling the world or doing yoga on a stand up

. . . sunrise or sunset, by land or sea or even in the pool. Dashama makes yoga look pretty cool.

Photo: Dashama/Christian de la Iglesias

paddleboard. Through the Internet, she continued the story and detailed how yoga flowed into SUP yoga:

I've been an athlete since age 12, a yogi since even before that. I was born at home and raised in a rural environment. I grew up swimming in rivers, lakes and oceans. Back in 2009, I was the first person to publicize the SUP yoga practice, with videos online. My friend Jesse Cors, who owns several surf shops in Fort Lauderdale, took me out paddle boarding since he felt I'd be a natural at it. My first thought when I stepped out on the paddle board was it looked like a perfect,

water-based yoga mat! I just started doing a full yoga sequence on the board and he filmed me with a waterproof Flip video camera. You can see most of that sequence on YouTube, and after six years it's still the highest-viewed SUP yoga video on YouTube.

From there, I was asked to teach at Waldorf Astoria Resort, in Boca Raton. The members loved it. When the water was too choppy, we did it in their pool. From there, I also taught and practiced it in other locations like Malibu, when I moved to California. I have been traveling the world teaching yoga since 2005 and teaching SUP yoga since 2009.

Dashama with her purpose-built, 10' × 35" Astro Yoga Dashama—the custom-made inflatable platform for SUP yoga. Easily transportable, then stable when inflated, Dashama uses this board to go around the world and do for SUP yoga what Duke Kahanamoku did for surfing.
Photo: Dashama/Margareta Engstrom

Prior to becoming a yoga teacher, Dashama was involved in a serious car accident that damaged her spine, causing scoliosis and the loss of her cervical curvature. Doctors told her there was not much that could be done and suggested chiropractic as a treatment to alleviate pain. Being unwilling to believe there was no hope to regain her alignment, Dashama began to seek solutions and eventually discovered a yoga teacher named Anna Forest, who had been known to heal and regain the alignment of her spine through the practice of yoga.

This gave Dashama hope, and she embarked upon the self-healing journey that took her around the world to learn from healers, teachers, and experts of many yoga and shamanic lineages and disciplines. She also studied Thai massage, Reiki, qi gong, martial arts, dance, and a variety of healing modalities along the journey and began to apply these techniques to herself and to teach them to her students. They were all gaining miraculous results. Dashama's spine was slowly regaining alignment, and pain was becoming a distant memory.

Dashama has found peace of mind and a calling in practicing and sharing yoga and SUP yoga. Her travels, projects, and accomplishments could fill a book, but can be seen in detail at www.dashama.com.

SUP is the Perfect Platform

There is a natural inclination toward yoga and stand up paddleboarding for people who are seeking new and effective ways to feel better and enhance health and happiness while releasing stress to improve the quality of their lives. And many people who love yoga and/or paddleboarding immediately fall in love with SUP yoga. It takes both practices to the next level.

For yogis, the challenge is increased dramatically by being on water. Even with the most calm water conditions, the board has a level of movement that is ever-present during the entire practice. This enhances the experience and increases the need to stabilize, recruiting additional core strength, balance, and focus. The board is your teacher in SUP yoga, as it will always let you know if you are out of alignment. You will simply wobble or fall in the water if you are not in alignment!

Although many people believe at first sight that SUP yoga must be much more difficult and can only be accessible to more advanced practitioners, this is a false perception. There are SUP yoga poses and practices for all levels and abilities. Classes are being taught worldwide to children, athletes, yogis, the elderly, and everyone in between. The most incredible benefit of SUP yoga is the ability to practice yoga while floating on water, with the open sky above, the fresh air, and the vast ocean beneath. It is truly an experience of a lifetime for some people, and for others, it is becoming a regular part of their regimen, as they fit it into their routine cross-training schedule.

Here are a few keys to starting a successful SUP yoga practice of your own.

- Always listen to your body and stay connected to your breath.
- If you are new to SUP yoga, take some instructional classes with a trained professional teacher to learn the proper form and alignment.
- Watch some instructional videos and study written material to gain the best grasp of how to do this practice safely and most effectively.
- Wear sunblock if you will be out on the water during the sunny part of the day.
- Wear a visor if you can, to keep the sun off your face.
- Bring a PFD (personal flotation device) on the board for safety.
- Take a water safety course.
- Use an anchor or leash to tie to a dock to keep from drifting out to sea.
- Drink plenty of water and stay hydrated.
- Go with a friend to make it more fun.
- Rent a board if you don't have one, to learn which styles you like best.
- The board you use will make a big difference. Make sure to get one that is stable and comfortable to practice on—the wider, the more stable. Soft grippy mat is best.

Dashama demonstrates the down dog splits, complementing Bali's Mount Agung, in July 2015. According to Dashama, the photo was "taken at [the] magic hour before sunrise the morning of the full moon—which was setting over the water simultaneously with the rising of the sun." She is riding the new release 2016 Starboard Dashama SUP yoga board in front of Hotel Lombok Sunset. Photo: Starboard/Mick Curley

- Consider an inflatable board—they take up less space and can be taken anywhere.
- Take care of your SUP yoga board and it will last a long time!
- Try seated, supine (lying down), and kneeling postures first, to gain confidence.
- Practice on calm flat water for greatest success.
- Don't be afraid to fall in and get wet! This is one of the best parts of SUP yoga.
- Have fun and keep it light! Don't take life too seriously.
- Focus on the positive and keep gratitude in your heart.
- Be kind to others on the water; it should be a friendly environment.
- Don't be self-critical if you can't do some poses: You will improve with practice!
- Always take some time at the end for quiet relaxation (savasana meditation).

Dashama and the Ten Poses

Dashama demonstrates and describes ten great poses you can try, at various levels, to increase your strength, flexibility, and overall well-being.

Crescent Lunge Pose
(Sanskrit: *Anjaneyasana*)

This is one of my favorite poses because it strengthens your core and legs, stretches your hip extensors, and improves your balance. Start with one foot forward and the other leg extended back, your front knee bent at 90 degrees. Tilt your tailbone down while lengthening the spine and engaging your core. Beginners should start with hands on the board by your front foot or at least one down and one up to stabilize until you have the core control to stay aligned on the board with arms extended above your head. Your back foot can be flipped over with toes pointed out to the side to stabilize your body. Lift your heart and lengthen your spine while reaching up toward the sky. Your *dhristi* (focus) is forward or slightly up. With a slight smile on your face, remember to breathe. Hold the pose for at least five breaths, then switch sides.

Starboard/Roi Bar David

Downward Dog, or Downward-Facing Dog (Sanskrit: *Adho Mukha Svanasana*)

This widely known yoga pose is a great place to start. With all four limbs grounded into the paddleboard, you should feel stable and balanced on all sides. Start on all fours with palms beneath shoulders and knees hip-distance apart. Spread your fingers wide, root down into the palms, and place equal pressure on your fingertips and the base of your hand. Extend your arms straight, wrap your shoulders down your back, and engage the stretch in your core, lats, shoulders, and upper back. Press your chest back toward your legs as you straighten your knees, and root down into the soles of your feet. Relax your neck, allowing the crown of your head to hang toward the yoga board. Take a few breaths in and out through your nose in this balancing, strengthening pose.

Starboard/Roi Bar David

Camel Pose
(Sanskrit: *Ustrasana*)

Camel pose is great for increasing spinal flexibility and core and leg strength. Begin by rooting your knees, shins, and the tops of your feet deeply into the board. If you feel stable, flip your toes under to lift your ankles higher if you don't yet have the deep spinal flexibility. Engage your core and lengthen from the lumbar spine as you shift your hips slightly forward. Lift your heart toward the sky and, if your neck is flexible, release your head back. Otherwise, maintain the integrity of your cervical spine and look forward past the front of the board. Your shoulder blades should draw down and back, remaining in the pose for five to ten breaths. Place your hands on your lower back for support and rise slowly back to the starting position. Repeat three times. Be sure to counterbalance this pose with a restorative forward bend like child's pose.

Starboard/Roi Bar David

Warrior II
(Sanskrit: *Virabhadrasana II*)

All standing poses require strength and balance, but on a floating platform, it becomes an additional challenge. As we move from the lower positions in which we incorporate all four limbs to stabilize us on the board, we are required to recruit a deeper sense of stability that comes from "grounding into the flow." This is where you feel the water and waves and become one with them. Being fluid and strong allows you to balance better.

For this pose, position yourself with right leg forward, knee bent at 90 degrees, and left leg back and straight. Feet are perpendicular—your front toes point forward and your heel lines up with back arch. Your tailbone is tilted down and your spine is long. Engage your core, spread your arms wide apart, lift the crown of your head, and focus your gaze forward past the front middle finger. Sink the hips low as you track your right knee forward. Hold for five to ten breaths and repeat on the other side.

Splits, or Monkey Pose
(Sanskrit: *Hanumanasana*)

Yogic splits are great for opening your hamstrings, inner thighs, and hip extensors. If you have not been able to do splits so far, you will want to focus on stretching those areas of your body first before going into this intermediate pose. On the paddleboard, you may wish to stabilize yourself with hands positioned on the board and connect to the waves beneath you. If you feel stable, you may increase the challenge by reaching your hands toward the sky. Lengthen your spine and keep your hips as square to the front of the board as possible to maintain a balanced, even stretch. Hold for five to ten breaths and repeat on the other side.

Starboard/Roi Bar David

Starboard/Roi Bar David

Scorpion Pose
(Sanskrit: *Vrschikasana*)

This is one of the most advanced inversions in yoga and requires great balance, core strength, stabilization, spinal flexibility, and focus. You can build up to this pose by practicing dolphin (downward-facing dog on your forearms) or other forearm balances. Starting on your hands and knees, place both of your forearms flat on the board with elbows and wrists shoulder-distance apart. You should be positioned directly in the center of the board. Extend your knees straight so you are in a forearm version of downward-facing dog. From there, walk your feet toward your face while rooting into your elbows and shoulders with your core engaged. You may find it easier to interlace your fingers to feel even more rooted. From there, lift one leg at a time or, if you can, both of them together, bend your knees, and point your toes toward your head. Remember to breathe as you lift your head, extending through your upper back and heart. To come down, lower one leg at a time and rest in child's pose for a counterbalance to soften the muscles of the spine.

Starboard/Roi Bar David

Side Plank
(Sanskrit: *Vasisthasana*)

This pose will challenge your core strength and balance. For beginners, start with the bottom knee down or the top leg bent to stabilize yourself on the board. Rooting down through your right palm and lifting your hips toward the sky, engage your oblique strength and lengthen the left side of the body as you make a rainbow arch with your body. Feet are either positioned heel to toes or, for a more advanced option, can be stacked. Your upper arm can be extended straight up over your head or on your left hip. Engage your lats and rely on your shoulder strength while holding for five to ten breaths. Repeat on the other side.

Starboard/Roi Bar David

Chin Stand Scorpion
(Sanskrit: *Shalabhasana Vrschikasana*)

This is another advanced pose that challenges balance, flexibility, focus, and strength. Start in chatarunga, which is like plank position with elbows bent 90 degrees and squeezed into your side. From there, shift your weight forward and place your chin down on the board; gaze forward down the tip of your nose. Raise one leg at a time, grounding into your palms and engaging your core. Then lift both legs toward the sky. The power in this pose comes from maintaining your focus. Squeeze your elbows into your side ribs, lengthen your spine, and bend your knees, allowing your toes to fall toward the crown of your head. Hold for a few breaths then slowly lower one leg at a time back to chatarunga.

Starboard/Roi Bar David

Hollow Back Wheel
(Hollow Back *Chakrasana*)

This is an advanced yoga pose that requires deep shoulder and spinal flexibility, stabilization, and core and leg strength. If you are not ready for this yet, you can try traditional wheel or bridge pose to build up to it. To get into this pose, start in full wheel (*chakrasana*) then lower onto the elbows one at a time so the forearms are on the board and palms come together into a prayer position. To alleviate some pressure and gain length in the lower back, lift your heels to tilt the tailbone down and create space in the lower back. Another option is to connect with the flow of the water beneath you. In this challenging pose, you will be upside down, so you must stabilize yourself by keeping your core engaged and legs strong. Your shoulder blades should wrap around your back, with your heart lifting toward the sky, neck relaxed, and crown of the head hanging free. Your gaze can be down toward your hands or the bottom of the yoga board. Take a few breaths. To come out of this pose, flip the palms one at a time to face down. Straighten your elbows and press back to full wheel then lower from there as you would normally. Be sure to counter the pose by squeezing your knees into your chest.

Starboard/Roi Bar David

Full Lotus Seated Meditation

This asana, or yoga pose, is best if you have very open hips. If your hips are not ready for this, simply sit in a comfortable seated position with your legs crossed. With a straight spine, and the crown of your head lifting toward the sky, close your eyes and focus your awareness on your breath. Touch your index and thumb together in a mudra to keep the energy circulating within yourself. Connect with your breath and the stillness within your mind, while feeling the breeze on your skin, the water moving gently beneath you, and the sunshine on your body. Take a few moments at the end of your practice for gratitude and appreciation for all of the blessings in your life. *Namaste*. (The light in me bows to and honors the light within you.)

Starboard/Roi Bar David

Where to Go from Here?

As the global yoga ambassador for Starboard International, Dashama has attracted an incredible SUP yoga ambassador team with leaders in Germany, Brazil, Holland, the United States, Costa Rica, Mexico, and many other countries worldwide. The team is expanding and welcoming new members who wish to spread the love of SUP yoga on waters in their region and lead retreats and SUP yoga trainings and events around the globe.

For more information about purchasing a SUP yoga board; to register for a SUP yoga retreat, event, or training; or to apply to join the ambassador team, visit www.sup-yoga.com. For any questions, comments, to sponsor an event, or for , media inquiries, e-mail contact@pranashama.com. For more information about Dashama, visit www.dashama.com.

At the end of the day, yoga is all about health and peace of mind. Photo: Dashama/Roi bar David.

Competitors and support crews gather on the beach at Kaluakoi on the west end of Molokai before the start of the 2014 Molokai 2 Oahu Paddleboard World Championships. The pre-race pule (prayer) connects the paddlers as the Ka'iwi channel awaits.

Photo: Johann / 808photo.me

CHAPTER 9

BUILT FOR SPEED

COMPETITIVE SUP

FROM WAVES TO WATERFALLS

Snowboarding goes back as far as the Snurfer in the 1960s, but the sport really began to bubble in the second half of the 1970s, then made the Olympics about twenty years later, in 1998.

Stand up paddleboarding goes back as far as

the 1930s, but the sport began to evolve from the second half of the 1990s to the first half of the first decade of the twenty-first century. Stand up paddling is really no more than twenty years old, and you have to wonder when competitive SUP

The starting line for the Standup World Series Air Elite event at Maceio, Alagoas, Brazil in 2014—won by Connor Baxter. Brazil is an ocean- and water-sports-crazed country, and Brazilians have taken to SUP like cariocas take to feijoada. Photo: Waterman League/Matty Schweitzer

Zane Kekoa Schweitzer is 21 years old and heir to the family of watermen and women who brought the sailboard into the world. Living on Maui, Zane does it all but he has been competing at SUP since 2009 and pushing himself every year to stay on top. Here, Zane is taking a speed run on a Starboard 2014 12'6" Sprint at Baby Beach, Sprecklesville, Maui.

Zane says: "It's amazing to see how fast the sport of SUP has grown globally. Everywhere I travel lately people know about SUP or are paddling! I see so much opportunity in the sport of SUP because it is so diverse, being able to SUP in any body of water in the world, not just coastal locations like surfing. I also know that anybody can learn in minutes and take it on—I have been teaching SUP and putting on clinics for the sport for eight years!! I see SUP going to the Olympics and being a lifestyle and action sport."

Photo courtesy Starboard

Two views of action from the Camp David SUP World Cup, a Stand Up World Series event held in the center of Hamburg in 2013. In the first shot we see Leonard Nika (IT) leading in front of Casper Steinfath (DK), Beau O'Brien (AUS), Paul Jackson (AUS), and Gaetan Sene (FR). In the second shot we see racers coming around the bend again at the Germany stop on the World Series, destined to be one of the biggest stops on the series. Photos courtesy Waterman League/Sebastien Schoffel

Credit: Reid Inouye

Credit: Waterman League

From any random lake, anywhere (this one is Race of the Lake of the Sky in South Lake Tahoe), to the exotically unique shadow of the Guggenheim Museum in Bilbao, Spain, SUP racing is the go for those in the know: social, adrenalized, healthy, and good fun— whether it's a casual race or going for a world title.

racing will follow snowboarding as a thoroughly modern discipline with the momentum to become an Olympic sport.

Stand up paddling is already extremely competitive, accelerating from a handful of races to multitudes in just over ten years. According to a post on www.supracer.com: "There were a lot of SUP races this year [2014]. We had over 400 listings on the Rogue Race Calendar. We sent 137 race results to the Results by Riviera archive. You couldn't go a week without your Facebook feed being flooded with photos of SUP races here, there and everywhere."

SUP racing isn't much more than ten or eleven years old, according to Ron House, who was one of the original SUP shapers. He remembers competitions as early as 2004:

The first stand up race I was aware of was in about 2003 or 2004. A few of us, including Jimmy Terrell and Kyle Mochizuki, contacted Russ Coble and Eric Smith at the Dana Point Outrigger Club about inclusion in their Outrigger-Prone Paddle races at Dana Point Harbor. Their response was that if we could get four to five guys we could have a stand up class at their event. We ended up with about eight or nine entries and the race was held. I don't remember who won, as Terrell, easily the fastest, went off course, taking Mochizuki with him. That having been done, there were a few more races, one every few months and then with increasing frequency up to the first Battle of the Paddle, which changed everything.

The Battle of the Paddle

In the 2014 *SUP the Mag Gear Guide*, a number of pioneering stand up paddlers point not to materials or construction, but to an event as a turning point in the evolution of stand up paddling: the Battle of the Paddle.

Sparky Longley is the owner of Rainbow Sandals and one of the founders of the Battle:

The Battle of the Paddle has brought more attention to the competitive side of SUP, and competition is always the driving force within any sport. The race through the surf has created a uniquely dynamic and original format that has been equally exciting, fun and competitive for the racers and spectators alike. Not only has this event helped spread the joy of SUP far and wide but it has also been a driving force within the industry in the innovation and development of specialized racing equipment including boards, paddles and accessories.

An October 2014 *Sports Illustrated* story on the 2014 Battle of the Paddle looked back to its origins, and how Ron House begat Sparky Longley, and Sparky and Gerry begat the Battle of the Paddle:

Yet eight years ago, there were no drums, no spectators, no racers. Eight years ago, Sparky, the owner of Rainbow Sandals—the Battle's name sponsor—had never even heard of this offshoot of surfing with ancient Polynesian roots.

Few others had. Big wave surfers Laird Hamilton and Dave Kalama only started to rekindle interest in the sport starting in the early 2000s.

Sparky got his first glimpse one afternoon in 2006 when he watched master surfboard shaper, Ron House, glide along wave after wave at Capistrano Beach. "He was catching everything and seemed like he was having a blast even though the waves were horrible and about two inches high," Sparky recalls.

Ron's secret?

He was standing—the whole time.

Instead of paddling with his arms then popping up to his feet once he caught the wave, Ron propelled himself using a six-foot single-bladed paddle.

"What's that?" Sparky asked his longtime friend and surfing legend, Gerry Lopez, who was sitting near him at Phillip (Flippy) Hoffman's beach front house.

The start/finish line for the 2014 Battle of the Paddle at Salt Creek. The rascal organizers threw a bit of surf at the beginning and end, to see how the racers would handle their speed-built boards. Kind of like adding whoop-de-doos at the start and finish of a Formula One race, or a steeplechase jump at the start of the Kentucky Derby. The results can be seen on YouTube. Photo: Reid Inouye

"That's SUP," said Lopez, who had seen Hamilton and Kalama stand up paddleboarding on a trip he took with them to the Mentawai Islands in Indonesia.

"I didn't care what the name was," Sparky says. "I just told Gerry we had to learn to do that."

They did. After a lesson from Ron, Sparky and Gerry found themselves spending more time on their SUPs than on their regular surfboards and soon dreamt up the idea of a contest that "celebrated the love of the ocean and paddling," says Sparky.

Lopez took up the cause and designed an event that combined flat-water paddleboard racing with a wave-catching component.

The result was a format that was the first of its kind: a four-mile circuit course, on which competitors complete four laps paddling through the surf zone and around a series of buoys. Between each lap racers also have to dismount their boards and run a short sprint on the beach.

In 2008 Lopez partnered with Rainbow Sandals to hold the first Battle of the Paddle at Doheny State Beach. Two-hundred and seventy five racers showed up.

"No way," Lopez says when asked about the inaugural event at which the lifeguards gave the paddlers confused stares. "We had absolutely no idea what we created."

Ron House confirmed that in an e-mail in March of 2015:

The Battle of the Paddle started like this: Sparky and Gerry and I were sitting in Sparky's house on

Beach Road and they had just caught the SUP bug. Sparky was saying he wanted to have a party-like event. He stated that he wanted it to be fun for everyone and not contentious. My response was "Don't have a contest, have a race." He wanted people to come from all over so I suggested prize money.

He said "Ten grand?"

I answered "Yes. For first."

He said "I'm in." There were two things I didn't like about previous races I had attended: having to walk far from parking and having the racers disappear into the distance, only to be seen an hour later for the finish. So I had the idea to create a short course where racers could be seen the whole time. I picked the venue, Doheny's Hole-in-the-Fence, for those reasons. Pat Huber came up with the name "Battle of the Paddle." Barrett added the chicane run to the format. Gerry remarked, at the event, that it would be good next year to hold it in the surf, which it was. Professional SUP began with the first Battle.

Chuck Patterson was the winner of the first Battle of the Paddle, and in the 2014 *SUP the Mag Gear Guide*, he said: "I would have to say that the vision and concept behind Battle of the Paddle really helped shape and evolve the future of racing to where it is today, highlighting the world's best

A D-Dayish sample of the in/out, in/out at the start and finish of the 2014 Battle of the Paddle at Salt Creek. Good fun for all involved—but especially the gladiatorial spectators. Photo: Reid Inouye

all-around paddler in surf sprint racing and long distance."

In that same Gear Guide, SUP racer Jenny Kalmbach said: "The deal in racing was when The Battle of the Paddle standardized the length of the race board in the elite class at 12'6". It seems like an arbitrary figure, but it went on to become the standard all over the world. It probably had a bigger influence on the international race scene than anything else. I'd love to know how they came up with that length."

Another women's SUP racer, Brandi Baksic, added her two cents about Battle of the Paddle: "A big moment was when the Battle of the Paddle introduced waves into racing. Before it was just flatwater paddling. But starting in 2009 you had to know how to surf, you had to perfect buoy turns at speed and race strategy became involved. The board manufacturers had to keep up, too, building boards that were both fast and stable, that you could race and surf. And that changed the shape of the sport, not just for racers but for recreational paddlers, too."

Barrett Tester is a 49-year-old originally from Atlanta, Georgia, who moved to Orange County as a teenager. Barrett has worn many hats in the water-sports industry. He has been involved in Battle of the Paddle since its genesis in 2008 and was also instrumental in evolving the Molokai-2-Oahu race.

Tester was kind enough to detail how Battle of the Paddle has evolved, and how that meeting of hundreds of dedicated stand up paddlers has evolved the sport:

Certainly Laird/Kalama/Keaulana/Bradley/Parmenter were the modern SUP pioneers and dabbled in fast boards/racing/distance through the early 2000s. I was lucky to be Dave Kalama's manager during that time period.

In my opinion, the first big SUP competitive moment was when Archie Kalepa did the Molokai crossing (2004). That showed the global paddling community there was a new craft . . . a new fun way to do it and it should be taken seriously. Up to that point, the prone paddleboard, multisport scene had been burgeoning with a plethora of California, Hawaii and Florida races/lifeguard/ocean festival type events.

From 2004 onwards, as a novelty, sometimes a SUP competitor would enter these events (such as Archie @ Molokai). By 2007 there were several noteworthy paddling events that included SUP as a racing category (Molokai to Oahu Race, San Clemente Ocean Festival, Maui Downwind events . . .).

In May of 2008, Rainbow Sandals hired me to produce the Battle of the Paddle. Up to that point I was an avid paddler, Quiksilver Marketing Director (Silver Edition/Waterman Collection), Dave Kalama et al. team manager, co-founder Molokai to Oahu Paddleboard Race (1996, Quiksilver event producer 13 years), Athletic Director of the San Clemente Ocean Festival (1996 onwards) and consultant to U.S. Canoe/Kayak.

October 11, 2008 was the first BOP at Doheny Beach, at "Hole-in-the fence" in the south parking lot day use area. Chuck Patterson won $10,000 for first place on a sleek Hobie carbon specifically designed for the race. There were 248 entries in the first Open Race & 55 entries (men & women) in the first-ever Elite Race. It was very windy and the race lacked a surf course. To make it interesting we set up the run transition through the banner fencing. This forced more athleticism into the race: in/outs, shorebreak riding, dismount/remount/running, and teamwork with board caddies.

Rainbow Sandals also invited eleven elite Hawaiians and paid their travel/hotels to race. The SUP expo was carefully invitee-only too. There was $25K in prize money, Tahitian drumming, Hawaiian music and a big banquet afterwards.

In 2009 Rainbow Sandals sponsored the Molokai to Oahu Paddleboard Race in July.

The 12'6" Elite Race Class Is Born

The 12'6" board measurement was agreed upon because we knew (at that time) that Surftech and a couple of other board manufacturers were going to have a bunch of new epoxy boards (from China) delivered to shops locally. Some of these new "touring/all around" boards were in the 12'–12'6" range, so we made it so these boards could be used in the competition. We set up a board measuring table, and as a gag, we had a saw there to trim any oversized boards—amazingly several were trimmed.

The second Battle of the Paddle was held in October of 2009 at Doheny Main Beach—first time raced on a surf course (Gerry Lopez' idea from the beginning). Event now a two-day format with the key events: Saturday = Elite Race and Open Race. Sunday = Distance Race, Kids Race and Relays.

In 2010 and 2011 we held the Battle of the Paddle Hawaii at Waikiki. These were amazing and historic BOP events on Duke Kahanamoku Beach. The Distance Race course was a 9.0 mile Hawaii Kai down-winder from Diamond Head.

The 2010, 2011, 2012 and 2013 Rainbow Sandals Battle of the Paddle events were all held at

The starting line for the Elite class at the 2009 Battle of the Paddle, held at Doheny Beach, California. Photo courtesy Battle of the Paddle/Rainbow Sandals

"The next images are showing the bulk of the competitors that were towards the front coming in on larger waves."

Fun, fun, fun at the 2014 Battle of the Paddle at Salt Creek. Pat Huber explains: "Those photos are showing people come in after rounding the last buoy of each lap before entering the beach where they run through the chicane then paddle back out to start the next lap. I designed the race course for both Doheny and Salt Creek and created the placement of the buoys to position the racers to be in the best spot to catch the wave if a set came through. At Salt Creek we had a significant south swell coming through and impeccable conditions. The last buoy was set up to line racers up to catch the left-hand break at a spot called 'The Point' at Salt Creek. These photos are from competitors trying to all come in on their second lap. The close-up of Connor, Kai, and Danny Ching: They were leading the race and this was the first wave of the set."

"The one that shows people possibly going out and bailing is actually a photo of all the competitors coming in. That wave in the set was the biggest and the people you see bailing and going out actually just turned around in an attempt to try to get back over the wave and not get taken out."

This kind of chaos is what made Boardercross so fun in the winter Olympics. A guy could wipe out and still win. The Olympics are missing out if they don't include an event like this, soon. Photos: © Pat Huber/Rainbow Sandals

Doheny State Beach. Each event bigger—registration & SUP Expo increase—with greater media coverage.

In 2012 Battle of the Paddle made the Guinness World Record for "World's Largest Paddleboard Race" with 404 participants in the BOP Open Race. The 2013 Open Race had 464 racers entered.

In 2013 the United States Anti-Doping Authority conducted doping tests at the Battle of the Paddle (sanctioned by the International Surfing Association). There were six tests on winners and random selects.

In 2013 Battle of the Paddle Brazil was held at Cabo Frio, Rio De Janeiro.

In 2014 the Rainbow Sandals Battle of the Paddle moved from Doheny Beach to Salt Creek Beach. The event played out in perfect overhead surf and saw Elite Racing elevated to new heights. Prone paddleboard events were added to the BOP format for first time.

The 2014 running of the Battle of the Paddle shows just how far and fast SUP racing has come. The venue for the race was changed from Doheny to Salt Creek, California, and the race was held during a pretty crunchy, head-high south swell. That created more than a few thrills and chills and spills as hundreds of racers on sleek, not entirely stable race boards dealt with the shorebreak and waves going out and coming in. There are lots of videos online if you want to check out the comedy and/or grace of the world's best paddlers at one of the most prestigious SUP races in the world.

The success of the Battle of the Paddle, which was attended by paddlers from several nations, spread the idea of competitive SUP around the world. In 2012 the International Surfing Association (ISA) held their first-ever World SUP and Paddleboard Championships at Mira Flores, Peru (see below for details on the ISA's involvement in SUP).

And since 2009 there has also been the emergence of SUP river racing (SUPcross style) on inflatable boards. Important events included the Teva Games and GoPro Games in Vail, Colorado, the Weber River events in Utah, and the Payette River games in Idaho. C4 and Boardworks brands were at the forefront of these events.

Downriver Racing

According to Charlie MacArthur, one of the pioneers of river SUP (and son of the original Danno on *Hawaii Five-0*):

The first river SUP race was actually in 2009 in Glenwood Springs, Colorado and was created in a partnership with C4 Waterman. We called it the Whitewater Stand Up Paddling Championship and it was a triple header: A 10 mile downriver, a slalom and a surf event all in one day! Paul Tefft had the idea and I was the co-coordinator. Dan Gavere took first and I was second. Coral Ferguson won the overall in the women's

events. The Teva Mountain Games added their first SUP event in 2010. Also in 2010 we dropped the slalom and we ran the world's first SUPcross competition as it is way more exciting.

Paul Tefft is a resident of Aspen, Colorado, who has been involved with stand up paddling on rivers going back to the beginning. For 2015, Tefft's company, EnviroAction Productions, was promoting the Rocky Mountain Surf Festival to be held at the world-famous Glenwood Springs Park in May. In addition to hosting the Whitewater Stand Up Paddling Championship, the surf festival includes short- and longboard river surfing competitions and other events.

According to an outline on the proposed 2015 festival, the river SUP events include the Downriver, a 3-mile timed event starting in the eddy above the whitewater park and charging through "Glenwood Springs' famous rip roaring river feature."

The timing of the Downriver events determines the seeding of the SUPcross, a crash-and-burn event similar to Boardercross, where stand up paddlers race in heats of four and have to maneuver around gates in the whitewater park, trying not to take each other out as the river tries to take them out.

The SUP River Surf will be the final, climactic event of the 2015 Rocky Mountain Surf Festival, "an amazing surfing contest on the world famous wave at the Glenwood Springs Whitewater Park. Each stand up paddler will get three, one-minute rides with the surfer's best score being counted towards their final results."

Tefft's proposal represents the state of the art for river SUP competition, and it includes a short history of stand up paddling competitions on rivers, which would be six years old in May of 2015:

The Whitewater Stand Up Paddling Championship, the first river stand up paddling competition/

Two views of river SUP racing.

The three racers going upriver—Dan Gavere, Noa Ginella, Ryan Guay—are competing in the SUPcross at the Rocky Mountain Surf Festival in Colorado.

RMSF photo courtesy RMSF/Paul Tefft/Cathy Corbett

The three going downriver are competitors in the female SUP-cross at the Payette River Games held in June of 2014 on the Payette River in Idaho.

Payette photo courtesy Pau Hana/Jake Albrecht

championship ever, was held in Glenwood Springs in 2009. It was created to share and showcase our love of this new twist of the sport and was supported and sponsored by C4 Waterman. We garnered some nice coverage for river SUP including an article in the Denver Post *and an article in* Standup Journal. *Since then whitewater stand up paddling has exploded in popularity and is now a staple of rivers everywhere. River SUP competitions are now held worldwide and*

are expanding at a remarkable rate each year. The format of the original Whitewater Stand Up Championship has been copied by other events around the country. Variations of these river SUP events are now a staple of most paddlesports festivals.

The 2015 Rocky Mountain Surfing Festival will be scheduled between two major events on the summer paddlesports circuit: Paddlefest and the GoPro Mountain Games. Next up on the circuit is Fibark. This is one of Colorado's signature summer events and draws massive crowds each year with the SUP competition one of the most popular.

Next up on the paddlesports summer circuit is the country's largest cash prize purse whitewater paddling event, the $50,000 Payette River Games held at Cascade, Idaho's Kelly's Whitewater Park. They recently announced that the 2015 event is dropping kayaking and going SUP-only for 2015 and beyond. Prize money is obviously a huge draw for competitors and the Idaho event draws a number of the world's best ocean surfing and sprint SUPers to vie for the booty.

Where organizers of ocean events have to worry about swell and waves, Tefft and other river SUP event organizers worry about river flow:

Always a wildcard, river flows can make or break events. For the 2011 Rocky Mountain Surf Festival the runoff was raging (26,000 cfs approx.) and we were not sure if we would have to cancel the event because the flow would be too high and the wave would flatten out (the park had never seen flows that high since its inception). It turned out to be epic and probably the best river surf session ever held in the world. The next year was the polar opposite with the river being at a record low (3,000 cfs approx.) for that time of year. In 2012 we had to cancel the surfing portion of the festival; however we were still able to run the event and SUP championship with a Circle SUP event (racing around multiple buoys and across numerous eddy lines) created as a replacement for the surfing portion of the competition.

As a comparison at the then called 2011 Teva Mountain Games in Vail, one of the SUP events had to be cancelled as Gore Creek was too high with bridge clearings being dangerous. Then in 2012 both of the SUP events were cancelled due to flows being too low. Regardless of river flows river SUP events are here to stay and will continue to increase in popularity. Simply put, river SUP is ridiculously fun and competitions are a natural evolution. Stand Up Paddlers will continue to challenge themselves and others on whitewater rivers around the world and will take this rapidly evolving twist of the sport to new dimensions.

Molokai-2-Oahu: King of the Downwinders

There are a lot of open-water crossing races around the world now, but the Molokai-2-Oahu Paddleboard World Championships is considered the mother of them all—a late July, 32-mile crossing of the treacherous, windy, swell-riddled Ka'iwi Channel, aka the Channel of Bones, aka the Molokai Channel.

Whatever you call the channel between Molokai and Oahu, it has been sinking ships and killing mariners going way back to prehistoric Hawaii. In 1978 it was the gale-force winds and 30-foot swells in the Molokai Channel that flipped the Polynesian oceangoing canoe *Hokule'a*, leading to the heroic but tragic death of Hawaiian lifeguard/surfer/paddler Eddie Aikau.

In the late 1990s top Hawaiian paddler Dawson Jones competed in the 32-mile Catalina Classic paddleboard race and thought Hawaii needed something similar. Jones teamed up with Mike Takahashi and Garrett MacNamara and they put their heads together to formulate a race from Molokai to Oahu across the Channel of Bones.

Every paddler in Molokai-2-Oahu goes with a support craft, in case of dehydration, sharks, water spouts, humpback whales, or any number of things than can happen in the Channel of Bones. This is Travis Baptiste and friends. Travis amended the caption: "During the time of Molokai 2 Oahu it's not our whale season so we don't see any. And the boats are for moral support, encouragement, nutrition and, of course, information." Photo: Molokai2Oahu/Kurt Hoy

The first Molokai-2-Oahu race was for prone paddleboarders only. It ran in 1997 with thirty-six competitors—both solo and team—with a winning time of 5:22:48 by Mick DiBetta, followed by Dawson Jones at 5:24:41.

Molokai-2-Oahu was an instant hit with prone paddlers, and the entrants grew to fifty-six for the 2004 race—plus one. That one was Archie Kalepa, a Maui waterman and lifeguard who chose to show his paces across the channel on one-a-them new-fangled stand up paddleboards.

According to Todd Bradley:

In 2004 Maui waterman and lifeguard Archie Kalepa was an unofficial entrant in the 2004 Quiksilver Molokai to Oahu paddleboard race. Stand up paddling a 12-foot EPS [expanded polystyrene]/epoxy board, Kalepa finished in six hours where the overall winner Jamie Mitchell finished in 4:56:03.

Original contest organizer Mike Takahashi added:

The first race had 36 race #'s. Of that 34 finished—26 finishers were solo and eight teams finished.

If you think the commute from Kapolei to Honolulu is tough . . . Kai Lenny sets his sights on Diamond Head, which doesn't get closer with any speed. Photo: Molokai2Oahu/Kurt Hoy

When Archie showed up in 2004, it was a real surprise, the sport was so new that we (Dawson Jones, Garrett MacNamara, and I) did not think anyone would do it solo, so we decided not to have an SUP category. If I recall, some people asked me if they could do team SUP, but I strongly felt than if there were no solo SUP entries, then, there should be no category.

As everyone knows, I am a real traditionalist, so Archie proved to us that SUP belongs in the race. Archie was not only the first person to cross the channel solo on a stand up, but his time of approximately six hours was over an hour faster than the winning times for the next two years.

I feel fortunate to have witnessed sport history. It is really incredible how much the sport advanced within a few years of Archie's feat. Can't help but wonder how he would have done on an unlimited board with a rudder.

In 2005 a team stand up division added to the Quiksilver Molokai-2-Oahu race brought three SUP teams and was won by Todd Bradley and Brian Keaulana, who finished eleventh overall in the Standup Paddleboard Relay field with a time of 5:42:31. Second place was the team of Archie Kalepa and Dave Parmenter, less than 3 minutes behind. Third place was a female team of Andrea Moller and Maria Souza at 6:56:33.

"There was one solo SUP entrant in 2005," Mike Takahashi said. "Kevin Horgan. His time of 9:27 was outside of the cutoff time, but if I recall correctly we did give him a trophy for first place."

In the 2010 race, Dave Kalama finished first on a stand up at 4:54:15, while Women's SUP division winner Andrea Moller did it in 6:00:00. Jamie Mitchell won the overall paddleboarding with a time of 4:52:52—a difference of 2 minutes between prone and stand up.

Shannon Delaney is one of the contest organizers and has been deeply involved with the

Connor Baxter, somewhere between Molokai and Oahu and hooking into a swell. This makes the whole ordeal a whole lot easier, and one of the keys to winning is making wind and swell work with you. Still, it's grueling. Photo: Molokai2Oahu/Kurt Hoy

evolution of SUP at M2O (the abbreviation for Molokai-2-Oahu):

The SUP aspect of the race really opened the event to a larger audience and additional sponsorship partners. The event has sold out the last five years due to the addition of SUP. It was not until last year [2014] that SUP overall numbers were larger than paddleboard. Partly due to the task at hand, it's taken awhile for a larger population ready for the channel. It's great to see the same athletes doing both disciplines through the years. Numerous high-profile SUP athletes raced the channel on paddleboards first: Kai Lenny at age 12 in paddleboard relay. Talia Gangini dominating the mixed and women's relays in paddleboard. Buzzy Kerbox, Dave Kalama and Brian Syzmanski did the

race paddleboard in the early 2000s. So in reality it was a natural progression to add SUP. Todd Bradley with C4 was involved with both additional sponsorship dollars and initiative to get his athletes racing starting officially in 2006.

Mike Takahashi added some thoughts to that:

I don't think that M2O legitimized SUP. By 2004 some paddleboard races were including SUP, and quite a few paddleboarders were converting to SUP. M2O did inspire the SUP athletes to push their limits and did bring about a new generation of young athletes like Connor Baxter and Kai Lenny.

The 2014 running of Molokai-2-Oahu included 187 official finishers with 108 SUP (team and

The start is big, the channel is big, the finish is big. Imagine battling wind and swell and chop for 32 miles, then dealing with the backwash off the cliffs at Portlock in the last couple hundred yards. Photo: Molokai2Oahu/Erik Aeder

solo), including 21 three-person teams. The first twelve finishers were on SUP, with Connor Baxter in the Men's Unlimited Overall SUP class winning it all with a time of 4:08:08. Australian Matt Poole was the top paddleboarder, finishing thirteenth overall with a time of 4:52:02.

The Stand Up World Tour

The documentary *That First Glide* shows highlights of the first Stand Up World Tour, which was five SUP-surf events in Hawaii, France, Tahiti, Brazil, and back to Hawaii. Maui surfer Kai Lenny came out on top of a field of more than one hundred surfers who competed in the inaugural year of a tour that has grown to six events, with several

hundred competitors and a total prize purse for surfing of $120,000 in 2014.

Tristan Boxford is a representative of the Waterman League, which produces the Stand Up World Surfing Tour and Racing Series:

The Surfing Tour was launched in 2009 with a Contenders Exhibition at the infamous Teahupo'o in Tahiti. That led to the launch of the World Tour with five events in four countries to provide the first global platform for the sport, crowning the sport's first ever World Champion.

This sparked the evolution of the surfing side of the sport dramatically, as board design transformed overnight and a global representation of athletes from all four corners of the world stepped up to do battle.

Kai Lenny secured the World Title in years 2010 and 2011, with the Brazilian Leco Salazar then capturing it in dramatic fashion in 2012, breaking the Hawaiian's dominance. However, Kai came back in 2013 to secure it again, and held it through 2014 as well, despite fierce competition from Brazilian Caio Vaz, the American Sean Poynter and the young Tahitian talent Poenaiki Raioha.

At the end of 2011, we launched the sister property of the World Tour to address the ever-growing racing side of the sport with a World Series of events that crowned a World Champion in 2012, with Kai Lenny stepping up to take the win in the first two years of the Series. Connor Baxter put on a dominant

performance to secure the World Title in 2014, and now stands as the reigning World Champion coming into 2015.

In the Women's it was Annabel Anderson who won in years 2012 and 2013 and then Lina Augaitis who stepped up in 2014 to take the win.

The World Series focuses on the two major racing disciplines: Sprint Racing and Long Distance. The sprint racing features fast-paced short course sprint racing, held in a heat format much like surfing, but in all types of conditions from surf to flat water. The long distance features either traditional downwind long distance courses depending on the location or lap racing either through the surf or around the contest location

Dylan Frick from South Africa cuts that jibe, competing at the Rome stop of the 2014 European Cup. Photo courtesy Waterman League

to provide the most challenging, competitive athlete and spectator-friendly racing.

In 2015, the World Tour and Series see premium events in all major regions, and a mix of iconic locations with prime global markets, from North and South America, Europe and Africa, to Asia, Australia and the Pacific, as the sport continues to skyrocket globally. We also celebrate regional growth with the European and US Cup, with foundations in place for an Asia Cup for 2016.

The World Series has visited the expected coastal venues of Hawaii, California and Brazil, but also more iconic destinations such as Chicago, Patagonia, Hamburg and Bilbao, showcasing the diversity and reach of the sport and creating media that embodies the allure and all-access appeal of this incredible sport.

The ISA: Racing to the Olympics?

Racing and wave competitions on stand up paddleboards go back to around 2004, but the sport has accelerated, pushed along by the sheer number of stand up paddlers who have taken it up in the last decade, riding a swell of popularity.

Are those gusts and swells of popularity enough to propel SUP racing into the Olympics? Fernando Aguerre and the International Surfing Association (ISA) believe so.

Founded in 1964, the ISA has a long history of overseeing surfing around the world. Recognized by the International Olympic Committee as the leader, authority, and governing body for all wave-riding activities, the ISA recognized that stand up paddleboarding evolved from surfing, and they got involved with the competition side of SUP in 2012, when they held the first ISA World Standup Paddle and Paddleboard Championships (WSUPPC) at Miraflores, Peru.

The first WSUPPC had 105 participants from 17 teams competing in Men's and Women's SUP Surfing, SUP Technical Race, SUP Distance Race, and prone paddleboarding disciplines.

The 2013 WSUPPC was held again in Miraflores, Peru, with 22 teams and 200 participants, and the 2014 version was held in La Boquita and Granada, Nicaragua, with 27 teams and 277 participants, a substantial increase in countries and participants in each year over the prior year.

The 2015 WSUPPC was scheduled for Sayulita, Mexico, in May 2015 and was expected to be the largest SUP event ever—as ISA SUP is exploding as SUP explodes in general.

As of March 2015 the ISA had ninety-five member nations, and it had applied for the inclusion of SUP and surfing competitions at the Pan American Games in Lima, Peru, in 2019. The ISA has filed applications for inclusion in the Central American and Caribbean Games, the South American Games, the Asian Games, the Commonwealth Games, and—off in the distance—the Mother of All Sporting Games.

The ISA along with its ninety-five National Federations are leading the effort for SUP's inclusion in the Olympic Games. Fernando Aguerre was one of the founders of Reef Brazil Sandals and has been involved with the ISA since 1994:

SUP is a sport that is totally ready for Olympic inclusion, just as surfing is. In fact, SUP and surfing will probably excel in fans following and numbers of participants with several currently Olympic Sports. SUP is a very universal sport, practiced in all continents, and over 100 countries in the world, even in remote places as Nepal, Bolivia, Latvia and Fiji.

The ISA intends to include SUP in the Olympic Games in 2020 (Tokyo), and is in the process for inclusion in the 2019 Pan Am Games in Lima, Peru, and the Central American Games in 2017. SUP has been approved for inclusion in the South American Beach Games, for late 2015. In all of these events, SUP racers

Competing nations show their true colors at the opening ceremonies for the 2014 World Standup Paddle and Paddleboard Championships in Ecuador. Photo courtesy ISA

will participate as members of their National Olympic Committee's teams, funded by each NOC.

When asked what hurdles/obstacles/backwash SUP faces for Olympic inclusion, Aguerre said, "Different hurdles in each of the Games. All are long and complex processes, in which the ISA has been professionally and consistently working for years."

When asked if SUP is more prepared and more likely to be included in the Olympic games, Aguerre replied, "SUP racing is ready to be included in the Olympic Games, if SUP were to be approved today."

With the demand from the International Olympic Committee to innovate and engage the youth, SUP brings these unique elements to the sporting world's greatest stage.

Olympic inclusion is a very important ISA goal, among several important ones. Through the tireless effort of longtime ISA president Fernando Aguerre, the ISA is actively and vigorously pursuing the inclusion of SUP and surfing in the Olympic Games.

With regards to these final two elements—SUP and surfing in Multi-sport and Olympic Games—as the IOC-recognized IF (International Federation) for SUP and surfing, the ISA will be the entity responsible for the sports' participation in the Games.

While the selection of the teams and athletes will be the responsibility of each National Olympic Committee (NOC) participating in most games, the qualification and eligibility process will be based on the ISA Rules and will therefore require a very close collaboration between the ISA's National Federations and the NOC. This is exactly the way it is in *all* sports included in games inside the Olympic Movement. Every sport's qualifications and competitions in those games is managed by the respective IF.

In addition, SUP's and surfing's inclusion in these Multi-sport Games will open up critical funding for the preparation of athletes, through either the NOC, governments, or the private sector, and most likely a combination of all three of them.

Aguerre said:

The promotion of SUP and surfing around the world, taking it to areas that have had the "playgrounds" but not the end users, will bring immense happiness, and a healthier future to millions of people. The personal and socio-economic benefits of promoting the creation of SUP and surf areas around the world, including in Latin America and the Caribbean, Africa, Asia and Eastern Europe, have already been proven and have been welcomed around the world in formerly non-SUPing, non-surfing nations.

I have personally seen these positive changes around the world, and have seen the happy faces of peoples that formerly did not even know that SUP or riding waves existed.

Sharing our happiness with them is the key reason that explains why I have been working as a volunteer at the ISA since 1994. Sharing the stoke is not just something that I believe in, it's something that I have been doing all my life, even as a teenage surf promoter in Argentina, despite a military dictatorship ban on surfing in my native Mar del Plata. Thousands of dedicated volunteers around the world, share this way of thinking and living, and strong passion for sharing our stoke.*

SUP Racing Organizations

Below are links to racing organizations for more information on when competitions are scheduled and how to enter.

Eaton Surf List of Events:
www.eatonsurf.com/Events.htm

Hawaii Paddleboard Association:
www.hawaiipaddleboardassociation.com

International Surfing Association:
www.isasurf.org

Stand Up Paddle Athletes Association:
www.supathletes.com

Stand Up World Tour and Stand Up World Series: www.watermanleague.com

***SUP the Mag* event calendar:**
www.supthemag.com/event-calendar

SUP Racer: www.supracer.com

World Paddle Association:
www.worldpaddleassociation.com

BUILT FOR SPEED
A SELECTION OF THOROUGHLY MODERN RACING AND DOWNWIND BOARDS

SUP racers and downwind thrill-seekers are serious about their equipment, because a solid, sturdy, fast, reliable course racer or downwind board can mean the difference between first and second—or life and death.

The engineering and R & D quest for Faster, Stronger, Better competitive stand up paddleboards has intensified with the ever-increasing competition in course races like Battle of the Paddle and downwinders like Molokai-2-Oahu. Where these races were informal, funky, and fun a decade ago, the races and the racers are now dead serious about winning and losing—there is prestige, money, sponsorships, and livelihoods at stake—with the faint, promising glow of Olympic gold hovering on the horizon like the green flash.

The Skunk Works of the major SUP companies are abuzz with materials, designs, technologies, and constructions to evolve the next generation of SUP racers from the course to the retail showroom. Most of the major SUP companies are in the game, and Surftech has been involved as long as most.

Surftech has a dozen choices in its 2015 line of SUP racers and downwinders. This is a sample to give an idea of length, width, thickness, and cost.

14' Bark Downwinder

Described in Surftech literature as a Palos Verdes shaper/firefighter/freediver/spearfisher/father/surfer/paddler/boardbuilder/husband/harbor patrolman, Joe Bark competed as a prone paddler in the resurrected Catalina Classic in 1983, and won the event in 1988 and 1989. He has been shaping paddleboards going back to the 1970s and evolved into stand up paddleboards when the bug hit him around Y2K.

The 14' Bark Downwinder is the result of a lot of water hours by Bark and others, and a lot of early mornings in the workshop for Bark. This board is 14' × 28" × 6.8" with a volume of 274.6 liters and weighing a shocking 28 pounds. (When people come into the Surftech warehouse and heft the thing, they often say, "What's this made of, Unobtanium?!")

Photo courtesy Surftech

The board is light, fast, and stable. Downwinders are built to catch "bumps"—swells and windswells that can pick up and propel a downwinder faster than he can paddle. For casual downwinders, riding bumps is nothing but fun. For racers, having the skill to catch and ride bumps can mean the difference between victory and defeat. The 14' Bark Downwinder sells for around $2,400.

14' Bark D2

Also shaped by Joe Bark, Surftech's 14' Bark D2 is 26.4" wide and 7" thick, with a volume of 238.7 liters and weighing 25.5 pounds. The D2 is an updated version of the Dominator, and it's made for paddlers weighing between 140 and 190 pounds.

Photo courtesy Surftech

12'6" Bark Contender

Twelve feet 6 inches is the standard size for course racing on stand up paddleboards. Course races can be held in flat water or in howling winds with bump coming from all directions, and race boards have to be built with both extremes in mind. The Contender's dimensions are 12'6" × 27" × 6.5" with a volume of 203.2 liters and weighing 24.3 pounds. Ideal for paddlers from 130 to 180 pounds.

Returning to distressedmullet .com, Julia Nicholls's review stated: "I chose the Contender after riding it twice. Once on flat glass, once in some choppy, swelly washing machine water with frequent boat wake. I never felt unstable and actually found the rough conditions fun. . . . What I think this board does is gives someone who's 130–180 pounds the same industry standard Bark performance of the Competitor which fits both small or large paddlers.

Photo courtesy Surftech

APPENDIX A

STAND UP PADDLING
MEDIA, COMPETITIONS and MANUFACTURERS

After attempting to gather a complete list of all known SUP institutions in the world—SUP shops, SUP schools, SUP tours, SUP races, SUP paddle manufacturers, SUP accessory manufacturers, and SUP board manufacturers—we gave up. On part of it, anyway.

We used "ClaysLists" as a base; that is, the alphabetical listing of *Who's Who in the SUP Biz* compiled by Clay Feeter and the editors of *Standup Journal* for the June 2011 issue. And also the *Standup Journal* list of SUP shops.

Clay Feeter sent that information with a caveat: "Just watch: A year from now (make that by the end of summer!) there will be twice as many companies and shops. The shops category grows by the day. I just learned that West Marine now carries SUP boards! And so does L.L.Bean."

And he was right. The list of SUP shops, schools, and tours was blossoming and exploding as we were putting it together, and so to save space and not risk leaving anyone out, here is a list of vital information which you can use to find a school, shop, tour, or race near you.

Manufacturers and media are all you need today to stay informed on a SUP market that is expanding faster than the universe after the Big Bang.

Stand Up Paddling Media

As of summer 2011, there were three major SUP magazines, along with a growing number of websites dedicated to spreading local and international news about the world of stand up paddleboarding. As expected, the number of magazines and websites grew four years later, so here is a list that is current as of March 2015.

Since we referred to these sites to gather a lot of information on races, shops, tours, and schools, we recommend you let your fingers do the surfing through these sites. Sign up for their e-mail alerts, and they'll keep your finger on the pulse of all that is happening in the world of SUP.

Distressed Mullet, www.distressedmullet.com: Straight outta Wilmington, North Carolina, John Beausang's website is "dedicated to Stand Up Paddleboarding. From racing, to surfing, to training, equipment and technique. . . ."

Paddlesurf, www.paddlesurf.net: "News, reviews—everything about stand up paddle surfing . . . get out and poach some!"

Samata, **www.samatamag.com:** The only women's magazine for stand up paddling, health, fitness, gear guide, apparel, and fashion.

Stand Up Global Magazine, **www.supglobal.com:** Covering the US, UK, and the world, look to their Stand Up Paddle Directory link to find all the shops we missed.

Stand Up Latino, **www.standuplatino.com:** La comunidad Latino del stand up paddle.

Stand Up Paddle Surf, **www.standuppaddlesurf .net:** Founded by Evan Leong, a dedicated SUPster since 2007, this online magazine is based out of Oahu, one of the centers of the SUP universe.

Standup Journal, **www.standupjournal.com:** "The Original Standup Paddling Mag" transitioned from *Wind Tracks* windsurfing mag to *Standup Journal* in June 2007. The journal is the cream of the crop of all stand up publications: high graphic and printing values with an emphasis on the top images of the sport. Published by Clay Feeter, who began his publishing career at *Wind Surf* mag in 1981, when he was handpicked by editor John Severson, founder/former publisher of *Surfer* magazine.

Standup Paddle Magazine, **www.standuppaddle magazine.com:** The second SUP publication and closest to the source (*Standup Paddle Magazine* is published in Honolulu), this mag has its finger on the pulse of what is happening from Waikiki to Maui to around the world.

Standup Zone, **www.standupzone.com:** One of the best social networking sites for stand up paddlers.

SUP Advisor, **www.supadvisor.com:** "At SUP Advisor you can find and read reviews from fellows, pros and manufacturers, post your own reviews, and rate any product in the SUP world, while being up to date on everything regarding stand up paddling."

SUP Instruction, **www.supinstruction.com:** Purchase SUP instructional DVDs here, including Dan Gavere's excellent *Ultimate Guide to Stand Up Paddling*.

SUP the Mag, **www.supthemag.com:** Straight outta the same building that gives the world *Surfer* and *Surfing* and *Bike* and *Snowboarder* and many other fine publications, *SUP the Mag* delivers the latest SUP news, gear, travel destinations, and more.

SUP Racer, **www.supracer.com:** The pulse of stand up paddle racing. Go directly to www .supracer.com/calendar to find SUP race events in your 'hood.

SUP–Stand Up Paddlers, **www.standuppaddlers .ning.com:** "Stand Up Paddlers is a community of enthusiastic SUP paddlers and surfers from around the world who want to share their love of SUP!"

SUPboarder Magazine, **www.supboardermag .com:** Get the latest stand up paddleboarding news, product reviews, SUPvideos, and features from *SUPboarder* online magazine.

Supconnect and My Local Lineup, **www.sup connect.com:** Part of the Andre Niemeyer communications empire, which also includes cable television shows and other websites. Tune in to supconnect.com for the very latest, up-to-the-second info on what is happening in the world of stand up paddleboarding.

supsurfmag.com: An online magazine to connect you minute by minute with what is happening in the SUP world.

Stand Up Paddling Competitions

The Eaton Surf website lists three grades of stand up paddleboard races. Beginner races are 0 to 6 miles, intermediate races are 7 to 15 miles, and advanced races are 16 miles or more. The number of SUP races is mutating as we speak, and it's impossible to list them all because they are being invented around the world, every day.

As of March 1, 2015, the supracer.com Rogue Race Calendar had 200 races listed from Alberta to Wisconsin, looking as far into the future as May of 2016. Supthemag.com also had a calendar of SUP races and other events, extending to December of 2015.

These lists are ever-changing, expanding and contracting, and it would be impossible to keep it all updated in print. Below are links to racing organizations for more information.

Eaton Surf List of Events, www.eatonsurf.com/ Events.htm: Eaton Surf keeps a detailed list of upcoming stand up paddleboard events.

Hawaii Paddleboard Association, www.hawaii paddleboardassociation.com: The HPA has a long and growing list of paddleboard competitions on its site.

International Surfing Association, www.isa surf.org: The International Surfing Association (ISA) is recognized by the International Olympic Committee (IOC) as the world governing authority for surfing and SUP racing, and all other wave-riding activities.

Stand Up Paddle Athletes Association, www .supathletes.com: Established in September 2013, the Stand Up Paddle Athletes Association is an international governing body for stand up paddleboard racing. With cooperation from athletes, race directors, sponsors, and SUP constituent groups, the association establishes standards for stand up paddleboard racing rules and execution while providing valuable SUP training and SUP racing tools and resources.

Stand Up World Tour, www.standupworldtour .com: Established in 2009 to provide a professional platform for the world's best stand up paddlers, the Stand Up World Tour has had two successful seasons of five events each. And that will grow as interest grows.

SUP Racer, www.supracer.com: The pulse of stand up paddle racing. Go directly to www .supracer.com/calendar to find SUP race events in your 'hood.

World Paddle Association, www.worldpaddle association.com: According to their website, the mission of the WPA is to provide a comprehensive voice, fair and equal access, and organizational structure to the sport of stand up paddling and its participants in a manner that benefits the collective paddling community. Their objective is to provide a consistent and fair experience for paddlers through established classes, guidelines, and safety.

Stand Up Paddleboard Competitions by State and Region

California

- Hennessey's SUP and Paddleboard Racing Series, Southern California, www.hennesseys paddleboarding.com.
- Malibu Downwinder, Malibu, www.malibudw .blogspot.com.

Colorado

- FIBArk, Salida, www.fibark.net. The weird name stands for First in Boating on the Arkansas River, and this event lays claim to being American's Oldest and Boldest Whitewater Festival. Going back to 1949, a wide variety of watercraft competed in the 57-mile run through the Royal Gorge Canyon to Canon City. The treacherous race was shortened to 25.7 miles and now includes stand up paddleboards.
- Go Pro Mountain Games, Vail, www. mountain games.com. America's largest celebration of adventure sports includes kayaking, rafting, biking, bouldering, climbing, fly fishing, and running along with a stand up paddling event.

- Whitewater Stand Up Paddling Championship, Glenwood Springs, www.facebook.com/pages/Whitewater-Stand-Up-Paddling-Championship/121866904494822. A three-event competition which includes the Downriver race, SUPcross, and the surf competition, held at the Glenwood Springs Whitewater Park, which is the first artificial whitewater feature built on the entire length of the Colorado River.

Florida

- Key West Paddleboard Classic, Key West, www.facebook.com/KeyWestClassic. Held off Smathers Beach, there is a 12-mile elite race and a 4-mile open race in a dozen divisions, along with SUP clinics, demonstrations, parties, and lots of fun.

Hawaii

- Buffalo Big Board Surfing Classic, Makaha, www.buffalosurfingclassic.com. Going back to 1975, this contest by Buffalo Keaulana and the westside Oahu crew has featured traditional Hawaiian *alaia* and outrigger canoe surfing, along with more traditional longboard and shortboard events. This was the first contest to have a SUP division (they call it beach boy surfing), and now it's one of the most respected SUP/BBS contests of the year.
- Duke's Ocean Fest, Waikiki, www.dukefoundation.org. This weeklong summer ocean festival at Waikiki has surfing, paddleboarding, volleyball, board polo, and other competitions, including a 10-mile stand up paddleboard race from Hawaii Kai.
- Molokai-2-Oahu Paddleboard Championships, Kai'wi Channel, www.molokai2oahu.com. Going back to 1996, this grueling 32-mile race begins on the north shore of Molokai and finishes on the south shore of Oahu, crossing the treacherous Kai'wi/Molokai/Channel of Bones.

- Olukai Ho'olaulea, Kahului, Maui, www.olukai.com. Also known as "The Maliko Downhill Run," this 8-mile race for OC1 and stand up paddlers has three SUP divisions: Elite Open has no board length or rudder restrictions and awards $15,000 in "gender equal" prize money. Recreational Open has no board length or rudder restrictions but doesn't award prize money. Recreational Under 14' Fixed allows only fixed fins, no rudders.

Mexico

- Punta Sayulita Longboard and SUP Classic, www.puntasayulita.com.

North Carolina

- The Carolina Cup, Wrightsville Beach, www.facebook.com/CarolinaCupSUP. A three-day event with several different races in Kids, Recreational, Open, and Elite divisions. Sanctioned by the World Paddle Association.

Virginia

- Steel Pier Classic, Virginia Beach, www.vbsurfartexpo.com.

Washington

- Round the Rock, Seattle, www.roundtherock.com. A yearly competition held at Seward Park in Seattle. The "Rock" in the title is Mercer Island.

Stand Up Paddleboard Companies

The roster of SUP manufacturers comes and goes, ebbs and flows. For a current list, check out the Stand Up Paddle Industry Association at www.supindustry.org. Also look for lists at www.supglobal.com and www.standupzone.com.

Here are some of the SUP manufacturers found online from 2011 to 2015.

404 SUP, San Clemente, CA, www.404sup.com.

Advanced Elements, Benicia, CA, www.advancedelements.com. Inflatable kayaks.

Amundson Designs/Aquaglide, White Salmon, WA, www.apaddlesurf.com.

Art in Surf, worldwide www.artinsurf.com. Responsible for Terry Chung's refined Kauai stand up paddleboards and a wide range from beginner to pro.

ATL Surfboards, Guadalajara, Mexico, www.atl surfboards.com. Marco Ortiz handcrafts custom SUPs and also distributes Kialoa Paddles, Zinka, and Sticky Bumps in Mexico.

August Surf Co., Huntington Beach, CA, www .robertaugust.com.

Badfish SUP, Salida, CO, www.badfishsurf.com. Mike Harvey and Zach Hughes got tired of surfing the Arkansas River on their behinds, so they got behind stand up paddling and make specialized short, stubby, wide boards for running and riding rivers and surfing river waves.

BIC SUP, France, www.bicsport.com. BIC is into everything from SUP to nuts and is now one of the leading manufacturers of stand up paddleboards.

Boardworks, Encinitas, CA, www.boardworkssurf .com. What began as Windsurfing Works in the early '90s became Acme Supply when they got into surf, windsurf, and kiteboards, and then Boardworks in 2003, when they branched into SUP. Their original partnership with C4 Waterman in 2007 now includes Surf Hawaii, Rusty, Dennis Pang, and Morrelli and Mevin race paddleboards.

BOGA, San Clemente, CA, www.bogaboards.com. BOGA makes a complete line of SUP using E11 epoxy construction, the next level of epoxy vacuum-bagged performance-based construction, which contains the benefits of flex and extended durability.

BOTE, Fort Walton Beach, FL, www.boteboard .com. BOTE designed the first SUP for fishing and now has a complete line of SUP for cruising, surfing, racing, and fishing.

C4 Waterman, Makaha, HI, www.c4waterman .com. The first dedicated SUP-only manufacturer and a pioneer in SUP for rivers and inland, the C4 Waterman retail showroom is at 515 Ward Avenue in beautiful downtown Kaka'ako.

Chandler Surf & Paddletech, North San Diego County, CA, www.chandlersurf.com.

Coreban, worldwide, www.coreban.com. Established in 2005, Coreban offers a complete range of SUP from 7' to 14' in six different technologies.

Crescent Kayaks, Carrollton, Georgia, www .crescentkayak.com.

Doyle SUP, Orange County, CA, www.scsiinc.us.

Eaton Surfboard and Paddleboards, Hawi, HI, www.eatonsurf.com.

Eboards, Dana Point, CA, www.ericksonpaddle boards.com.

Fanatic, Munich, Germany, www.fanatic.com. A longtime maker of sailboards, surfboards, skateboarding and other boards, now making a line of a half-dozen stand up paddleboards, and growing.

F-ONE, France, www.f-onesup.com. Founded in 1989 by sailboarder and now SUPer Raphael Salles, F-ONE has been making SUPs since 2011.

Foote Maui Designs, Haiku, Maui, HI, http:// foote-surfboards.com/.

Imagine Surf, Miami, FL, www.imaginesurf.com. Founded in 2002 by kayaker-turned-surfer-turned-stand up paddler Corran Addison, since 2007 Imagine Surf has been pioneering the use of ecological and sustainable materials to make stronger, longer-lasting stand up paddleboards.

Gerry Lopez Surfboards, Bend, OR, www.gerry lopezsurfboards.com.

Glide SUP, Salt Lake City, UT, www.glidesup.com.

Global Surf Industries, San Clemente, CA, www .surfindustries.com. A leading manufacturer of molded surfboards using epoxy, carbon, and other high-tech materials and processes, GSI makes SUPs for McTavish, Walden, NSP, 7S, and Surf Series, among others.

Harbor Outfitters, Ocean City, NJ, www.harbor outfitters.com.

Hobie SUP, Orange County, CA, www.hobie.com.

Hooked SUP, Maui, HI, www.hookedSUP.com. Founded by Maui resident Alex Aguera, this company specializes in wide, thick, stable SUPs that make a great platform for ocean or freshwater fishing: ono to steelhead.

Infinity Surfboards, Dana Point, CA, www.infinity surf.com.

Jason Polakow SUP and Windsurf Boards, Innsbruck, Austria, www.jp-australia.com.

Jeff Clark Surfboards, Half Moon Bay, CA, www .maverickssurfshop.com.

Jimmy Lewis, Haiku, Maui, HI, www.jimmylewis .com.

Joe Bark Paddleboards, Palos Verdes, CA, www .joebarkpaddleboards.com.

JP Australia, Maui, HI, www.sup.JP-australia.com.

Kainoa McGee Board Company, North Shore, Oahu, HI, www.kainoamcgee.com.

Kazuma Surfboards, Haiku, Maui, HI, www .kazumasurf.com.

King's Paddle Sports, San Marcos, CA, www .kingspaddlesports.com.

Kings Surf, Honolulu, HI, www.kingsurfhawaii .com. Richard and Jolly King manufacture custom boards for Hawaiian kahuna Ben Aipa, as well as Akila Aipa, Triple Witch, Standup Hawaii, China Uemura, Maui Longboards, Endless Summer, and Hulakai.

Ku Hoe Hawaii / RJ Surfboards, Oahu, HI, www .kuhoe.com and www.rjsurf.com.

Lakeshore Paddleboard Company, Reno, NV, www.lpc-sup.com. Straight outta Reno, Nevada, Lakeshore Paddleboard Company makes stable, quality boards specifically for flatwater touring and recreation.

Mahana Surfboards, www.mahanasurfboards.com.

McKinnon Shapes and Designs, Huntington Beach, CA, www.McKinnonSurfboards.com.

Nahskwell, Tridden County, France, www .nahskwell-sup.com.

Naish International, North Shore, Oahu, HI, www.naishsurfing.com. Many thanks to Naish for their help with this book. When stand up paddling resurfaced in Hawaii in the early 2000s, Naish developed prototypes for three years before launching its initial product line in 2007—two boards by Harold Iggy. By 2009 Naish had 19 different boards in their range, then 23 in 2010 ranging from 7"3" to 17'. The innovators behind Naish SUP include Robby Naish, Dave Kalama, Michi Schweiger, Harold Iggy, and Kai Lenny.

Paddle Surf Hawaii, North Shore, Oahu, HI, www.paddlesurfhawaii.com.

Paddle Surf Warehouse, Costa Mesa and Dana Point, CA, www.paddlesurfwarehouse.com.

Pangasurf, The Woodlands, TX, www.pangasurf .com.

Pau Hana Surf Supply, Santa Clarita, CA, www .pauhanasurfco.com.

Rendezvous River Sports, Jackson Hole, WY, www.jacksonholekayak.com.

Riviera Paddle Surf, San Clemente, CA, www .rivierapaddlesurf.com. Manufacturer of boards designed by Ron House, Gerry Lopez, Nectar, 404, and Riviera as well as Danny Ching Signature Riviera Paddles.

Rogue Stand Up Paddleboards, San Clemente, CA, www.roguesup.com.

Rogue Wave Custom Ltd., Wasaga Beach, Ontario, Canada, www.roguewaveboards.com.

Sandwich Island Composites, San Clemente, CA, www.SICMaui.com.

Sea Eagle Boats, Port Jefferson, NY, www.sea eagle.com.

Siren SUP, Rheine, Germany, www.sirensirensiren .com.

Smooth Stand Up Paddleboards, San Clemente, CA, www.smoothsup.com.

Starboard SUP, Norway, Sweden, Thailand, the World, www.star-board-sup.com. Many, many thanks to Svein Rasmussen and Margareta Engstrom in 2011 and Caren in 2015 for their help with this book. Starboard boards are considered by many to be the most cutting-edge SUP boards on the market these days, made for everything from cruising the fjords to charging Backdoor.

Suplove Inc., Huntington Beach, CA, www.sup love.com. As a SUP instructor in Sydney, Australia, Matt Johnston saw a need for affordable, well-made boards. And now he spins out hand-shaped, light-but-strong boards in California.

Surftech, Santa Cruz, CA, www.surftech.com. Many thanks to Randy French, Duke Brouwer, John Griffith, Sean Burke, Ty Zulim, and everyone at Surftech for their help with this book. One of the pioneers of stand up paddleboarding, with their 12' Mickey Munoz surfboards and then the 12'1" Laird, Surftech now has one of the widest varieties of stand up paddleboards, in every possible material, for every kind of use.

Tahoe Paddle and Oar, Kings Beach, North Shore, Lake Tahoe, CA, www.tahoepaddle.com. The original stand up shop on Lake Tahoe, Tahoe Paddle is dialed in to the fast-changing world of stand up paddleboarding equipment and technique.

Tahoe SUP, Lake Tahoe, NV, www.TahoeSUP.com.

Tower Stand Up Paddle Boards, San Diego, CA, www.towerpaddleboards.com.

ULI Boards, San Diego, CA, www.uliboards.com. A pioneer in inflatable surfboards and stand up paddleboards, ULI makes an increasingly more sophisticated and refined line of stand up paddleboards that can be folded up for transporting, then blown up for . . . blowing up in the surf or on the river.

Wild Rock Outfitters, Peterborough, Ontario, www.wildrock.net. They've been "Countering Couch Culture since 1992" at this extensive outdoor goods store in Peterborough, and now they have an extensive supply of stand up paddleboards and accessories.

YOLO Board, Santa Rosa Beach, FL, www.yolo board.com.

Stand Up Paddle Manufacturers

Likewise, the roster of SUP paddle manufacturers comes and goes, ebbs and flows. For a current list, check out the Stand Up Paddle Industry Association at www.supindustry.org and also www.sup global.com and www.standupzone.com. Here are some of the SUP paddle manufacturers found online from 2011 to 2015.

Carbonerro SUP Training Rails and Paddles, Santa Barbara, CA, www.carbonerro.com. Hot paddles with cool names for every size paddler: Tad Pole, Bambino, Honey Girl, Mamacita, Bombora, and Bamboocha.

Kialoa Paddles, Bend, OR, www.kialoa.com. Cool, these guys make Dragon Boat paddles, but also a full range of SUP paddles for everything from running rivers to double-overhead.

Malama Paddles, Paia, Maui, HI, www.malama paddles.com. Many thanks to Malama and his spokeskahuna Karen Chun for their help with this book. Malama was one of the first people Laird Hamilton went to when he was starting to suss out SUP. If you're looking to get the feel of an all-wood paddle, dis is da guy.

Outside Reef, La Grand Motte, France, www.out sidereef.com. *Pagaie* is the word for "paddles" in France, and Outside Reef have become the word for "pagaie" in France and across Europe with a line of stand up paddles from *bois et carbone.*

Paddle Hawaii, Big Island, HI, www.paddlehi.com. Abraham Shouse makes innovative, quad-bent designs out of poplar and tropical hardwoods.

Pure Paddles, Big Island, HI, www.purepaddles .com. Odie K. Sunni lives on the Big Island of Hawaii and makes custom wood paddles for cruising, surfing, and racing.

Quickblade Paddles, Costa Mesa, CA, www.quick bladepaddles.com. A dedicated canoe paddler and Olympian, Jim Terrell and his wife, Elizabeth, now manufacture some of the world's finest stand up paddles. Thanks to both of them for their help with this book.

Sawyer Paddles and Oars, Talent, OR, www .paddlesandoars.com.

Werner Paddles, Sultan, WA, www.wernerpaddles .com. They come from the land of ice and snow, and have been making quality paddles for canoeing and kayaking since 1965. SUP is new to them, but they are approaching it with more than fifty years of experience with quality and customer service.

Whiskey Jack Paddles, Whitefish, MT, www .facebook.com/whiskeyjackpaddles. Owner Dan Brown spends the summer fishing and paddling around the nature-blessed waters of Montana, and in the winter he crafts beautiful paddles for canoes, kayaking, and now SUP.

Stand Up Paddle Accessories Manufacturers and Distributors

Better Surf Than Sorry and **Surfer Baby,** San Diego, CA, www.bettersurfthansorry.com and www.surferbaby.com.

Blue Planet Surf Gear, Honolulu, HI, www .blueplanetsurf.com. Robert Stehlik started surf gear company Blue Planet in 1993, got hooked on SUP in 2008, finished second in his age group in the Molokai-2-Oahu race, and now makes gear and accessories for his new fascination.

BoardFisher Products, Cardiff, CA, www.board fisher.com. Calvin Tom likes to combine fishing with his SUPping, and he has designed the first full stowaway SUP travel pack fishing system.

Carbonerro SUP Training Rails and Paddles, Santa Barbara, CA, www.carbonerro.com.

Creatures of Leisure, San Diego, CA and Australia, www.creatures.com.au. Leashes, board bags, and other surf accessories to meet the SUP sensation that is sweeping the nation.

FCS Fins, San Diego, CA, www.surfFCS.com.

Fuacata Sports, Miami, FL, www.fuacatasports .com. Distributor of Jimmy Lewis SUPs for the US, the Caribbean, and Latin America and also the organizers of the Orange Bowl Paddle Championships. Fuacata also distributes Puka Patch ding repair and rail savers, Surf Nano ceramic board coatings, and the Supper Tray fishing application.

Graphite Master, Los Angeles, CA, www.graphite master.com and www.surfxglass.com.

Hyperflex Wetsuits, Millville, NJ, www.hyper flexusa.com.

Icon Sports Group, Okanagan, BC, Canada, www
.iconsports.ca.

Indo Board Balance Trainer, Indian Harbour
Beach, FL, www.indoboard.com.

Kelp Farmer, Cayucos, CA, www.kelpfarmer.com.
Clothing and accessories for the SUP lifestyle.

KP2 Rail and Paddle Tape, Encinitas, CA, www
.kp2surf.com. Matt Kidd and Micah Peters
make durable and almost invisible material to
protect rails from dings.

Monster Paint Traction, San Clemente, CA,
www.facebook.com/pages/Monster-Paint
-Traction/89365366123.

NE Surf n' Sales, Cape Cod, MA, www.NESurf
nSales.com.

North Shore Inc., Hood River, OR, www.North
ShoreInc.com.

Ocean Minded, California and the world, www
.oceanminded.com. A footwear, apparel, and
accessories company that has been supporting
Chuck Patterson, Candice Appleby, and SUP
events from the early days.

Resin Research, Tucson, AZ, www.resinresearch
.net. Greg Loehr was a top pro surfer in the
1970s, a pro sailboarder in the 1980s, and
began producing quality, specialty epoxy systems for the boarding industry in 1982.

Standup Paddle Sports, Santa Barbara, CA, www
.paddlesurfing.com. The website for Standup
Paddle Sports in Santa Barbara, the first dedicated stand up paddleboard dealer in the world,
offering just about everything you can imagine
in the world of stand up.

Sweet Waterwear, Oahu, HI, www.sweetwater
wear.com. Owner Sean Sweet became a SUP
addict and then began using his years of experience in the rag trade to make functional,
fashionable clothing and accessories for stand
up paddling.

Watershed Sales Agency, Ottawa, Ontario, www
.markscriver.wordpress.com. Run by Mark
Scriver and Johno Foster, Watershed supplies
quality SUP equipment to eastern Canada, and
the two founders are deeply involved in providing beginner to advanced SUP instruction to
that part of the world.

Wax Research (Sticky Bumps), Carlsbad, CA,
www.stickybumps.com. Owner John Dahl has
been surfing and making surf wax since the
1960s. He got into SUP in the twenty-first
century, and his company produces SUP accessories and the first SUP grip wax.

X-Trak and Seadek, Rockledge, FL, www.xtrak
.com.

APPENDIX B
SAFETY INFORMATION
EVERYTHING'S OKAY
UNTIL IT ISN'T

Safety information is included throughout this book in the form of wind and weather warnings, etiquette guidelines, and anecdotes about people who got in trouble while stand up paddling. If you've read this book, you're already well aware of the major safety issues confronting stand up paddlers—for the most part, they are similar issues to those confronted by other folks who take to the water on their own power, such as surfers and kayakers.

Dealing with extreme safety issues such as tidal currents, rip tides, and whitewater river features is beyond the scope of this book, and I suggest you refer to numerous other books and seek expert instruction to safely navigate those hazards. But some safety issues are especially pertinent to stand up paddlers, and we've included this list as a quick reference to safety information throughout the book.

1. Keep a weather eye on weather, wind, and water conditions: Is there a big swell coming, a calving glacier up this fjord, gale warnings? Know what weather is coming, so you don't get stuck in it. Know where you are going, and how to get back.

2. The buddy system from scuba should also be applied to SUP. Having someone keeping an eye on you could save your life if something goes south.

3. Wearing a personal flotation device and a helmet is a good idea from Pipeline to your pool. But when running rivers, a PFD and helmet are mandatory.

4. Leashes aren't always a good idea for running rivers, but if you do attach yourself to your board, the leash should attach to your PFD and not your ankle. A leash snagged on a tree or rock will pull you down like an anchor, and you might not be able to reach an ankle leash.

5. When running rivers, scout your route. If you fall, keep your feet in front of you and off the bottom, trees, or rocks. You could get pinned in the current and drown.

6. Beginning ocean paddlers should learn in flat water and stay far from the surf zone until their skills are solid. A beginner on a SUP in the surf can be like a bull in a china shop.

7. When transporting stand up paddleboards on the exterior of a vehicle, let your "racknophobia" grip you: Triple check the racks, because you don't want your boards taking out a big rig or low-flying jet. When the wind catches all that area, they take off.

8. When going into the ocean, always wear a leash so the winds or currents or waves don't separate you from your board and possibly endanger others. Don't strap your leash under your wetsuit—you might need to get to it fast.

9. Try to give a wide berth to orcas, alligators, white sharks, and other large aquatic animals. You just never know what you're gonna get.

10. Keep your eyes up when paddling. Don't look at your feet—look for waterfalls, ocean liners, tsunami, and fins. Situational awareness is crucial.

INDEX

ABOUT THE AUTHOR

Originally from Santa Cruz, California, Ben Marcus was an editor at *Surfer Magazine* from 1989 to 1998. As a freelance writer, Ben has had twenty books published and has written for a wide variety of websites and publications, including *The Surfer's Journal, Standup Journal, LA Weekly, Malibu Magazine, LA Times, Muscle and Fitness,* www.swell.com, and surf and SUP media around the world. Check out www.benmarcusrules.com for a complete resume.